Find It Quick
Handy Bible Encyclopedia

Ron Rhodes

HARVEST HOUSE™ PUBLISHERS

EUGENE, OREGON

Cover by Terry Dugan Design, Minneapolis, Minnesota

FIND IT QUICK HANDY BIBLE ENCYCLOPEDIA
Copyright © 2003 by Ron Rhodes
Published by Harvest House Publishers
Eugene, Oregon 97402

Library of Congress Cataloging-in-Publication Data
  Rhodes, Ron
    Find it quick handy Bible encyclopedia / Ron Rhodes.
        p. cm.
      ISBN 0-7369-0559-6 (pbk.)
    1. Bible—Encyclopedias. I. Title.
      BS440 .R487 2003
      220.3—dc21   2002012508

    03 04 05 06 07 08 09 10 11 / DP-CF / 10 9 8 7 6 5 4 3 2

To Bible lovers everywhere!

Acknowledgments

A special thanks to the team at Harvest House Publishers for their creative input on this book. And, as always, a deeply heartfelt thanks to my wife, Kerri, and our two children, David and Kylie, for their never-ending love and support.

Introduction

Many Bible encyclopedias contain well over 5000 articles, and most of them are in small print (hard to read). Besides covering a variety of articles of interest, they also contain a multitude of obscure place names and people names—which, in my experience, are rarely read.

The "handy" encyclopedia you are holding in your hands is different. It does not contain obscure place names and people names, and the print is very user-friendly (easy to read). This *Find It Quick Handy Bible Encyclopedia* focuses more on the "big picture" of life in Bible times, providing only the primary information that most Bible students want to have at their disposal.

My prayer is that this encyclopedia would further enlighten your understanding of, and enhance your love for, the Word of God. May the Lord truly bless you as you study His Word!

Abraham

1. *God's Call.* Christians consider Abraham an important ancestor of Jesus Christ (Matthew 1:1) and the father of the faithful (Romans 4:16). Abraham, whose name means "father of a multitude," lived around 2000 B.C. He originated from the city of Ur, in Mesopotamia, on the River Euphrates. He was apparently a very wealthy and powerful man.

God called Abraham to leave Ur and go to a new land—the land of Canaan (literally, "belonging to the land of the red purple"), which God was giving to Abraham and his descendants (Genesis 12:1). Abraham left with his wife, Sarah, and his nephew, Lot. Upon arriving in Canaan, his first act was to construct an altar to worship God. This was typical of Abraham; God was of first importance to him.

Abraham's sojourn to Canaan was, in itself, an act of great faith. After all, Canaan was already occupied by the fearsome Canaanites. But Abraham never doubted God's promise. The land would someday belong to Abraham and his descendants. It was just a matter of time.

2. *God's Covenant.* God made a covenant with Abraham in which He promised him that his descendants would be as numerous as the dust of the earth (Genesis 12:1-3; 13:14-17). The promise may have seemed unbelievable to Abraham since his wife was childless (11:30). Yet Abraham did not doubt God; he knew God would faithfully give what He had promised. God even reaffirmed the covenant in Genesis 15, perhaps to emphasize to Abraham that even in his advanced age, the promise would come to pass. God also promised Abraham that he would be personally blessed, that his name would become

A

great, that those who bless him would be blessed and those who curse him would be cursed, and that all the families of the earth would be blessed through his posterity.

At one point, an impatient Sarah suggested that their heir might be procured through their Egyptian handmaiden, Hagar. Ishmael was thus born to Abraham, through Hagar, when he was 86 years old. But Ishmael *was not* the child of promise. In God's perfect timing, the child of promise was finally born when Abraham and Sarah were very old (Abraham was 100), far beyond normal childbearing age. Their son was named Isaac (Genesis 21), and, as promised, an entire nation eventually developed from his line. "Isaac" means "laughter" and is fitting because it points to the joy derived from this child of promise.

3. *Abraham's Test of Faith.* In a famous episode in the Bible, Abraham's faith was stretched when he was commanded by God to sacrifice his beloved son of promise, Isaac. Abraham obeyed God's command without hesitation. In his heart, Abraham believed God would provide a substitute lamb for the burnt offering (Genesis 22:8). God, of course, intervened before Isaac was actually sacrificed, but the episode served to demonstrate the tremendous faith Abraham had in God. Many theologians have noted that Abraham prefigures the heavenly Father, "who did not spare his own Son, but gave him up for us all" (Romans 8:32).

Abraham lived 175 years, and then "breathed his last and died at a good old age" (Genesis 25:7-8).

Abrahamic Covenant—See *Covenants.*

Acts

The book of Acts may be considered "Part Two" of Luke's Gospel, for Luke is the author of both. He wrote Acts in A.D. 61, shortly after he wrote his Gospel.

A

While Luke's Gospel contains an orderly account of the accomplishments of Jesus during His earthly life, the book of Acts contains an orderly account of the accomplishments of Jesus, through the Holy Spirit, in the 30 years or so of the early church following His resurrection and ascension. The book covers events beginning with the ascension of Jesus into heaven and ending with the apostle Paul's imprisonment in Rome. It serves as a link between the four Gospels and the Epistles.

Though the book of Acts focuses primarily on the "acts of the apostles" (such as Paul and Peter), in reality the book predominantly focuses on the "acts of the Holy Spirit" through different people. It focuses on how Paul and Peter and others empowered by the Holy Spirit were used to spread Christianity among both Jews and Gentiles around the northern Mediterranean, including Samaria (Acts 8:5-25), Phoenicia, Cyprus, and Antioch (9:32–12:25), Phrygia and Galatia (13:1–15:35), Macedonia (15:36–21:16), and Rome (21:17–22:29). Despite persecution by Roman authorities, Jewish authorities, and others (2:13; 4:1-22; 5:17-42; 6:9–8:4), Christianity spread like wildfire.

Adam and Eve

Adam and Eve were our first parents, the first human beings created by the hand of God (Genesis 1:26-27; 2:7,22-23). The Hebrew word for "Adam" literally means "humanity" and is an appropriate term for the first man since he represents the human race. The Hebrew word for "Eve" means "giver of life" and is appropriate since it was through her body that the rest of humanity was given birth.

The words translated "man" and "woman" in Genesis 2:21-22 are based on a play on words in the Hebrew. "Man" in Hebrew is *ish*, while "woman" is *ishshah*. The name indicates that woman has the same nature as man *(ish)*, but also is different in some way *(shah)*. The woman is a perfect companion of the opposite gender for man.

It is highly revealing that man was formed from the very soil that God entrusted him to cultivate (Genesis 2:15; 3:17). Woman, on the other hand, was created from a rib taken from man's side, and she was called to be his helper. It would thus seem that their different modes of creation are closely related to their respective tasks in life.

It is also interesting that when God was giving instructions about moral responsibility, He gave these instructions to Adam alone. After the Fall, God first summoned Adam, not Eve, even though *she* was the one who had led him into sin (Genesis 3:9). Adam, the head of the family, was held responsible for what had happened. Indeed, Romans 5:12 ascribes the guilt to Adam.

Adultery—See *Sex and Sexuality.*

Agriculture and Farming—See *Farming.*

Almsgiving and Charity

The New Testament is replete with admonitions to give freely to others. Hebrews 13:16 instructs us to do good and share with others. We are admonished to give to the poor (Matthew 19:21; Luke 11:41; 12:33; 1 John 3:17) and to those who ask (Matthew 5:42). We are called to share food with the hungry (Isaiah 58:7,10), to share money generously (Romans 12:8), and to use money for good (1 Timothy 6:17-18). The early church certainly showed charity as an evidence of Christian love (Acts 9:36; 10:2,4; Romans 12:13; Ephesians 4:28). Jesus advises us to give to others secretly, instead of openly in order to win the praise of men (Matthew 6:1-2).

The New Testament often describes such generous activities as almsgiving. The word "alms" derives from the Greek word *eleos,* which means "mercy." "Almsgiving" thus means "mercy-giving." We are called to show mercy and kindness to others whenever the opportunity arises.

In Old Testament times, the Mosaic Law encouraged charity among the people. For example, Leviticus 25:35 instructs: "If one of your countrymen becomes poor and is unable to support himself among you, help him as you would an alien or a temporary resident, so that he can continue to live among you." Likewise, Deuteronomy 15:7 encourages: "If there is a poor man among your brothers in any of the towns of the land that the LORD your God is giving you, do not be hardhearted or tightfisted towards your poor brother." (See also Psalm 41:1.) Old Testament law stipulated that farmers should leave the corners of their fields unharvested so that poor people who walked by could pick some food to eat (see Leviticus 19:9-10; Deuteronomy 15:11; Ruth 2:2).

Altar

1. Definition ◆ 2. Altar of Burnt Offering ◆
3. Incense Altar ◆ 4. Other Altars

1. *Definition.* The Hebrew noun for "altar," *mizbeah*, means "place of sacrifice." Altars played a prominent role in the religious history of the Israelites.

2. *Altar of Burnt Offering.* The altar of burnt offering was made of wood and was covered by bronze. It was placed in front of the entrance to the tabernacle (Exodus 40:6). On the altar of burnt offering were sacrificed all the offerings by fire (Exodus 29:13-34). A burnt offering consisted of an animal (without defect) that was to be completely consumed by the fire (Leviticus 1:3-17). Perpetual fire was kept on the altar so that whenever a person sinned he could immediately offer a sacrifice to God (Leviticus 6:13). This altar was also called the altar of God (Psalm 43:4) and the altar of the LORD (Malachi 2:13).

A

Such altars were not to be built with dressed stones—that is, with hewn stones (Exodus 20:25). Only natural stones were to be used, for using tools on the stones to shape them would defile them and thus defile the altar.

The altar was also to be without steps (Exodus 20:26). This would prevent indecent exposure while climbing up to the altar. This is in noted contrast to pagan rituals, which often included nudity.

3. Incense Altar. The incense altar was the place where incense was burned morning and evening when the priest tended to the lamp. This altar was a small movable table made of acacia wood and overlaid with gold (Exodus 37:25-26). It was placed inside the tabernacle before the veil that separated the most holy place from the rest of the worship area (40:26-27). Incense in the Bible is often representative of the prayers of God's people (see Psalm 141:2).

4. Other Altars. Other altars mentioned in the Bible include those built by Noah (Genesis 8:20), Abraham (Genesis 12:7), Isaac (Genesis 26:25), Jacob (Genesis 33:20), Moses (Exodus 17:15), Saul (1 Samuel 14:34), David (2 Samuel 24:15-25), Solomon (2 Chronicles 4:1), and a pagan altar to an unknown God (Acts 17:23).

Amos, Book of

The book of Amos was written by a prophet of the same name about 755 B.C. Amos, whose name means "burdenbearer," was a prophet to the northern kingdom of Israel (Amos 7:14-15). By trade, he was a lowly shepherd and a dresser of fig trees. He lived in Tekoa, south of Jerusalem (1:1). He was a contemporary of Jonah, Hosea, and Isaiah, and prophesied during the reigns of Uzziah and Jeroboam II.

Amos focused heavy attention on the social injustice of his day (see Amos 5:24). During his time the land was prosperous

A

and there were many rich people. Yet the rich did not aid those who were disadvantaged. This was not as it should have been. Amos, the farmer-turned-prophet, therefore prophesied that a day of judgment was forthcoming in which destruction would be inevitable (7:1–9:10).

Ironically, the rich people of Amos's day thought they were given such great wealth because they were so religious. They had it backward: They did not use their wealth to do God's work of caring for the poor and disadvantaged. Rather, they exploited the poor to become even richer. From the vantage point of Amos, these rich people were nothing more than hypocrites. It was not long after Amos wrote his book that the Assyrians invaded the land and took the people into captivity. Judgment came just as Amos had prophesied.

Angels

1. Created Beings ◆ 2. Characteristics ◆
3. Innumerable ◆ 4. Roles

1. *Created Beings.* Angels are created beings. They have not existed forever. Nor were they formerly humans. They were created *as angels*. Psalm 148:2-5 affirms that God spoke the word and the angels were created at a specific point in time. Theologians believe the angels were created some time prior to the creation of the earth. After all, Job 38:7 makes reference to the "sons of God" (who are angels—see Job 1:6; 2:1 NASB) singing at the time the earth was created.

2. *Characteristics.* We learn a great deal about the nature of angels by studying what the Bible says about their characteristics.

A. *Angels Are Incorporeal and Invisible* (Hebrews 1:14). The word "incorporeal" means "lacking material form or substance." Angels, then, are not material, physical beings; they are invisible spiritual beings.

13

A

B. *Angels Are Localized Beings.* Scripture portrays them as having to move from one place to another. An example of this is when the angel Gabriel had to engage in "swift flight" to travel from heaven to Daniel's side (Daniel 9:21-23).

C. *Not All Angels Have Wings.* Many angels in the Bible are described as having wings (Isaiah 6:1-5; Ezekiel 1:6; Revelation 4:8). But some Bible verses about angels make no mention of wings (for example, Hebrews 13:2). We conclude that though it is possible all angels have wings, this is not a necessary inference. There is no explicit reference indicating that angels *as a whole* are winged.

D. *Angels Can Appear as Men.* Though angels are by nature incorporeal and invisible, they can nevertheless appear as men (Genesis 18). Their resemblance to men can be so realistic that the angel is actually taken to be a human being (Hebrews 13:2).

E. *Angels Are Powerful Beings.* Scripture portrays angels as being extremely powerful and mighty beings. Psalm 103:20 calls them "mighty ones who do his [God's] bidding." Second Thessalonians 1:7 makes reference to God's "powerful angels." Yet, none of them are omnipotent (all-powerful)—only God is. Angels are creatures with creaturely limitations.

F. *Angels Are Holy.* The word "holy" comes from a root that means "set apart." God's angels are set apart from sin and set apart to God, to serve Him and carry out His assigned tasks. Angels are often called God's "holy ones" (Job 5:1; 15:15; Psalm 89:7).

G. *Angels Are Obedient.* The angels do not do their own bidding. They do only God's bidding (Psalm 103:20).

H. *Angels Have Great Knowledge.* Though angels are not all-knowing, they nevertheless possess great intelligence. Angels were created as a higher order of creatures than humans (see Psalm 8:5) and innately possess a greater knowledge. Beyond this, angels gain ever-increasing knowledge through long observation of human activities.

I. *Angels Are Immortal.* Angels are not subject to death (Luke 20:36). Since angels are immortal and do not die—and

14

since they do not propagate baby angels (Matthew 22:30)—
it seems obvious that the number of angels is and always will
be the same.

3. Innumerable. Scripture makes reference to "a great company of the heavenly host" (Luke 2:13), and the angels are spoken of as "tens of thousands and thousands of thousands" (Psalm 68:17). Their number is elsewhere described as "myriads of myriads" (Revelation 5:11 NASB). (The word "myriad" means "vast number," "innumerable.") Daniel 7:10, speaking of God, says that "ten thousand times ten thousand stood before him." The number "ten thousand times ten thousand" is 100,000,000 (100 million). This is a number almost too vast to fathom. Job 25:3 understandably asks, "Can his forces be numbered?"

4. Roles. Angels are engaged in fulfilling various roles:

A. *Messengers.* The word "angel" literally carries the meaning, "messenger." Angels serve as God's messengers—bringing revelation, announcements, warnings, and other information to the people of God. For example, angels appeared to the prophet Daniel to reveal the future (Daniel 9). An angel appeared to Joseph and to Mary to announce the birth of the Savior, Jesus Christ (Matthew 1).

B. *Guardians.* God has assigned angels to watch over believers. Psalm 91:9-11 affirms that the angels guard believers in all their ways. (See 2 Kings 6:17.)

C. *Ministry at Death.* At the moment of death, when the soul separates from the body, angels are there to escort the believer's soul into his or her eternal inheritance (Luke 16:22).

D. *Restraining Evil.* Angels sometimes restrain evil among humans. For example, in Genesis we read about angels that struck some wicked men with blindness so they could not carry out their evil intentions when they came to Lot's house (Genesis 18:22; 19:1,10,11).

E. *Executing Judgments.* Angels are sometimes found in Scripture executing God's judgments. A prime example is found in Acts 12 where an angel executed Herod in judgment (Acts 12:22-23). (See *Satan* and *Demonology*.)

Animals and Birds

1. Animals ◆ 2. Birds

1. *Animals*. There are a variety of animals mentioned in the Bible. Among the more common animals were sheep and goats, which often grazed through the rough hills of Israel. They were a good source of food—not just meat but also milk and cheese (see, for example, Exodus 23:19). The wool from sheep was often used to make clothing. Goat hair woven together was used to make tents. Both sheep and goats were sacrificed in the temple in Jerusalem (Genesis 22:8; Exodus 20:24). Jesus often compared His followers to sheep because sheep are intrinsically helpless creatures (John 10:1-16).

Shepherds in Old and New Testament times tried to keep sheep safe from wolves. Wolves were fierce hunters that sought to feed on sheep and other small animals (Jeremiah 5:6). In the New Testament, Jesus metaphorically spoke of evil leaders as wolves (Matthew 7:15).

Camels were often used by desert nomads. One reason for this is that camels can go for days without water. These "beasts of burden" were great for carrying people and heavy loads. Indeed, they can carry a load of some 400 pounds in addition to their rider. Camels are mentioned in the stories of Abraham and Job (see, for example, Genesis 12:16; Job 1:3).

Donkeys and mules were common pack animals often used to carry heavy loads (Numbers 22:21). Jesus rode into Jerusalem on Palm Sunday on a donkey (Matthew 21:1-11). The best animal for riding *without* a load was a horse. Horses were also used to pull chariots.

While the Bible does not speak often of bears, we read that bears attacked some youth who were mocking Elisha the prophet (2 Kings 2:24). Bears typically live in the hilly and wooded areas of Israel.

2. Birds. Birds were common in Israel too, including the vulture, eagle, sparrow, quail, dove, partridge, crow, pigeon, raven, crane, stork, and owl. Besides resident birds in Israel, other birds would pass through the land during the spring and autumn when migrating from one country to another.

Doves and pigeons are prominent in the Bible as these birds were used as sacrifices when people could not afford to purchase a sheep or goat. In the Old Testament, we read that a dove brought a green leaf to Noah after the flood, indicating there was dry land (Genesis 8:8-12). In the New Testament we read that the Holy Spirit descended upon Jesus like a dove (Matthew 3:16).

Owls are nighttime animals that sit silently waiting for prey to come along so they can swoop down and eat it. The Bible often portrays owls as being inhabitants of desolate and barren areas (Isaiah 34:10-15).

Sparrows, mentioned occasionally in the Bible, are small birds that could be cooked and eaten. In the New Testament Jesus emphasized the love of God by showing that He cares even for the sparrow. If God cares for the smallest of birds, certainly He will take care of human beings who are created in His image (Matthew 10:29-31; Luke 12:6-7).

Eagles are portrayed in the Bible as creatures of strength and vigor. For this reason, Isaiah promises that those who wait on the Lord will rise up with the strength of eagles (Isaiah 40:31; Psalm 103:5).

Ravens are black, flesh-eating birds. In Scripture, we read that following the Flood, Noah dispatched a raven to see if the land had dried yet (Genesis 8:7). We also read that ravens were used by God to provide food for Elijah during a famine (1 Kings 17:4).

All the animals and birds in the world were part of God's original creation (Genesis 1:24-25).

A

Antichrist—See *End Times.*

Apocrypha

1. The Case for the Apocrypha ◆ 2. The Case Against the Apocrypha

1. *The Case for the Apocrypha.* The Apocrypha refers to 14 or 15 books of doubtful authenticity and authority that were written between the time of the Old and New Testaments. These include Tobit, Judith, the Additions to Esther, the Additions to Daniel (the Prayer of Azariah and the Three Young Men, Susanna, and Bel and the Dragon), the Wisdom of Solomon, Ecclesiasticus (also called Sirach), Baruch (also called 1 Baruch), the Letter of Jeremiah, 1 Maccabees, and 2 Maccabees.

Roman Catholics decided these books belonged in the Bible sometime following the Protestant Reformation. The Catholic Council of Trent (A.D. 1545–1563) canonized these books. This canonization took place largely as a result of the Protestant Reformation. Martin Luther had criticized the Catholics for not having scriptural support for such doctrines as praying for the dead. By canonizing the Apocrypha, the Catholics obtained "scriptural" support for this and other distinctively Catholic doctrines (see 2 Maccabees 12:45-46).

Roman Catholics argue that the Septuagint (the Greek translation of the Hebrew Old Testament that predates Christ) contained the Apocrypha. As well, church fathers like Iraneaus, Tertullian, and Clement of Alexandria used the Apocryphal books in public worship and accepted them as Scripture. Further, it is argued, St. Augustine viewed these books as inspired.

2. *The Case Against the Apocrypha.* Protestants have responded by pointing out that no New Testament writer ever quoted from any of these books as Holy Scripture or gave them the slightest authority as inspired books (they *often* quoted from the Old Testament). Jesus and the disciples virtually ignored these books, something that would not have been the case if they had considered them to be inspired. Moreover, even though certain church fathers spoke approvingly of the Apocrypha, there were other early church fathers—notably Origin and Jerome—who denied their inspiration. Further, even though the early Augustine acknowledged the Apocrypha, in his later years he rejected these books as being outside the canon and considered them inferior to the Hebrew Scriptures.

The Jewish Council of Jamnia, which met in A.D. 90, rejected the Apocrypha as Scripture. In addition, there are clear historical errors in the Apocrypha, such as the assumption that Sennacherib was the son of Shalmaneser instead of Sargon II (see Tobit 1:15). Further, unlike many of the biblical books, there is no claim in any Apocryphal book in regard to divine inspiration. (See *Canon of Scripture*.)

Apostasy

The word "apostasy" comes from the Greek word *apostasia* and means "falling away" or "defection from the faith." In the New Testament, Judas Iscariot and his betrayal of Jesus for 30 pieces of silver is a classic example of apostasy and its effects (see Matthew 26:14-25,47-57; 27:3-10). The apostles often warned of the danger of apostasy (see, for example, Hebrews 6:4-8; 10:26-29).

Apostles

1. Identification ◆ 2. Agents of Revelation ◆
3. Foundation Builders ◆ 4. Unique

1. *Identification.* The apostles were chosen messengers of Jesus Christ, including specifically the 12 disciples Jesus sent out to spread the good news of the Gospel. "These are the names of the twelve apostles: first, Simon (who is called Peter) and his brother Andrew; James son of Zebedee, and his brother John; Philip and Bartholomew; Thomas and Matthew the tax collector; James son of Alphaeus, and Thaddaeus; Simon the Zealot and Judas Iscariot, who betrayed him" (Matthew 10:2-4). Once Judas Iscariot betrayed Christ and committed suicide, the number of apostles was brought back up to 12 when they chose Matthias (Acts 1:23-26). Paul and James (the brother of Jesus) were also considered apostles in the New Testament (1 Corinthians 1:1; Galatians 1:19).

2. Agents of Revelation. Just as the prophets were God's representatives in Old Testament times, so the apostles were God's representatives in New Testament times. They were specially handpicked by the Lord or the Holy Spirit (Matthew 10:1-4; Acts 1:26). They were the special recipients of God's self-revelation and were aware that God was providing revelation through them (1 Corinthians 2:13; 1 Thessalonians 2:13; 1 John 1:1-3). It is clear that they recognized their special divine authority (1 Corinthians 7:10; 11:23).

3. Foundation Builders. Ephesians 2:19-20 (NASB) refers to God's household as "having been built upon the foundation of the apostles and prophets," whom Christ had previously promised to guide into "all the truth" (John 16:13; see also 14:26; 15:27). It is particularly significant that God's household was founded on the apostles (Ephesians 2:20). Obviously, once a foundation is properly constructed, the foundation never needs to be laid again. A second foundation is out of the question.

4. Unique. Two key factors show the utter uniqueness of the apostles. First, they were all authenticated by miraculous signs. In Acts 2:43 we read that "everyone was filled with awe, and many wonders and miraculous signs were done by the apostles" (see also Acts 3:3-11; 5:12; 9:32-42; 20:6-12).

Second, the apostles (that is, the "Twelve") were granted an eternal place of honor. In the description of the New Jerusalem in Revelation 21, we read: "And the wall of the city had twelve foundation stones, and on them were the twelve names of the twelve apostles of the Lamb" (verse 14).

Scripture indicates there can be no apostles today. An apostle had to be an eyewitness of the resurrected Christ. When Paul was proving his apostleship in 1 Corinthians 9:1, he said, "Am I not an apostle? Have I not seen Jesus our Lord?" Later in the same book, Paul said that the resurrected Christ appeared to James, then all of the apostles, and finally to Paul himself (1 Corinthians 15:7-8). Obviously, no one living today can claim to have witnessed the resurrected Christ, and hence there can be no apostles. Further, as noted above, the church was built on the foundation of the apostles and prophets (Ephesians 2:20), and once a foundation is built, it does not need to be built again.

Archaeology

1. Significance ◆ 2. Uncovering Ancient Ruins ◆
3. Significant Discoveries

1. Significance. The word "archaeology" literally means "study of ancient things." Biblical archaeology, then, involves a study of ancient things related to biblical people, places, and events. Such studies prove to be very beneficial in better understanding the historical context of the Bible.

The Bible's accuracy and reliability have been proved and verified over and over again by archaeological finds produced by both Christian *and* non-Christian scholars and scientists. This includes verification for numerous customs, places, names, and events mentioned in the Bible.

2. Uncovering Ancient Ruins. Homes and buildings in ancient cities were generally constructed of bricks, which

A

could be easily knocked down by an enemy, a flood, or an earthquake. Whenever that happened, those who lived in the city would typically level the rubble and rebuild atop the old city, using more bricks. Then, over time, the process would repeat itself all over again. City would be built upon leveled city, on and on through history.

As this continued over time, the city eventually took on the appearance of a mound, for it had been rebuilt—layer upon layer—many times through the years. Archaeologists call these mounds "tells" (Arabic for "mounds"). Some of these tells could rise as high as 75 feet.

In the process of uncovering ancient cities, archaeologists excavate one layer at a time, with each layer representing a certain period of occupation. As archaeologists go through each successive layer, they steadily uncover the progressive history of the city.

3. Significant Discoveries. To date, over 25,000 sites in biblical lands have been discovered that date back to Old Testament times and have established the accuracy of innumerable details in the Bible.

A. *The Hittites.* For many years the existence of the Hittites, a powerful people who lived during the time of Abraham (Genesis 23:10-20), was questioned because no archaeological digs had uncovered anything about them. Critics claimed the Hittites were pure myth. But today the critics are silenced. Abundant archaeological evidence for the existence of the Hittites during the time of Abraham has been uncovered. One can even obtain a Doctorate in Hittite Studies from the University of Chicago.

B. *Handwriting During the Time of Moses.* It was once claimed that Moses could not have written the first five books of the Bible (Genesis, Exodus, Leviticus, Numbers, and Deuteronomy) because handwriting had not been invented yet. But archaeological discoveries of ancient inscriptions have silenced critics by now conclusively proving that there indeed was handwriting during the time of Moses.

22

C. *Sodom and Gomorrah.* Critics used to say that Genesis 10, 13, 14, 18, and 19 are full of myth because of a lack of evidence that Sodom and Gomorrah ever existed. But these critics have now been silenced in view of the abundant archaeological evidence for the existence of these cities.

D. *Floors of Ancient Homes.* It has now been discovered that many ancient floors in homes were cobbled. On such a floor, it would be quite easy for someone to lose a small object, such as a coin, between the stones on the floor. This archaeological discovery helps us to better understand Jesus' parable of the lost coin in Luke 15:8.

In view of such discoveries, we can conclude that archaeology is a true friend of the Bible. Archaeological discoveries have never controverted a biblical fact, but rather have always seved to support the veracity of the Bible.

Ark of the Covenant

The Ark of the Covenant was constructed from the wood of an acacia tree (which grows in the Sinai desert) and was coated with gold. It had rings at the four corners through which poles were inserted to make it easier to carry. It measured about 45 by 27 by 27 inches. It was built by a talented craftsman named Bezalel (Exodus 37:1).

In the Ark were placed the two stone tablets of the law written by the finger of God on Mount Sinai, which were a continual reminder of the covenant between God and Israel (Exodus 25:16,21). It also contained the pot of manna which symbolized the bread of God from heaven (Exodus 16:33; Hebrews 9:4). Aaron's rod was later placed in it as a witness to Israel of God's choice of the priesthood (Numbers 17:10).

Scripture indicates that the Ark symbolized God's presence (1 Samuel 4:3-22). It was kept in the Holy of Holies, the innermost shrine, of the tabernacle and the temple (Exodus 26:33).

The lid of the Ark held great significance. It was known as the Mercy Seat or Atonement Cover. On each annual Day of

Atonement, the high priest sprinkled the blood of a sacrificial animal on it to symbolize the nation's repentance for the sins committed the previous year. Israel's guilt was transferred to the animal (Leviticus 16:14-15).

Eventually, the Ark disappeared following the days of Jeremiah (Jeremiah 3:16). It may be that the Ark was destroyed when the Babylonians wrecked the temple in 586 B.C. Others believe the Ark has not been destroyed, but that it is hidden somewhere. Some suggest it may be hidden on Mount Nebo. Others suggest it may be hidden in a cave beneath Jerusalem. Many archaeologists—both Christian and non-Christian—have continued to search for its whereabouts.

Armageddon—See *End Times.*

Arms—See *Weaponry and Arms.*

Assyria

The Assyrians were a Semitic people who lived along the Tigris River in what is now the northern part of Iraq. Their language was quite close to that of the Babylonians. Archaeologists have discovered many clay tablets containing records of Assyrian administration, letters, and various legal documents. Such documents give us great insight into Assyrian culture.

Assyria was a prosperous nation by any measure. They enjoyed abundant crops of barley, wheat, grapes, olives, cherries, apricots, and a variety of other fruits. Hence, there was always plenty of food, except during times of widespread famine. Having built trade relationships with other nations, Assyria was able to generate significant wealth. This wealth was used for various building projects, including temples for their pagan gods and great palaces in major cities such as Nineveh and Asshur. Even the furniture within the palaces and temples was exuberant, involving engravings and sometimes gold plating.

Assyrians were pagans in their belief in many gods. Assyrian art often exalted the Assyrian gods, who were believed to be the key to military victory. The national god of Assyria was Asshur, the king of the gods. Asshur and various other deities were believed to control all natural phenomena, including the sun, the moon, and the weather. The patron god or goddess of each individual city was worshiped in a local temple. Assyrians also practiced divination, consulted astrologers, and engaged in other forms of occultism in seeking to predict the future.

A famous example of Assyria in the Bible relates to Jonah, a prophet of the northern kingdom, who was commanded by God to witness to the inhabitants of Nineveh, the capital of Assyria. Since the Assyrians had previously destroyed Israel (in 722 B.C.), Jonah resisted the idea of preaching to them and tried to run from God to get out of this assignment. But in God's providence, Jonah was brought back to Nineveh, where he preached, and the Ninevites repented (Jonah 1:17; 3:6 10; 4:1-3). Just a century later, however, the Ninevites were back in full swing with their idolatry, paganism, and brutality (see Nahum 3:1-4). The city was judged and destroyed by God in 612 B.C.

Astrology

1. Predictions Based on the Stars ◆ 2. Biblical Denunciation

1. *Predictions Based on the Stars.* Astrologers believe that man's evolution goes through progressive cycles corresponding to the signs of the zodiac. Each of these cycles allegedly lasts between 2000 and 2400 years. It is believed by astrologers that man is now moving from the Piscean Age (the

25

A

age of intellectual man) into the Aquarian Age (the age of spiritual man).

Astrology can be traced back to the religious practices of ancient Mesopotamia, Assyria, and Egypt. It is a form of divination—an attempt to seek paranormal counsel or knowledge by occultic means. It is believed that the study of the arrangement and movement of the stars can enable one to foretell events and determine whether they will be good or bad (see Daniel 1:20; 2:2,10,27; 4:7; 5:7,11).

2. Biblical Denunciation. In the Bible, we find a strong denunciation of astrologers and their craft. Isaiah 47:15 explicitly states that "each of them goes on in his error," and "there is not one that can save you." The book of Daniel confirms that astrologers lack true discernment, and that the only source of accurate revelation is God Almighty (Daniel 2:2,10).

It is noteworthy that there is no uniform zodiac constellation. Some astrologers of the past have claimed there are 24 zodiac signs, while others have counted 8, 10, or 14. This makes it impossible to interpret the stars in a uniform, objective way. Moreover, there is no uniform message behind the stars. The star-formed zodiac signs can be assigned whatever meaning the interpreter subjectively decides upon; the purported messages behind the signs are completely arbitrary.

Some astrologers have tried to claim that the story of the Magi seeing a star in the sky that led them to the house of the infant Jesus shows that the Bible supports astrology (Matthew 2:1-12). This is an incorrect interpretation. The star in this biblical account was to *announce* the birth of Christ, not to *foretell* this event. God gave the star to the Magi to proclaim to them that the divine child had already been born. We know the child was already born because, in Matthew 2:16, Herod gave a command to kill all the boys in Bethlehem and vicinity that were two years old or younger in accordance with "the time he had learned from the Magi."

A

The only sense in which the stars give revelation is that they reveal the existence of God in a general way. Psalm 19:1-6 affirms that the heavens declare God's glory, and Romans 1:18-20 teaches that creation reveals God's existence. Further, in relation to the end times, Christ indicates there will be cosmic disturbances in connection with His Second Coming (Matthew 24:29-30).

Atonement

1. Necessity ◆ 2. Nature ◆ 3. Benefits

1. Necessity. God did not just subjectively or arbitrarily decide to overlook man's dire sin or wink at his unrighteousness (Ecclesiastes 7:20; Romans 3:23; 5:18; 6:23; Colossians 1:21). Scripture says an atonement was necessary in order to make salvation possible. Jesus thus died on the cross for us. He died in our stead and paid for our sins. He ransomed us from death by His own death on the cross (2 Corinthians 5:21).

2. Nature. Jesus affirmed that it was for the very purpose of dying that He came into the world (John 12:27). Moreover, He perceived His death as being a sacrificial offering for the sins of humanity. He said His blood was "poured out for many for the forgiveness of sins" (Matthew 26:26-28). Jesus took His sacrificial mission with utmost seriousness, for He knew that without Him, humanity would certainly perish (Matthew 16:25; John 3:16) and spend eternity apart from God in a place of great suffering (Matthew 10:28; 11:23; 23:33; 25:41; Luke 16:22-28).

Jesus therefore described His mission this way: "The Son of Man did not come to be served, but to serve, and to give his life as a ransom for many" (Matthew 20:28). "The Son of Man came to seek and to save what was lost" (Luke 19:10).

"God did not send his Son into the world to condemn the world, but to save the world through him" (John 3:17).

In John 10, Jesus compared Himself to a good shepherd who not only gives His life to save the sheep (John 10:11) but lays His life down of His own accord (John 10:18). This is precisely what Jesus did at the cross: He laid His life down to atone for the sins of humanity.

Certainly this is how others perceived His mission. When Jesus began His three-year ministry and was walking toward John the Baptist at the Jordan River, John said: "Look, the Lamb of God, who takes away the sin of the world!" (John 1:29). John's portrayal of Christ as the Lamb of God is a graphic affirmation that Jesus Himself would be the sacrifice that would atone for the sins of humanity (see Isaiah 53:7).

3. Benefits. In Romans 3:25 we read that God presented Jesus as a "sacrifice of atonement." The Greek word for "sacrifice of atonement" is rendered more literally *propitiation*. This word communicates the idea that Jesus' sacrificial death on the cross provided full satisfaction of God's holy demands against a sinful people, thereby averting His just wrath against them (Romans 1:18; 2:5,8; 3:5). Because of this propitiation, we can freely and justly be "declared righteous" or saved (Romans 3:4,20,24,28).

Christ's work of atonement is marvelous indeed, for it makes possible the forgiveness of sins for all who trust in Him for salvation. Hebrews 10:17-18 says, "'Their sins and lawless acts I will remember no more.' And where these have been forgiven, there is no longer any sacrifice for sin." Ephesians 1:7 likewise says, "In him we have redemption through his blood, the forgiveness of sins, in accordance with the riches of God's grace" (see also Psalm 32:1-2; 103:11-12; Micah 7:19).

Baptism—See *Sacraments.*

Babylon

Babylon lay in the land of Shinar (Genesis 10:10). This influential civilization, ruled by kings and priests, was situated on the banks of the Euphrates River, a little over 50 miles south of modern Baghdad. Because of its ideal location, Babylon was an important commercial and trade center in the ancient world. It became a powerful kingdom under the leadership of Hammurabi (1792–1750 B.C.).

Archaeologists have discovered a variety of Babylonian documents. For example, Babylonian collections of wisdom literature include *Counsels of Wisdom* (ca. 1500–1000 B.C.), *Akkadian Proverbs* (ca. 1800–1600 B.C.), and *The Words of Ahiqar* (ca. 700–400 B.C.). Many of the proverbs contained in these works are secular in nature, and some are even quite crass in their moral tone.

Like other pagan nations of the Ancient Near East, the Babylonians believed in many false gods and goddesses. These gods were thought to control the entire world of nature, and so to be successful in life, one would do well to placate the gods. In Babylonian religion, the behavior of the gods was considered unpredictable at best.

Each city in Babylon had a patron god with an accompanying temple. There were also a number of small shrines scattered about each city where people often met to worship various other deities. The chief of the Babylonian gods was Anu, considered the king of heaven, while the patron god of Babylon was Marduk.

Belief in an afterlife permeated the thinking of the Babylonians. The dead were thought to live in the underworld and were sustained by offerings made by their living descendants.

B

If no offerings of food or drink were made by descendants, the ghosts of the dead would allegedly return to haunt them. Hence, there was strong motivation to make such offerings.

The Babylonians were well known for their practice of divination. For example, astrologers in Babylon would observe the movements of the stars to obtain information about the will of the gods (see Daniel 1:20; 2:2,10,27; 4:7; 5:7,11,15). Modern astrology is largely rooted in the religious practices of the ancient Babylonians.

Babylon is often represented in Scripture as being arrayed against God and His people (2 Kings 24:10). In 597 B.C., for example, some 3000 Jews went into exile in Babylon by Nebuchadnezzar. Jerusalem and the temple were obliterated (Lamentations 1:1-7). Though God sovereignly used Babylon as His powerful whipping rod in chastening Israel, Babylon was to be utterly destroyed by God's hand of judgment for its continual standing against His people (Isaiah 13:1-16).

Beatitudes

The word "beatitudes" comes from the Latin word *beatus,* which means "blessed." The word is an appropriate one to describe the eight blessings Jesus pronounced at the beginning of the Sermon on the Mount in Matthew 5:1-12, each beginning with "Blessed are..."

The word "blessed" literally means "happy," "fortunate," or "blissful." Blessing involves a divinely bestowed sense of well-being, which constitutes a little foretaste of heaven itself. In the beatitudes, then, Jesus depicts the means of a person attaining a divinely bestowed sense of well-being in daily life. True happiness is found in following Jesus' wisdom.

The actual literary form of the beatitudes is rooted in wisdom literature, especially the Psalms. Indeed, in the Psalms one often finds the words, "Blessed are..." (see, for example, Psalm 2:12; 65:4; 84:4-5; 89:15; 106:3; 119:1).

Behavior—See *Ethics and Behavior.*

Betrothal—See *Marriage.*

Bible

1. Theme ◆ 2. Divisions ◆ 3. Inspiration ◆
4. Authority ◆ 5. Reliability

1. *Theme.* The Bible is not a single volume, but is rather an entire library of books, including letters, histories, poems, prayers, and other kinds of writing. These writings were penned by numerous different authors, living in different lands, in a variety of different circumstances. Yet, from Genesis to Revelation, the Bible tells one primary story of redemption. It is a thread that runs through the entire Bible. Though God deals with different people in each of the biblical books, in each case we read of God's interaction among them for the purpose of bringing redemption to them.

2. *Divisions.* Most fundamentally, the Bible divides into the Old Testament, written predominantly in Hebrew, and the New Testament, written in Greek. Beyond this, we can break the Bible down into a number of key divisions, as shown on page 32.

(For information on how we know which books belong in the Bible, see *Canon of Scripture.)*

3. *Inspiration.* The biblical Greek word for "inspired" literally means "God-breathed." Biblical inspiration may be defined as God's superintending of the human authors so that, using their own individual personalities—and even their writing styles—they composed and recorded without error His revelation to humankind in the words of the original autographs.

31

B

THE BIBLE
The Old Testament

Law	History	Poetry	Major Prophets	Minor Prophets
Genesis	Joshua	Job	Isaiah	Hosea
Exodus	Judges	Psalms	Jeremiah	Joel
Leviticus	Ruth	Proverbs	Lamentations	Amos
Numbers	1 and 2 Samuel	Ecclesiastes	Ezekiel	Obadiah
Deuteronomy	1 and 2 Kings	Song of Solomon	Daniel	Jonah
	1 and 2 Chronicles			Micah
	Ezra			Nahum
	Nehemiah			Habakkuk
	Esther			Zephaniah
				Haggai
				Zechariah
				Malachi

The New Testament

Gospels	History	Paul's Epistles	General Epistles	Apocalyptic
Matthew	Acts	Romans	Hebrews	Revelation
Mark		1 and 2 Corinthians	James	
Luke		Galatians	1 and 2 Peter	
John		Ephesians	1, 2, and 3 John	
		Philippians	Jude	
		Colossians		
		1 and 2 Thessalonians		
		1 and 2 Timothy		
		Titus		
		Philemon		

In other words, the original documents of the Bible were written by men, who, though permitted to exercise their own personalities and literary talents, wrote under the control and guidance of the Holy Spirit, the result being a perfect and errorless recording of the exact message God desired to give to man.

The writers of Scripture were thus not mere writing machines. God did not use them like keys on a typewriter to mechanically reproduce His message. Nor did He dictate the words, page by page. The biblical evidence shows that each writer had a style of his own. (Isaiah had a powerful literary style; Jeremiah had a mournful tone; Luke's style had medical overtones; and John was very simple in his approach.) The Holy Spirit infallibly worked through each of these writers, through their individual styles, to incrrantly communicate His message to humankind.

4. *Authority.* The Bible teaches that Scripture alone is the supreme and infallible authority for the church and the individual believer (2 Peter 1:21; 2 Timothy 3:16-17; 1 Corinthians 2:13; 1 Thessalonians 2:13). Certainly Jesus and the apostles often gave testimony to the absolute authority of the Bible as the Word of God. Jesus affirmed the Bible's divine inspiration (Matthew 22:43), its indestructibility (Matthew 5:17-18), its infallibility (John 10:35), its final authority (Matthew 4:4,7,10), its historicity (Matthew 12:40; 24:37), and its factual inerrancy (John 17:17; Matthew 22:29).

Scripture has final authority because it is a direct revelation from God and carries the very authority of God Himself (Galatians 1:12). What the Bible says, God says. The Scriptures are the final court of appeal on all doctrinal and moral matters. We need no other source, and indeed there *is* no other source that is authoritative and binding upon the Christian.

Jesus said, "Scripture cannot be broken" (John 10:35). He also said, "I tell you the truth, until heaven and earth disappear, not the smallest letter, not the least stroke of a pen, will by any means disappear from the Law until everything is

B

accomplished" (Matthew 5:18). He said, "It is easier for heaven and earth to disappear than for the least stroke of a pen to drop out of the Law" (Luke 16:17). Jesus appealed to Scripture in every matter under dispute. To the Sadducees He said, "You are in error because you do not know the Scriptures or the power of God" (Matthew 22:29). He told some Pharisees that they invalidated the Word of God by their tradition that had been handed down (Mark 7:13). To the devil, Jesus consistently responded, "It is written..." (Matthew 4:4-10). Following Jesus' lead, we must conclude that Scripture alone is our supreme and final authority.

5. *Reliability.* The Bible is not based on myth or hearsay. It is rather based on eyewitness testimony. John, who wrote the Gospel of John, said in his first epistle: "That which was from the beginning, which we have heard, which we have seen with our eyes, which we have looked at and our hands have touched—this we proclaim concerning the Word of life" (1 John 1:1). Peter, an eyewitness, wrote in one of his epistles: "We did not follow cleverly invented stories when we told you about the power and coming of our Lord Jesus Christ, but we were eyewitnesses of his majesty" (2 Peter 1:16). It is noteworthy that the Bible writers gave up their lives defending what they wrote, and no one gives up their lives in defense of a lie! Further, history and archaeology give a convincing stamp of approval to the reliability of the Bible. (See *Archaeology.*)

Bible Versions

1. Today's Versions ◆ 2. Ancient Versions

1. *Today's Versions.* Today we possess thousands of Greek and Hebrew manuscripts, which have been translated into numerous languages around the world. In English alone, there are many translations, including the King James

B

Version, the New King James Version, the New American Standard Bible, the New International Version, the New Revised Standard Version, and the New Living Translation.

Today's translators generally base their work on either "formal equivalence" or "dynamic equivalence." Formal equivalence advocates as literal a rendering of the original text as possible. The translator attempts to render the exact words (thus the word "formal"—"form for form," or "word for word"). The advantage to this type of translation is that it is excellent for serious Bible study. A disadvantage is that it can sometimes be harder to read. An example of this type of translation is the New American Standard Bible.

Dynamic equivalence advocates a more readable translation that does not provide an exact rendering of the text but rather focuses on communicating the *meaning* of the text. It is a "thought for thought" translation that seeks to produce the same dynamic impact upon modern readers as the original had upon its audience. The advantage to this type of translation is that it is easier to read. The disadvantage is that it might incorporate too much of the translator's personal interpretations (though unintended) and be less suitable for serious Bible study. An example of this type of translation is the New Living Translation.

A few modern Bibles are not translations at all, but rather are paraphrases. To paraphrase a statement is to say it in different (and simpler) words than the author used. It involves more literary license than does dynamic equivalence. The Living Bible is an example of a paraphrase.

2. Ancient Versions. In the third century B.C., the Jews produced a Greek translation of the Old Testament Scriptures for the Jews living in Alexandria, a Greek-speaking city. This translation was called the Septuagint, and was used for reading aloud in synagogues in Greek-speaking cities, including Corinth and many in Rome. Many of the Jews who grew up in these cities could no longer speak Hebrew, so a

B

translation in their native language of Greek became necessary.

Later, Christians produced a variety of translations in different languages so they could fulfill their assignment by
Jesus to make disciples of all nations (Matthew 28:18-20).
The Bible was translated into Latin between A.D. 150 and 220,
into Syriac in about A.D. 160, and into Coptic (an Egyptian
language) in the third century A.D. Translations into new
languages have continued ever since.

Blessing

To "bless" someone is to pronounce goodness or favor upon
them. In Scripture we find God blessing people, people
blessing other people, and people blessing God. Examples of
God blessing people abound in Scripture (for example, Genesis 1:22,28; 12:2; 22:17; 24:35; 32:29; Exodus 20:24; Job
42:12; Psalm 45:2). Examples of people blessing people are
well illustrated in several famous biblical personalities,
including Isaac (Genesis 27:26-40), Jacob (Genesis 49:1-28),
Moses (Deuteronomy 33:1-29), Joshua (Joshua 22:6-7), and
Jesus (Luke 24:50). Scripture indicates that human beings
bless God when they recognize and thank Him for His wonderful acts of mercy and grace in their lives (see Psalm 63:4
NASB; 103:1-2 NASB; 104:1 NASB; 145:1-2 NASB).

Building Houses—See *Houses and Tents.*

Burial—See *Crucifixion and Burial.*

Burnt Offering—See *Altar* and *Offerings.*

C

Calendar, Israel's

Most ancient calendars, including that of ancient Israel, were based on the farmer's year. These are the twelve months of Israel's calendar:

JEWISH MONTH	FARMING ACTIVITY	JEWISH FESTIVALS	OUR MONTH
Nisan	Flax harvested	Passover and Unleavened Bread	April
Iyyar	Flax and barley harvested		May
Sivan	Grain harvested	Harvest (Weeks, First Fruits, or Pentecost)	June
Tammuz	Vines tended		July
Ab	Summer fruit harvested		August
Elul	Grapes and olives harvested		September
Tishri	Grapes and olives harvested	Trumpets, Day of Atonement, Ingathering	October
Marchesvan	Plowing and planting		November
Kislev	Plowing and planting	Dedication (Hanakkuh)	December
Tebet	Plowing and planting		January
Shebat	Late planting		February
Adar	Late planting	Purim	March

Canaanites

C

The Canaanites were the inhabitants of Canaan (present-day Israel and Jordan) who first settled there in about 2000 B.C. and remained until ousted by the Israelites. Because they lived on the coast, it was inevitable that they would eventually become great traders. From Canaanite ports, such goods as oil, wine, and cedar wood were transported to other parts of the world, including Egypt, Greece, and Crete. They were a fairly advanced culture for the time.

Historical studies reveal that there were many skilled craftsmen in Canaan. Such skills came in handy in the many building projects of the Canaanites.

The religion of the Canaanites was polytheistic. Like other pagan nations, they believed that behind the world of nature were numerous gods and goddesses that controlled various events. El was considered the chief among the Canaanite deities. Likened to a bull in a herd of cows, the people referred to him as "father bull" and regarded him as creator. Asherah was the wife of El.

Chief among the 70 gods and goddesses that were considered offspring of El and Asherah was Hadad, more commonly known as Baal, meaning "lord." As reigning king of the gods, Baal controlled heaven and earth. As god of rain and storm, he was responsible for vegetation and fertility, and his blessing was critical to the Canaanites in obtaining good harvests. Anath, the goddess who loved war, was his sister as well as his spouse. In the ninth century B.C., Ashtoreth, or Astarte, goddess of the evening star, was worshiped as his wife. Mot, the god of death, was the chief enemy of Baal. Yomm, the god of the sea, was defeated by Baal. These and many other gods were part and parcel of the Canaanite pantheon.

The Canaanites often gave sacrifices to their gods—sometimes involving an animal, but at other times humans (Hosea 13:2). This, of course, was considered an abomination to God in Scripture (Deuteronomy 12:13).

Canon of Scripture

1. Definition ◆ 2. Emergence of the Canon ◆
3. Tests for Canonicity

1. *Definition.* The word "canon" comes from a Greek word that means "measuring stick." Over time, the word eventually came to be used metaphorically of books that were "measured" and thereby recognized as being God's Word. When we talk about the "canon of Scripture" today, we are referring to all the biblical books that collectively constitute God's Word.

2. *Emergence of the Canon.* Many books written during New Testament times were recognized as being the Word of God *at that time.* It is highly revealing that in 1 Timothy 5:18, the apostle Paul joined an Old Testament reference and a New Testament reference and called them both (collectively) "Scripture" (Deuteronomy 25:4 and Luke 10:7). It would not have been unusual in the context of first-century Judaism for an Old Testament passage to be called "Scripture." But for a New Testament book to be called "Scripture" so soon after it was written says volumes about Paul's view of the authority of contemporary New Testament books.

To be more specific, only three years had elapsed between the writing of the Gospel of Luke and the writing of 1 Timothy (Luke was written around A.D. 60; 1 Timothy was written around A.D. 63). Yet, despite this, Paul (himself a Jew—a "Hebrew of Hebrews") does not hesitate to place Luke on the same level of authority as the Old Testament book of Deuteronomy.

Further, the writings of the apostle Paul were recognized as Scripture by the apostle Peter (2 Peter 3:16). Paul, too, understood that his own writings were inspired by God and therefore authoritative (1 Corinthians 14:37; 1 Thessalonians 2:13). Paul, of course, wrote nearly half of the New Testament books.

3. Tests for Canonicity. When the church formally recognized which books belonged in the canon at the Council of Carthage in A.D. 397, there were five primary tests that were applied. Here they are, listed in question format:

C

A. *Was the book written or backed by a prophet or apostle of God?* The reasoning here is that the Word of God, which is inspired by the Spirit of God for the people of God, must be communicated through a man of God. Deuteronomy 18:18 informs us that only a prophet of God will speak the Word of God. Second Peter 1:20-21 assures us that Scripture is only written by men of God. In Galatians the apostle Paul argued support for the book of Galatians by appealing to the fact that he was an authorized messenger of God, an apostle.

B. *Is the book authoritative?* In other words, can it be said of this book as it was said of Jesus, "The people were amazed at his teaching, because he taught them as one who had authority, not as the teachers of the law" (Mark 1:22)? Put another way, does this book ring with the sense of, "Thus saith the Lord"?

C. *Does the book tell the truth about God as it is already known by previous revelation?* The Bereans searched the Old Testament Scriptures to see whether Paul's teaching was true (Acts 17:11). They knew that if Paul's teaching did not accord with the Old Testament canon, it could not be of God. Agreement with all earlier revelation is essential. Paul certainly recognized this, for he said to the Galatians: "But even if we or an angel from heaven should preach a gospel other than the one we preached to you, let him be eternally condemned!" (Galatians 1:8).

D. *Does the book give evidence of having the power of God?* The reasoning here is that any writing that does not exhibit the transforming power of God in the lives of its readers could not have come from God. Scripture says that the Word of God is "living and active" (Hebrews 4:12). Second Timothy 3:16 indicates that God's Word has a transforming effect. If the book in question did not have the power to change a life, then, it was reasoned, the book could not have come from God.

E. *Was the book accepted by the people of God?* In Old Testament times, Moses's scrolls were placed immediately into the Ark of the Covenant (Deuteronomy 31:24-26). Joshua's writings were added in the same fashion (Joshua 24:26). In the New Testament, Paul thanked the Thessalonians for receiving the apostle's message as the Word of God (1 Thessalonians 2:13). Paul's letters were circulated among the churches (Colossians 4:16; 1 Thessalonians 5:27). It is the norm that God's people—that is, the majority of them and not simply a faction—will initially receive God's Word as such.

Interestingly, some 30 years prior to the Council of Carthage, the great champion of orthodoxy, Athanasius (a bishop of Alexandria), wrote his *Paschal Letter* in A.D. 367 in which he listed all the books of our present New Testament canon and all the Old Testament books except Esther. It is true that he mentioned some of the apocryphal books such as the Wisdom of Solomon, the Wisdom of Sirach, Judith, and Tobit, but he said these are not to be included in the Canon, but rather were used for instruction purposes.

Captivity and Exile

In the book of Deuteronomy, God through Moses promised great blessings if the nation lived in obedience to the covenant. God also warned that if the nation disobeyed His commands, it would experience the punishments listed in the covenant—including exile from the land (Deuteronomy 28:15-68).

Old Testament history is replete with illustrations of how unfaithful Israel was to the covenant. The two most significant periods of exile for the Jewish people began with the fall of Israel to the Assyrians in 722 B.C. and the destruction of Judah by the Babylonians in 597–581 B.C. As God promised, disobedience brought exile to God's own people.

It is interesting to observe that the first chapter of Isaiah takes the form of a lawsuit against Judah. Judah was indicted by the Lord (through Isaiah) because of Judah's "breach of contract" in breaking the Sinai Covenant, which had been given to the nation at the time of the Exodus from

C

Egypt. In this courtroom scene, the Lord called upon heaven and earth to act as witnesses to the accusations leveled against the nation (Isaiah 1:2). The whole universe was to bear witness that God's judgments are just.

The Lord indicted Judah for rebelling against Him. It is noteworthy that the Hebrew word for "rebel" in Isaiah 1:2 was often used among the ancients in reference to a subordinate state's violation of a treaty with a sovereign nation. In Isaiah 1, the word points to Judah's blatant violation of God's covenant. Hence, Israel went into captivity.

In this case, the Babylonian captivity was God's means of chastening Judah. This punishment, of course, was intended as a corrective. Throughout both the Old and New Testaments, we find that God disciplines His children to purify them. Just as an earthly father disciplines his children, so God the Father disciplines His children to train and educate them (Hebrews 12:1-5).

Charity—See *Almsgiving and Charity.*

Children

In biblical times children were considered a gift from God (Psalm 127:3). The inability to have children was, by contrast, considered a disgrace (Luke 1:24-25; see also Genesis 16:1-2; 30:1). Jesus had a very high view of children and said that to such belongs the kingdom of God (Matthew 19:14).

Among the ancient Jews, having baby boys was especially coveted. There were several reasons for this. First, a boy would be needed to carry on the family name. Further, a boy would eventually be able to assist the father in the family trade, thereby contributing to the family income.

Scripture has a lot to say about good children versus wicked children. Good children are said to be pleasing to the Lord (Colossians 3:20), bring joy to a father (Proverbs 23:24), and typically live long (Ephesians 6:2-3). Wicked children, by contrast, despise and defy their parents (Deuteronomy 27:16; Micah 7:6), mistreat their parents (Exodus 21:15; Proverbs

19:26), curse their parents (Exodus 21:17; Proverbs 20:20; 30:11), are disobedient (Romans 1:30; 2 Timothy 3:2), foolish (Proverbs 10:1; 15:5), rebellious (Deuteronomy 21:18), and are shameful (Proverbs 17:2 NASB).

In view of such a contrast, the Bible strongly urges parents to discipline their children (Proverbs 13:24; 19:18; 29:17). Discipline is said to produce wisdom in the child (Proverbs 29:15). It is also said to drive away foolishness (Proverbs 22:15) and to save a child from death (Proverbs 23:14). Parents are to teach their children about God (Deuteronomy 11:19), about God's laws (Deuteronomy 4:10), and about the right path (Proverbs 22:6).

Chosen People

The Jews are God's "chosen people" (Exodus 19:4-6; Deuteronomy 7:6-8; Psalm 105:43), not only because the divine Messiah would be born a Jew (see Genesis 12:1-3; 2 Samuel 7:12-14; Matthew 1:1) but also because the Jews were chosen of God to share the one true God with all the nations of the earth—a light unto the Gentiles (Isaiah 42:6). Though the Jews have failed at this task (they did not even recognize the true Messiah), many Bible expositors believe the 144,000 Jews mentioned in Revelation 7 and 14 will, in the end times, finally fulfill the task to which the Jewish nation was called; they will indeed be a "light" unto the entire world, sharing the truth of Jesus Christ.

Christ—See Jesus Christ.

Christ, Ancient Errors About

1. Docetists ◆ 2. Ebionites ◆ 3. Arians ◆
4. Apollinarians ◆ 5. Nestorians ◆ 6. Eutychians

1. Docetists. There were a number of ancient heresies about the person of Jesus Christ. The Docetists, for example, believed in a form of dualism—the view that matter is evil and

43

C

spirit is good. Because of this, the incarnate Jesus could not have had a real material human body because that would involve a union of spirit and matter (good and evil). Jesus therefore must have had a phantomlike body—that is, He only had the appearance of flesh, without substance or reality. ("Docetism" comes from a Greek word, *dokeo*, meaning "to seem" or "to appear.")

2. *Ebionites*. The Ebionites denied the Virgin Birth and the deity of Jesus Christ. They said Jesus was a mere man, a prophet who was the son of Joseph and Mary. Jesus allegedly distinguished Himself by strict observance of the Jewish law, and was accordingly chosen to be the Messiah because of His legal piety. The consciousness that God had selected Him to be the Messiah came at His baptism, when the Holy Spirit came upon Him. Jesus' mission as the Messiah was not to save humankind but to call all humanity to obey the law.

3. *Arians*. According to Arius, the founder of Arianism, Jesus was created out of nothing before the world began and is thus not an eternal being. Arius reasoned that since Jesus was "begotten," He must have had a beginning. Arius did not believe Jesus possessed a truly divine nature (like the Father). Rather, Jesus was simply the first and greatest of all created beings. Jesus was allegedly brought into being by the Father so that the world might be created through Him.

4. *Apollinarians*. The Apollinarians believed in a trichotomous view of man—that is, man has a body, soul, and spirit. In their view, Jesus possessed a human body and soul, but not a human spirit (which Apollinarius considered to be the seat of sin in the human being). In place of a human spirit was the divine Logos or divine reason. Jesus was considered human because He possessed a human body and soul; He was considered divine because He possessed divine reason in place of the human spirit. This Logos or divine reason dominated the passive human body and soul.

Apparently, Apollinarius's interest was in securing the unity of the person of Jesus Christ without sacrificing His deity, and guarding the sinlessness of Christ. The big problem was that even though he believed in Christ's deity, he virtually denied the complete humanity of Christ. The Council of Constantinople rightly condemned this view in A.D. 581, for Jesus in the incarnation was 100 percent God and 100 percent man.

5. *Nestorians.* According to the Nestorians, Jesus was a Mediator consisting of two persons, not just two natures. Instead of two natures in one Person, the Nestorians placed two persons—the human and the divine—alongside each other with a mere moral and sympathetic union but without a real union. Nestorius believed that Christ suffered only in His humanity, not in His deity. Ultimately, Nestorius's teaching constituted a denial of a genuine incarnation.

6. *Eutychians.* The Eutychians taught that the human and divine in Christ merged to form a third composite nature. In their view, the human attributes of Christ were assimilated in the divine nature. This view says the divine nature was so modified and accommodated to the human nature that Christ was no longer truly divine. Likewise, the human nature was so modified and changed by assimilation to the divine nature that He was no longer truly human. The result of this teaching was that Christ was neither truly human nor divine.

(For the correct view, see *Jesus Christ.*)

Christians and Christianity

1. Christian ◆ 2. Christianity

1. *Christian.* The word "Christian" is used only three times in the New Testament, the most important of which is Acts 11:26 (see also Acts 26:28 and 1 Peter 4:16). In Acts 11:26,

C

we are told simply and straightforwardly, "The disciples were called Christians first at Antioch." This would have been around A.D. 42, about a decade after Christ died on the cross and resurrected from the dead.

Up until this time the followers of Jesus had been known among themselves by such terms as "brothers" (Acts 15:1,23), "disciples" (Acts 9:26), "believers" (Acts 5:14 NASB), and "saints" (Romans 8:27). But now, in Antioch, they were called Christians.

What does the term mean? The answer is found in the "ian" ending, for among the ancients this ending meant "belonging to the party of." "Herodians" belonged to the party of Herod. "Caesarians" belonged to the party of Caesar. "Christians" belonged to Christ. And Christians were loyal to Christ, just as the Herodians were loyal to Herod and Caesarians were loyal to Caesar (see Matthew 22:16; Mark 3:6; 12:13).

The significance of the name Christian was that these followers of Jesus were recognized as a distinct group. They were seen as distinct from Judaism and as distinct from all other religions of the ancient world. We might loosely translate the term Christian, "those belonging to Christ," "Christ-ones," or perhaps "Christ-people." They are ones who follow the Christ.

Those who have studied the culture of Antioch have noted that the Antiochans were well known for making fun of people. It may be that the early followers of Jesus were called "Christians" by local residents as a term of derision, an appellation of ridicule. Be that as it may, history reveals that by the second century Christians adopted the title as a badge of honor. They took pride (in a healthy way) in following Jesus. They had a genuine relationship with the living, resurrected Christ, and they were utterly faithful to Him, even in the face of death.

The fact that followers of Jesus were first called Christians in Antioch is highly significant. After all, this city was a mixture of Jews and Gentiles. People of both backgrounds in this city were followers of Jesus. And what brought these believers unity was not their race, culture, or language. Rather, what brought them unity was the fact that they had a common relationship with Jesus the Christ. Christianity crosses all cultural and ethnic boundaries.

2. Christianity. If a "Christian" is one who has a personal relationship with Jesus Christ, then "Christianity" is a collective group of people who all have personal relationships with Jesus Christ. This may sound simplistic, but from a biblical perspective, this is the proper starting point.

It should be noted that no instance is recorded in the New Testament of the early Christians referring to their collective movement as "Christianity," even though the term "Christian" was used with greater frequency as the movement grew in numbers. By the time of Augustine (A.D. 354–430), the term "Christianity" appears to have become a widespread appellation for the Christian movement.

Chronicles, 1 and 2

First and Second Chronicles were written by an unidentified author between 450 and 425 B.C. Originally, these were a single book, but they were divided around 200 B.C. when the Septuagint translators divided the long scroll into two books. (The Septuagint is a Greek translation of the Hebrew Old Testament that predates the time of Christ.)

These books draw most of their information from the books of Samuel and the books of Kings, covering the period from the time of the Judges to the time of the Exile. As was true in the previous books, 1 and 2 Chronicles emphasize that the nation is blessed by God when it is obedient to Him, but it is punished by Him when it is disobedient. While the material is essentially the same as in these other books, it is presented from the vantage point of Jewish exiles returning from Babylon to Jerusalem.

The problem for these returning exiles was that the future looked bleak, especially in contrast to Israel's glorious past (the David-Solomon years). On the one hand, they were glad

C

to be back in the Promised Land. On the other hand, they were grieved at the hurtful memories of what they had lost as a result of their ancestor's sins. It is in this context that the books of Chronicles become so meaningful, for they served to give hope to the Jews by reminding them of truths about God's promises to them, their land, their temple, their priesthood, and especially the fact that they were from the line of David and were therefore God's chosen people. These reminders were intended to encourage the Jews to remain faithful to God during difficult times. God's covenant with them was still in place, and their obedience would result in blessing.

Church

1. The Universal Church ◆ 2. Local Church Attendance

1. *The Universal Church.* The universal church may be defined as the ever-enlarging body of born-again believers who comprise the universal body of Christ, over which He reigns as Lord. Although the members of the church may differ in age, sex, race, wealth, social status, and ability, they are all joined together as one people (Galatians 3:28). All of them share in one Spirit and worship one Lord (Ephesians 4:3-6). This body is comprised of only believers in Christ. The way one becomes a member of this universal body is to simply place faith in Christ.

The word "church" is translated from the Greek word *ekklesia.* This Greek word comes from two smaller words. The first is *ek,* which means "out from among." The second is *klesia,* which means "to call." Combining the two words, *ekklesia* means "to call out from among." The church represents those whom God has called out from among the world and from all walks of life. All are welcome in Christ's church.

The church did not exist in Old Testament times. Indeed, Matthew 16:18 cites Jesus as saying that "I will build my church" (future tense). This indicates that at the moment He spoke these words, the church was not yet existent. This is consistent with the Old Testament, for there is no reference there to the "church." The church is clearly portrayed as distinct from Israel in such passages as 1 Corinthians 10:32, Romans 9:6, and Hebrews 12:22-24.

Scripture indicates that the church was born on the Day of Pentecost (see Acts 2; compare with 1:5; 11:15; 1 Corinthians 12:13). We are told in Ephesians 1:19-20 that the church is built on the foundation of Christ's resurrection, meaning that the church could not have existed in Old Testament times. The church is called a "new man" in Ephesians 2:15.

2. *Local Church Attendance.* Though there is one *universal* church, there are many *local* churches scattered all over the world (see, for example, 1 Corinthians 1:2; 1 Thessalonians 1:1). While most who attend a local church are believers, some unbelievers are inevitably present. Attending local churches is strongly urged in the New Testament. Hebrews 10:25 specially instructs us not to forsake "our own assembling together" (NASB).

The Christian life as described in Scripture is to be lived within the context of the family of God and not in isolation (Acts 2:42-47; Ephesians 3:14-15). Moreover, it is in attending church that we become equipped for the work of ministry (Ephesians 4:11-16). Further, it is within the context of attending church that we can receive the Lord's Supper (1 Corinthians 11:23-26). The Bible knows nothing of a "lone-ranger Christian." As the old proverb says, many logs together burn very brightly, but when a log falls off to the side, the embers quickly die out (see Ephesians 2:19-21; 1 Thessalonians 5:10-11; and 1 Peter 3:8).

Circumcision

C

"Circumcision" comes from the Greek word *peritome*, which means a "cutting around." The Old Testament ceremony of circumcision consisted of cutting away the foreskin of the male organ with a sharp knife or stone (Exodus 4:25; Joshua 5:2). The son's father usually performed the ritual, although any Israelite could do it (but never a Gentile).

After God made a covenant with Abraham (Genesis 15), He commanded that every male should be circumcised as a token of the covenant. Everyone not so circumcised was to be "cut off from his people" as having broken the covenant (Genesis 17:10-14).

Circumcision fell into disuse during the wilderness sojourn. However, upon entering Canaan, Joshua circumcised the generation that had been born in the wilderness (Joshua 5:3). The ritual secured to those subjected to it all the rights of the covenant and participation in all its material and spiritual benefits. Of course, the circumcised person was bound to fulfill all the covenant obligations.

Christ has freed us from the ritual requirements of the Old Testament law, including circumcision (Acts 15:5-19; Galatians 5:2). Christians are said to be circumcised *in Christ*—a putting off not of a body part, but of an entire "body of flesh" (Colossians 2:11 NASB).

Citizenship

National citizenship in Bible times provided rights and privileges for each and every citizen. While there are not many mentions of citizenship in the Bible, the few times it is mentioned indicate it was a valued thing. We are told in Scripture that the apostle Paul was a citizen of Rome (Acts 22:28). He appealed to his rights as a Roman citizen when he was beaten without a trial (see Acts 16:35-39). He got some fast results from this appeal.

The most important citizenship mentioned in the Bible is the Christian's citizenship in heaven. We are told in Ephesians 2:19 that "you are no longer foreigners and aliens, but fellow citizens with God's people and members of God's household." As "fellow citizens," Christians enjoy all the privileges of God's new people. They are united with all the saints of the past (see verse 18) as well as with contemporary Christians (see verses 21-22).

The apostle Paul exults that "our citizenship is in heaven" (Philippians 3:20). We may be earthly citizens too, but in terms of our ultimate destiny, we are pilgrims passing through, on our way to another country, another land, another city. And we behave ourselves here below as citizens of that city above.

Clean and Unclean

The ancient Jews believed there were a number of things that could quickly render a person unclean. For example, a woman was rendered ceremonially unclean during menstruation and following childbirth (Leviticus 12:2-5). Touching a dead animal rendered one unclean (Leviticus 11:24-40), as did touching any dead body (Numbers 19:11). A person with a skin infection was considered unclean (Leviticus 13:3). Sexual discharges rendered one unclean (Leviticus 15:2). The Samaritans of New Testament times were considered unclean because they were a mixed breed, with Israelite and Assyrian ancestry (see John 14:9).

Once a person was rendered unclean, he or she had to go through the purification rituals prescribed by the Mosaic Law. For example, one could go through a purification ritual for skin diseases (Leviticus 13–14), sexual discharges (Leviticus 15), or contact with a dead body (Numbers 19:11-22). Of course, Jesus taught that the true "unclean" part of the human being is the heart, and the only possible cleansing for this condition comes by following Him (Mark 7:14-23; John 15:3) and being reborn (John 3:1-5; Titus 3:5).

Climate in Palestine

C

In Palestine the summers are painfully hot and dry, whereas the winters are cool and wet. There is considerable diversity in temperature in the Palestine area due to the varied elevation and wind direction. Sometimes searing hot winds blow in from the south out of Arabia, and other times cool breezes can blow in from the Mediterranean Sea. During the winter months it is coolest in the Lebanon mountains and warmest near the oceans.

In terms of rainfall, there is generally more rain at the higher levels of the land than at sea level. Significant rain falls during the winter months, especially December and January. Some rain continues through March and April, while the dryer weather begins to set in. The summer months are generally very dry.

Despite the fact that there are some parts of Palestine that have little rain, a morning dew always moistens areas near the coast. This is caused by moisture that comes inland off the Mediterranean Sea, which then falls to the ground during the night as temperatures fall.

Clothing and Dress

1. Men's Clothing ◆ 2. Women's Clothing ◆
3. Footwear ◆ 4. Coats ◆ 5. Materials

1. _Men's Clothing._ Dress in ancient days generally involved inner and outer clothing. A man's undergarment (tunic) generally consisted of a piece of cloth with holes for the arms and head, generally made of wool, haircloth, linen, or sometimes leather. His outer clothing (mantle) consisted of a shirt made of wool or linen that went down to his calf. This basically amounted to what looked like a big sack with a slit in the middle for the head and holes on the sides for the arms. The shirt was then fastened around the waist with a belt or girdle.

This was generally a long strip of cloth folded in such a way that it could hold small items such as coins. If a man was involved in tedious or heavy work, he might "gird up the loins" by tucking his shirt into his belt (see 1 Kings 18:46 NASB). This made it much easier for him to maneuver and get around.

2. Women's Clothing. Women also wore inner and outer garments. The outer garment looked like a long shirt, but instead of going down to the calf, it went all the way down to the ankle. If a woman was working and, for example, was carrying vegetables or some other food item, she could lift up the hem of her garment and put the vegetables in it for easy transport.

3. Footwear. Sandals were the footwear of choice in Palestine (Isaiah 5:27; Mark 1:7). Poor people, however, often went barefoot. It was traditional for people to always remove their sandals before entering a person's home, or before eating (see John 13:5-6).

4. Coats. If there was cold weather, people wore coats or cloaks. Wealthier people often wore coats made from fine material, while the common people wore simple wool coats or cloaks. These were generally made from stitching two pieces of material together at the shoulder, wrapped around the body, with slits made in the sides for arms.

5. Materials. Most clothing in ancient Israel was made from flax (from the flax plant), goat hair, animal skins, and, most commonly, the wool of sheep. Later in Israel's history, imported cotton was used as well. After sheep were shorn of their wool, it was washed, cleaned, and spread out to be dried. Such wool was also often dyed so that colorful clothes could be made. Popular colors among the ancient Israelites included blue, purple, and scarlet. (Blue dye came from pomegranate plants, purple dye came from Mediterranean shellfish, and scarlet dye came from insects taken from oak trees.) This wool would be combed thoroughly and then spun into yarn. Clothes could then be woven from this yarn.

C

Coins—See *Money.*

Colossians

The epistle to the Colossians was written by the apostle Paul in A.D. 61. Colossae was about 100 miles east of Ephesus. While Paul had never been to the city, he had heard about the church there from his associate Epaphras (see Colossians 1:7-8). Some of the news he heard, however, bothered him, so he wrote this epistle to the Colossian believers while he was in prison.

One of the problems the Colossians had in their church was a tendency to mix Christianity with other philosophies and religions. Within the church were both Greeks and Jews, and it seems that some of them—especially the Jews—incorporated some of their Jewish and gnostic religious ideas into Christianity. This was unsettling to Paul. By holding on to Jewish food laws and festivals (Colossians 2:16), circumcision (2:11), mysticism (2:18), and an over-elevated view of angels (2:18), these Jewish Christians had brought distinctly un-Christian elements into the church. They were also ultimately teaching that without such ideas, Christianity was incomplete. Such an idea was heresy to Paul.

Paul answered such ideas by urging the Colossians not to let anyone judge them in regard to food laws, holy days, or festivals (Colossians 2:16). He noted that we have a spiritual circumcision in Christ and do not need a physical circumcision (2:11). He warned believers against the "idle notions" that can result from mysticism (2:18). And he strongly argued for the absolute supremacy of Jesus Christ over all things—including the world of angels. He did this by pointing out that it was Christ Himself who had created the angelic realm, and so He was to be worshiped, not the angels (Colossians 1:16; 2:18-19). Paul further argued that Jesus was the "firstborn" of creation, a biblical term indicating that Jesus was supreme and preeminent over all creation (1:15). This makes sense, for He who created the creation is surely supreme over it.

C

Commerce and Trade

1. Old Testament Times ◆ 2. New Testament Times

1. *Old Testament Times.* Early in Israel's history, international trade was limited because of its impractibility. After all, at that time there were no established corridors of transportation, either by land or by sea, so it was difficult to get around. In addition, there was not a whole lot to trade, so the lack of commerce is quite understandable.

In early biblical times, most families produced just enough food and clothing to meet their own immediate needs. There was little need to buy items from other merchants, and, in fact, most people had little or no money to make such purchases anyway.

Eventually, however, local trading began to take place at the gates of various cities. At these gates vendors would set up shop, selling such products as fruit, vegetables, pottery, clothing, and various other goods. Often items could be purchased by bartering instead of using money.

As Israelite civilization continued to mature and government became more effective, international trade developed. Much improved transportation was a great impetus. Solomon was probably the most successful Israelite king in opening up international trade agreements (see 1 Kings 5:10; 9:26-28; 10:22). Ahab and Jehoshaphat were also involved in international trade (1 Kings 20:34; 22:48).

In Old Testament times, Israel exported a variety of items, including but not limited to myrrh, wool, oil, fruit, nuts, honey, and cereal. Israel imported various items as well,

C

including metals like silver, copper, and lead, as well as dyed cloth, spices, ivory, precious stones, wood, and linen. Such trading greatly benefited Israel's economy.

2. New Testament Times. In New Testament times, the Jews continued to trade, and one of their most popular products was olive oil (Egypt purchased *huge* quantities). Salt mined from the Dead Sea was also a hot export item. Imports included foods (like cheese, salted fish, and apples), clothing materials (high-grade linen and silk), and a variety of other items. Lydia is mentioned in Acts 16:14 as a "dealer in purple cloth" who was from Thyatira in Asia Minor.

To ensure honest business, regulations on buying and selling were instituted. Market inspectors made sure that all the trade and commerce rules of each community were enforced.

An unfortunate development in Israel's "commerce" relates to temple worship. When people came to Jerusalem from various cities to offer sacrifices, they had to buy animals from vendors in order to sacrifice them. Sometimes families would bring their own animals, only to be told that they had impurities on them and were unacceptable for sacrifice. They were forced to purchase suitable ones in Jerusalem, often at exorbitant prices. Further, because people came to Jerusalem from various cities, their money had to be converted into local currency. People were charged extra money for this conversion. In this way, the temple turned into "big business." This is why Jesus was so offended and made a whip of cords, driving the money changers out of the temple (Matthew 21:12).

Confession—See *Prayer.*

Corinthians, 1 and 2

For the apostle Paul, Corinth was a strategic center in Greece. Important north-south and east-west trade routes intersected there. Its population included Romans, Egyptians,

56

Greeks, and Asians. A Gospel message proclaimed in Corinth was likely to find its way to the distant regions of the inhabited earth.

Corinth's moral character also made it a fertile field for the Gospel. The city contained the Temple of Aphrodite, the Greek goddess of love, where 1000 sacred prostitutes (priestesses) were made available to its cultists. This led to sexual debauchery all over the city. The Greek word *korinthiazomai*, meaning literally "to act the Corinthian," came to mean "to practice fornication." Truly, Corinth was a city noted for everything depraved, dissolute, and debauched.

Paul had done missionary work in Corinth for 18 months during A.D. 50–51 (see Acts 18) and had moved on to Ephesus when he received notice that there were problems in Corinth. There were divisions in the church (1 Corinthians 1–4), and there were questions about morality, Christians and litigation, sex within marriage, food sacrificed to idols, payment for those involved in ministry, distinctive ministries of men and women, the Lord's Supper, charismatic gifts, and the resurrection from the dead (5–11). Hence, these believers were in need of detailed instruction, and Paul provided that instruction in 1 Corinthians, which he wrote in A.D. 55.

Paul wrote his second epistle to the Corinthians in A.D. 56 to defend his ministry and his God-given authority as an apostle of God. Apparently, false prophets had penetrated the Corinthian church and had assaulted Paul's character and authority. Some of the Corinthians had apparently believed their lies and rebelled against Paul. These false teachers were leading the people astray, and unless Paul acted decisively, the entire church might become engulfed in demonic doctrines.

Paul thus intervened and made a "painful visit" to them (2 Corinthians 2:1). He followed up this visit with a "severe letter" (no longer in our possession, 2:4). Later, Titus was able to pass on news to Paul that the majority of Corinthian believers had repented of their rebellion against him (7:7). Grieved at past strained relations, Paul, in his second epistle

C

to the Corinthians, sought to clarify his ministry and his calling and authority as an apostle. He also sought to bring unity to the church. It is clear from what he wrote that he had a strong love for the Corinthian believers. He sought to see them grow spiritually.

Cosmetics—See *Jewelry and Cosmetics.*

Covenants

1. Biblical Covenants ◆ 2. Abrahamic Covenant ◆ 3. Davidic Covenant ◆ 4. Sinai Covenant ◆ 5. New Covenant

1. *Biblical Covenants.* A covenant is simply an agreement between two parties. Covenants were used among the ancients in the form of treaties or alliances between nations (1 Samuel 11:1); treaties between individual people (Genesis 21:27); friendship pacts (1 Samuel 18:3-4); and agreements between God and His people.

In the Bible, God made specific covenant promises to a number of people, including Noah (Genesis 9:8-17), Abraham (Genesis 15; 17:1-14), the Israelites at Mount Sinai (Exodus 19:5-6), David (2 Samuel 7:13; 23:5), and God's people in the new covenant (Hebrews 8:6-13). God is a God of promises.

2. *Abrahamic Covenant.* A very famous covenant is God's covenant with Abraham (Genesis 12:1-3; 15:18-21), which was later reaffirmed with Isaac (17:21) and Jacob (35:10-12). In this covenant, God promised to make Abraham's descendants His own special people. More specifically, God promised Abraham:

- I will make you a great nation.

- I will bless you.

- I will make your name great.

- You will be a blessing.

- I will bless those who bless you.

C

- I will curse those who curse you.

- All peoples on earth will be blessed through you.

These covenant promises were "unconditional" in nature. As a backdrop, there were two kinds of covenants in biblical days: conditional and unconditional. A conditional covenant is a covenant with an "if " attached. This type of covenant demanded that the people meet certain obligations or conditions before God was obligated to fulfill His promise. If God's people failed in meeting the conditions, God was not obligated in any way to fulfill the promise.

As opposed to this, an unconditional covenant depended on no such conditions for its fulfillment. There were no "ifs" attached. That which was promised was sovereignly given to the recipient of the covenant apart from any merit (or lack thereof) on the part of the recipient. The covenant God made with Abraham was unconditional in nature.

3. Davidic Covenant. God later made a covenant with David in which He promised that one of his descendents would rule forever (2 Samuel 7:12-16; 22:51). This is another example of an unconditional covenant. It did not depend on David in any way for its fulfillment. David realized this when he received the promise from God, and he responded with an attitude of humility and a recognition of God's sovereignty over the affairs of men. This covenant finds its ultimate fulfillment in Jesus Christ, who was born from the line of David (Matthew 1:1).

4. Sinai Covenant. God's covenant with Israel at Mount Sinai, following Israel's sojourn through the wilderness after being delivered from Egypt, constituted the formal basis of the redemptive relationship between God and the Israelites (Exodus 19:3-6). It is fascinating to observe that this covenant was couched in terms of ancient Hittite suzerainty treaties made between a king and his subjects. In such treaties, there would always be a preamble naming the author of the treaty, a historical introduction depicting the relationship between the respective parties, a list of required stipulations explaining the responsibilities of each of the parties, a promise of blessing and warning of judgment based on faithfulness or unfaithfulness to the treaty, a solemn oath, and a ritual of ratification of the treaty. In such treaties, the motivation for obedience to the stipulations was the undeserved favor of the king making the treaty. Out of gratitude, the people were to obey the stipulations.

Such parallels between ancient treaties and God's covenant with Israel show that God communicated to His people in ways they were familiar with. Key parallels between such treaties and the Sinai Covenant are that God gave stipulations to the people explaining their responsibilities (the law, Exodus 20:1-17), a promise of blessing for obeying the law, and a warning of judgment for disobeying the law (see Exodus 19:8; 24:3,7). Sadly, Israel was often disobedient to God's covenant (Exodus 32; Jeremiah 31:32). In this covenant, blessing was conditioned on obedience.

5. *New Covenant.* The new covenant is an unconditional covenant God has made with humankind in which He has promised to forgive sin because of the sacrificial death and resurrection of Jesus Christ (Jeremiah 31:31-34; 2 Corinthians 5:21). Under the old covenant, worshipers never enjoyed a sense of total forgiveness. Under the new covenant, however, Christ our High Priest has made provisions for such forgiveness. When Jesus ate the Passover meal with the disciples in the Upper Room, He spoke of the cup as "the new covenant in my blood" (Luke 22:20; see also 1 Corinthians 11:25). Jesus has done all that is necessary for the forgiveness of sins by His once-for-all sacrifice on the cross. This new covenant is the basis for our relationship with God in the New Testament.

Crafts and Trades

C

1. *Few Skilled Craft Workers*. There were few skilled craft workers in Old Testament times. The reason for this is that the people were poor, and most of the time they were busy just taking care of their daily needs—food, clothing, and shelter. Little time was left over for the development of craft skills. As time passed, however, society became more settled, more and more families lived near each other, and people came to depend on each other for specialized services. Crafts and trades emerged as a means of benefiting all of society.

2. *Fishing*. Fishing became a thriving industry, especially in New Testament times (Mark 1:16). The Sea of Galilee was brimming with fishermen making a good living. Often members of an entire family would be involved in the fishing business.

One particularly effective means of fishing utilized a large net, known as a dragnet, which had floats on top and weights to drag it to the bottom. This effectively meant that as the boat moved, the net moved through the water and was used to bring fish to the boat or perhaps to the shallow water where the fish could then be captured.

3. *Leather Working*. Leather working was another popular trade (Acts 10:6). Obviously a number of clothing items utilize leather, such as footwear (sandals), belts, and pouches. Further, animal skins were sewn together in order to hold wine, water, or other liquids. Leather was also used in making shields for the army.

C

4. Pottery. Pottery became an increasingly popular trade among many people (Isaiah 41:25; Jeremiah 18:1-6). Red clay was in plentiful supply in Palestine, so materials were readily available.

There were a number of ways that potters molded the clay. A widespread method was simply to press the clay into a mold. This was a common way of making lamps in New Testament times. Other potters were skilled enough to mold the clay freehand. But perhaps the most popular means of shaping clay was placing it on a wheel. The potter's wheel was simply a disk that rotated on a vertical shaft.

A common item produced by pottery was the bowl, both large and small. After the bowl or pot was made, it would be fired in a kiln where it would be hardened. In order for the pot or bowl to withstand heat, limestone would sometimes be ground and mixed into the red clay.

In learning this trade, an apprentice potter would generally work with a professional potter for a time until the necessary skills were obtained.

5. Other Crafts and Trades. There are a variety of other crafts and trades evident in the Bible. For example, there were shipbuilders (1 Kings 9:26-27), bakers (Genesis 40:2), stoneworkers (1 Kings 5:15-16), cupbearers (1 Kings 10:5), merchants (Ezekiel 17:4), heralds (Daniel 3:4), bankers (Matthew 25:27), cooks (1 Samuel 8:13), brickmakers (Genesis 11:3), builders (Exodus 1:11), watchmen (2 Samuel 18:24), professional mourners (Matthew 9:23), embalmers (Genesis 50:26), shepherds (Genesis 13:7), farmers (Isaiah 28:24), hunters (Genesis 27:3), basketmakers (Acts 9:25), innkeepers (Luke 2:7), servants (Joel 2:29), barbers (Ezekiel 5:1), midwives (Genesis 35:17), secretaries (Jeremiah 36:26), tentmakers (Acts 18:2-3), and woodworkers (1 Kings 5:6). All of these served to enhance life in Israel.

Creation

1. God Is the Creator ◆ 2. Divine Revelation ◆
3. Means ◆ 4. Evolution

1. *God Is the Creator.* God said in Isaiah 44:24 (NASB): "I, the Lord [Yahweh], am the maker of all things, stretching out the heavens by Myself, and spreading out the earth all alone." Clearly, God is the sole Creator of the universe.

Many Old Testament references to the Creation attribute it simply to God rather than to the individual persons of the Father, Son, or Holy Spirit (for example, Genesis 1:1; Psalm 96:5; Isaiah 37:16; 44:24; 45:12; Jeremiah 10:11-12). Other passages relate the Creation specifically to the Father (1 Corinthians 8:6), to the Son (John 1:3; Colossians 1:16; Hebrews 1:2;), or to the Holy Spirit (Job 26:13 KJV; 33:4; Psalm 104:30; Isaiah 40:12-13 NASB).

How do we put all these passages together into a coherent whole? It has been suggested that creation is "from" the Father, "through" the Son, and "by" the Holy Spirit. A passage that has bearing on this issue is 1 Corinthians 8:6, which describes the Father as the One "*from* whom all things came" and the Son as the One "*through* whom all things came."

Based on this, many have concluded that while the Father may be considered Creator in a broad, general sense, the Son is the agent or mediating Cause of creation. Through the Son, all things came into being. Creation is said to be "in" or "by" the Holy Spirit in the sense that the life of creation is found in the Holy Spirit.

2. *Divine Revelation.* Since obviously there were no human spectators to the Creation, and since the first man and woman were placed in an already existing universe, we must accept whatever God has revealed about the Creation by faith. Otherwise we will know nothing with certainty about the origin of the universe. Hebrews 11:3 tells us, "By faith we

C

understand that the universe was formed at God's command, so that what is seen was not made out of what was visible." Even if a human observer had been present at the Creation, he could not have understood fully what he saw apart from God's own interpretation. Therefore, divine revelation is a necessity for those truly desiring to understand the origin of the universe.

3. Means. God created the universe *ex nihilo* (out of nothing) in an instantaneous fashion. Psalm 33 tells us, "By the word of the Lord were the heavens made, their starry host by the breath of his mouth" (verses 6,9; see also Genesis 1:3,6,9,14,20,24). Hebrews 11:3 likewise tells us "the universe was formed at God's command." When God said, "Let there be light" (Genesis 1:3), at one moment there was no light, and the next moment there was!

4. Evolution. Though many today believe in evolution instead of creation, there are many problems with the evolutionary hypothesis:

A. Scientists by and large agree that the universe had a beginning. They may disagree as to *how* that beginning happened, but they largely agree there was a beginning. The fact that there was a beginning implies the existence of a *Beginner*—a Creator. As Scripture says, "Every house is built by someone, but God is the builder of everything" (Hebrews 3:4).

B. By observing the universe around us, it becomes apparent that a Designer was involved. Everything is just perfect for life on earth—so perfect and so "fine tuned" that it gives every evidence of coming from the hands of an intelligent Designer (God). The earth's size, composition, distance from the sun, rotational period, and many other factors are all just right for life. The chances of there being even one planet where all of these factors converge by accident are almost nonexistent.

C. As one examines the fossil records, one not only finds no evidence supporting evolution, one finds evidence against it. If evolution were true, one would expect to see in the fossil records progressively complex evolutionary forms, indicating transitions that took place. But there is no such evidence. No transitional (species to different species) links have been discovered in the fossil records.

D. The theory of evolution assumes a long series of positive and upward mutations. In almost all known cases, however, mutations are not beneficial but are harmful to living beings, and often end up in death. Deformities typically lessen the survival potential of an animal, not strengthen it. Even if there were a few good mutations that took place, the incredible number of damaging mutations would utterly overwhelm the good ones.

E. The first and second laws of thermodynamics are foundational to science and have never been contradicted in observable nature. The first law says that matter and energy are not created nor destroyed; they just change forms. The second law says that in an isolated system (like our universe), the natural course of things is to degenerate. The universe is running down, not evolving upward.

F. False claims are often made by evolutionists. Some have claimed that there is scientific evidence that evolution is true. These individuals generally appeal to the fact that mutations *within* species is a proven scientific fact *(microevolution)*. But it requires an incredible leap of logic to say that mutations within species prove mutations or transformations into entirely new species *(macroevolution)*. You cannot breed two dogs and get a cat!

Creeds

1. Statements of Orthodoxy ◆ 2. Nicene ◆ 3. Athanasian ◆ 4. Chalcedonian ◆ 5. Westminster ◆ 6. Man-Made Documents

1. *Statements of Orthodoxy.* Throughout church history, a number of important creeds—formal, authoritative statements of belief based on Holy Scripture—have been formulated as

C

statements of orthodoxy. The word "creed" derives from the Latin word *credo*, which means "I believe." Among the more important creeds are the Nicene Creed, the Athanasian Creed, the Chalcedonian Creed, and the Westminster Confession of Faith.

2. Nicene. The Council of Nicea convened in A.D. 325 to settle a dispute regarding the nature of Christ. Arius, a presbyter of Alexandria who was the founder of Arianism, argued that the Son was created from the nonexistent and was of a different substance than the Father. There was a time, Arius argued, when the Son was not. But Christ was the highest of all created beings.

Athanasius of Alexandria, the champion of orthodoxy, stressed the oneness of God while maintaining three distinct persons within the Godhead. He maintained that the Son was the same substance as the Father (and therefore fully divine). Athanasius argued for the eternally personal existence of the Son. After considerable debate, Athanasius won out and Christ was recognized by the council as equal with the Father as an uncreated Being. The Nicene Creed thus affirms belief that Jesus Christ was "begotten, not made, being of one substance [essence] with the Father; by whom all things were made."

3. Athanasian. The Athanasian Creed is essentially an amplification of the Nicene Creed. It came to be generally adopted among the Western churches. This creed contains the words: "We worship one God in trinity, and trinity in unity, neither confounding the persons nor dividing the substance. For the person of the Father is one; of the Son, another; of the Holy Spirit, another. But the divinity of the Father and of the Son and of the Holy Spirit is one, the glory equal, the majesty equal."

4. Chalcedonian. Eutichus, the founder of Eutichianism, argued that Christ's human and divine natures merged to form a third composite nature. In this view, the human attributes of Christ were assimilated into the divine nature. The result of this teaching was that Christ was neither truly human nor divine.

C

The Council of Chalcedon condemned this view in A.D. 451. The Chalcedonian Creed affirms that Jesus in the Incarnation was "perfect in Godhead and also perfect in manhood; truly God and truly man." Christ is "to be acknowledged in two natures, inconfusedly, unchangeably, indivisibly, inseparably; the distinction of natures being by no means taken away by the union, but rather the property of each nature being preserved, and concurring in one Person."

5. *Westminster.* The Westminster Confession arose out of the stormy political scene in England during the reign of Charles I. The short story is that in 1643 the English parliament commissioned the Westminster Assembly to develop the creed of the Church of England. The confession was written by 121 English Puritan ministers and was completed in 1646 after over a thousand sessions. The creed is strongly Calvinistic. It affirms that "there is but one only living and true God, who is infinite in being and perfection, a most pure spirit, invisible, without body, parts, or passions, immutable, immense, eternal, incomprehensible, almighty, most wise, most holy, most free, most absolute, working all things according to the counsel of His own immutable and most righteous will, for His own glory."

6. *Man-Made Documents.* The above creeds, and all other creeds, are man-made documents. None of them is inspired as Scripture is inspired. Neither are they authoritative as Scripture is authoritative. Creeds are merely statements of faith that are true insofar as they accurately reflect what Scripture teaches. They are helpful "measuring sticks" for orthodoxy.

Crime and Punishment

C

Crimes were committed and punishments were administered in Bible times just as they are today. If one committed a criminal act, then one suffered the appropriate punishment.

Both murder and adultery carried the death penalty in ancient Israel (see Numbers 35:16,18,21,31; Leviticus 20:10; 24:17). Other crimes that were punishable by death include striking a parent (Exodus 21:15,17), breaking the Sabbath (Exodus 31:14; 35:2; Numbers 15:32-36), rape (Deuteronomy 22:25), incest (Exodus 22:19; Leviticus 20:11,14,16), blasphemy against God (Leviticus 24:14,16,23), witchcraft (Exodus 22:18; Leviticus 20:27; Deuteronomy 13:5; 18:20), and idolatry (Leviticus 20:2; Deuteronomy 13:6-18; 17:2-7). The Mosaic Law also stipulated that it was lawful to kill a burglar taken at night in the act, but unlawful to do so after sunrise (Exodus 22:2-3). Two witnesses were always required in any capital punishment case (Numbers 35:19-30; Deuteronomy 17:6-12).

Capital punishment was often by stoning (Exodus 17:4; Acts 14:5). On other occasions it was by burning (Leviticus 21:9) or being pierced by a sword (Exodus 19:13; 32:27; Numbers 25:7).

Lesser crimes, such as destruction of property, brought lesser forms of punishment. These include simple compensation for lost time or property (Exodus 21:18-36; Leviticus 24:18-21; Deuteronomy 19:21), being scourged with thorns (Judges 8:16), being whipped (Deuteronomy 25:3; 2 Corinthians 11:24), being mutilated (Judges 1:6), and having one's hair plucked out (Isaiah 50:6). Such punishment in biblical times served as a deterrent to crime.

Criticism, Biblical

There are a variety of forms of biblical criticism, including textual criticism, source criticism, form criticism, tradition criticism, and redaction criticism.

A. *Textual criticism* seeks to uncover the most reliable Hebrew and Greek manuscripts for the Old and New Testaments. The problem is that none of the original autographs penned by the original writers have survived. All we have are manuscript copies. By comparing the manuscripts with each other, scholars can classify them into groups or families that exhibit common characteristics. An attempt is then made to determine their age and what gave rise to those distinct characteristics. The ultimate goal is to examine all the families of manuscripts with a view to discovering the original wording of the original autograph.

B. *Source criticism* seeks to discover the sources that lay behind the biblical text. Since the Gospels were written 30 or more years after the time of Jesus, source criticism seeks to find pre-Gospel sources closer to His time. It is clear that such biblical books as Luke and Acts used earlier sources. Luke even acknowledged that "many have undertaken to draw up an account of the things that have been fulfilled among us" (Luke 1:1). Source criticism seeks to uncover information about such sources.

C. *Form criticism* investigates the "form" or genre of individual units of text—parables, miracle stories, legal sayings, discourses, and so forth—that are a part of the larger biblical text. Form criticism also seeks to investigate the influence of the "setting in life" (its place in the community) on such forms.

D. *Tradition criticism* studies how biblical themes and stories were passed from one generation to another. The word "tradition" refers to "that which is passed down." Generally, traditions were passed down orally for a time before they were written down.

E. *Redaction criticism*, popular among liberal theologians, focuses on how the biblical text was allegedly edited or "redacted" into its final shape. The theory here is that the Gospel writers were essentially compilers of earlier traditions who edited their Gospels according to their particular purpose or theology.

Crucifixion and Burial

C

1. Prediction ◆ 2. The Act of Crucifixion ◆ 3. Symptoms ◆ 4. Burial

1. *Prediction.* Jesus was prophesied to be executed by crucifixion several centuries before crucifixion was even used by the Romans as a means of execution (see Psalm 22:14-18; 34:20; 69:21; Isaiah 53:5,12; Zechariah 12:10). Crucifixion was considered a horrible and degrading way to be put to death.

2. *The Act of Crucifixion.* According to Scripture, Jesus was beaten and scourged beyond recognition; He was forced to carry His crossbeam to the place of execution (which He was not able to complete by Himself); He was stripped of His clothing; huge spikes were then driven through His wrists by the blow of a heavy mallet; immediately after, with one foot placed over the other, another huge spike tore its way through the quivering flesh into the wood beneath; and the cross, with the body attached by spikes, was then heaved up and firmly put into a hole in the ground (Matthew 27:35-50; Mark 15:23-37; Luke 23:33-46; John 19:18-30).

3. *Symptoms.* Jesus would have experienced a variety of horrible symptoms upon the cross, including (but not limited to) blood loss and the accompanying dizziness, extreme pain, growing infection at the wounds caused by the spikes, fever due to the infection, great thirst and hunger as time slowly passed, difficulty breathing as a result of hanging by the arms, deep shame as those below watched the horror, and an ever-present anticipation of the moment of death. Scripture tells us that at one point, a Roman soldier thrust a spear into Jesus' side so that blood and water came out, thus confirming Jesus' death (John 19:34). Once He died, four Roman executioners pronounced Him dead, and He was taken to be buried.

4. *Burial.* Following His crucifixion, the body of Jesus was buried in accordance with Jewish burial customs. He was wrapped in a linen cloth. Then, about 75 pounds of aromatic spices—mixed together to form a gummy substance—were applied to the wrappings of cloth around His body.

After His body was placed in a solid rock tomb, an extremely large stone was rolled against the entrance by means of levers. This stone would have weighed somewhere around two tons (4000 pounds). It is not a stone that would have been easily moved by human beings.

Roman guards were then stationed at the tomb. These strictly disciplined men were highly motivated to succeed in all they were assigned by the Roman government. Fear of cruel punishment produced flawless attention to duty, especially in the night watches. These Roman guards would have affixed on the tomb the Roman seal, a stamp representing Roman power and authority.

Of course, all this makes the situation at the tomb following Christ's resurrection highly significant. The Roman seal was broken, which meant automatic crucifixion upside-down for the person responsible. Furthermore, the large stone was moved a good distance from the entrance as if it had been picked up and carried away. The Roman guards had also fled. The penalty in Rome for a guard leaving his position was death. We can therefore assume that they must have had a substantial reason for fleeing!

D

Daniel, Book of

1. *Apocalyptic Literature.* Like the book of Revelation, the book of Daniel is known as apocalyptic literature. It contains Bible prophecy of the end times. One critically important reference involves the "seventieth week of Daniel" (Daniel 9:24-27), which speaks of the future Tribulation period that precedes the Second Coming of Christ (see *End Times* for an explanation of this). The book was written by Daniel in about 537 B.C.

Daniel was a Jewish youth who had been deported to Babylon along with many other Jews in exile as a result of Nebuchadnezzar's siege of Jerusalem in 605 B.C. In Babylon Daniel rose to a position of prominence because of his commitment to God and the skills God had given him.

There is a great deal of hope in Daniel's writing. Even though God's people were presently suffering great persecution in their exile in Babylon, God was nevertheless in control, and He had not abandoned them. There would come a day when He would deal with Israel's oppressors and set Israel free (Daniel 12). There would be justice in the end. God is sovereign over human history.

2. *Rescue in a Lion's Den.* There are several beloved stories in the book of Daniel that illustrate God's sovereignty. One of these is God's rescue of Daniel after he was thrown into the lion's den at the hands of King Darius (Daniel 6). Though the king personally liked Daniel, the governmental leaders under Darius were jealous of Daniel's position and they despised him. These unscrupulous men tricked the king into signing an irrevocable edict that decreed that no one could pray to any god or man except Darius for the next 30 days. Undaunted, Daniel continued his practice of praying three times a day to the true God. Upon being discovered by the scheming governmental leaders, Daniel was thrown into the lion's den overnight. Due to the irrevocable nature of the edict, Darius could not intervene. But the king admonished Daniel: "May your God, whom you serve continually, rescue you!" (verse 16).

The following morning, the king rushed to the lion's den and shouted, "Daniel, servant of the living God, has your God, whom you serve continually, been able to rescue you from the lions?" (Daniel 6:20). Daniel responded: "O king, live forever! My God sent his angel, and he shut the mouths of the lions" (verse 22).

3. Rescue in a Fiery Furnace. Another favorite story in Daniel is God's rescue of three of Daniel's friends who were thrown into a flaming furnace (Daniel 3). When Daniel's companions refused to worship the image of gold set up by King Nebuchadnezzar, they were threatened with being thrown into a blazing fire (verse 15). But the three brave lads responded: "If we are thrown into the blazing furnace, the God we serve is able to save us from it, and he will rescue us from your hand, O king" (verse 17). This comment made the king so mad that he heated the furnace seven times hotter than usual and commanded his strongest soldiers to toss Daniel's friends into the flames (verses 19-20).

As the king was observing what should have been an instant incineration, he was startled by what he saw and exclaimed: "Look! I see four men walking around in the fire, unbound and unharmed, and the fourth looks like a son of the gods" (Daniel 3:25). The king then commanded the three to come out of the flames, and after seeing that they were completely unharmed, exclaimed: "Praise be to the God of Shadrach, Meshach and Abednego, who has sent his angel and rescued his servants! They trusted in him and defied the king's command and were willing to give up their lives rather than serve or worship any god except their own God" (verse 28).

D David

David was the last of eight children born to Jesse and became a shepherd in Bethlehem. His story is told in 1 Samuel 16–31, 2 Samuel 1–24, 1 Kings 1–2, and 1 Chronicles 10–29.

From a human vantage point, David probably would not have been selected as the individual most likely to succeed in life by his peers. After all, David, as Jesse's youngest son, was just a humble shepherd boy. (Shepherding was considered a lowly job.) However, under God's sovereign plan, David was to become Israel's second king.

David became instantly famous for killing Goliath, the giant Philistine warrior (1 Samuel 17). The fact that David as a young boy would go up against such a gargantuan warrior shows David's tremendous trust in God. Of course, during his years as a shepherd boy, David had become increasingly proficient in using a slingshot, which he was able to providentially use, with God's blessing, in defeating Goliath. Even in his younger years, then, God was preparing David for his future role, though David was unaware of it at the time.

David was a gifted harpist (see 1 Samuel 16:15-23). He often played music to soothe the nerves of King Saul, who suffered from spells of madness and depression, having been forsaken by God and afflicted by an evil spirit. David was also a proficient poet, as evidenced by the many Psalms he wrote, many of which were accompanied by music. He was known as the "sweet psalmist of Israel" (2 Samuel 23:1 NASB).

Because of David's growing fame, King Saul became jealous of him and even sought to kill him. This resulted in David having to live as an outlaw for a number of years. It is to David's credit that he did not respond in like manner and seek to take Saul's life. Meanwhile, David developed a close friendship with Saul's son, Jonathan (1 Samuel 20).

David finally became king of Israel when he was 30 years old (2 Samuel 2:1-7). He assumed leadership following Saul's death. He was a good king and united the kingdom. He made Jerusalem his capital and ruled for 40 years.

David earnestly desired to build a temple for God. But it was not to be. God told David through the prophet Nathan that he could not build the temple because he was a warrior. So the task would be left to his son and successor, Solomon (1 Kings 6–8). Nevertheless, David did gather a great deal of material that would be used for the building of the temple.

In his old age, David summoned his son Solomon and anointed him king. He died at 71 years of age in his own bed.

D

Davidic Covenant—See *Covenants*.

Day of Atonement

The Day of Atonement was annually celebrated on the tenth day of the seventh month of the Jewish calendar—the month of Tishri (September/October). Only once a year could Aaron (or the high priest) enter into the Holy of Holies, the innermost part of the tabernacle, where the Ark of the Covenant was located. Before doing this, however, he had to secure forgiveness for his own sins. He did this by sacrificing a bull as a sin offering for himself, and he would sprinkle some of the blood in front of the Ark of the Covenant (see Leviticus 4:5; 16; 23:27). So insecure was the high priest that a rope would be tied around his leg so that if he entered the Holy of Holies without taking care of all his sin and then died, the other priests could pull him out by the rope.

Only after the high priest's sin had been forgiven could he then go on to offer sacrifices on behalf of the people of Israel. He would first kill a goat for the sins of the people. Then he laid his hands on a second goat, symbolically transferring the guilt of the people to it. The goat was then driven into the desert to symbolize that Israel's sins had been carried away.

Since these sacrifices took place annually, the Israelites were reminded year in and year out that sin cut them off from God and that there was a regular need for atonement. This makes the sacrifice of Christ all the more important, for His sacrifice was once and for all, never again having to be repeated (see Hebrews 9:9,23-28).

Dead Sea Scrolls

1. Discovery of the Scrolls ♦ 2. The Essene Community ♦ 3. Significance

1. *Discovery of the Scrolls.* Khirbet Qumran, on the western shores of the Dead Sea, lies in one of the lowest parts of the earth, on the fringe of the hot and arid wastes of the wilderness of Judea. Today, Qumran is silent, empty, and in ruins. But in that place, devout members of an ancient Jewish sect—the Essenes—hurried out one day from their commune and, in haste and secrecy, climbed the nearby cliffs to hide their precious writings in caves. This likely happened when Roman soldiers overran the Qumran community at the time of the Jewish revolt prior to A.D. 70. These scrolls remained undisturbed for some 2000 years.

An Arab shepherd boy accidentally discovered the first of these long-hidden writings in the spring of 1947. Since then, thousands of fragments belonging to 800 manuscripts have been discovered in 11 different caves in Qumran. Generally speaking, these include Old Testament books, commentaries on Old Testament books, apocryphal and pseudepigraphal texts, thematic collections of Old Testament passages, hymns, and sectarian writings of the Qumran community.

Among the specific manuscripts discovered are Isaiah, Exodus, Leviticus, Numbers, Deuteronomy, The Manual of Discipline, The Thanksgiving Psalms, The War Scroll, Pesher on Habakkuk, The Genesis Apocryphon, Tobit, Ecclesiasticus, the Book of Jubilees, the Book of Enoch, Testaments of the Twelve Patriarchs, the Sayings of Moses, the Vision of

Amram, the Psalms of Joshua, the Prayer of Nabonidus, the Book of Mysteries, the Hymn of the Initiates, Poems from a Qumran Hymnal, Lament for Zion, and Hymns of Triumph. This is one of the greatest manuscript discoveries of all time.

2. The Essene Community. Though scholars are unclear on the etymology of "Essene," the word seems to be related to the Aramaic *hasya* (meaning "pious") and the Hebrew title *hasidim* (meaning "the pious ones"). There is no reason to assume that "Essenes" was a self-designation for this group. It may have been a title or label applied by outsiders, pointing to the manner in which the Essenes were perceived by their contemporaries.

Pliny tells us that one Essene community lived on the northwest shore of the Dead Sea, but this was clearly not an exclusive settlement since other Essene communities were known to have existed in towns throughout Palestine. Josephus discloses that there were different orders of Essenes with a total of more than 4000 adherents. Both Pliny and Josephus viewed the Essenes as ascetic, semimonastic Jews who withdrew themselves from the pagan, materialistic world to pursue a life of righteousness and virtue, which they believed was impossible apart from such seclusion.

Admission to the Essene community was restricted, the discipline was rigid, and punishment for disobedience was severe. Because of their belief in the detrimental effects of evil, the Essenes engaged in constant purification rituals and performed their own sacrifices for sin. Too, they engaged in regular instruction and study of the Old Testament Law. By obedience to the Law and mutual love for one another, they attempted to live in an environment of peace and purity.

The Essenes were highly exclusive. They viewed themselves as the final remnant of God's people on earth. They believed they alone interpreted the Scriptures rightly, and they devoted their exile in the wilderness to the constant study of Scripture.

Essene life was also communal. Not only was property held in common, but the meals were taken together as well. Because of this, Essene travelers could always count on free lodging wherever other Essenes lived.

D

3. Significance. The Dead Sea Scrolls are an incredible source of information about the beliefs, habits, lifestyle, and understanding of Scripture of the Essene community, so they provide much valuable background for biblical studies. The scrolls certainly help scholars to clarify how Jewish religion influenced Christianity when Christianity first emerged.

Beyond this, Bible-believing Christians also find great significance in the scrolls because they verify the great accuracy with which biblical manuscripts were copied. In these scrolls, discovered at Qumran in 1947, we have Old Testament manuscripts that date about a thousand years earlier (150 B.C.) than the other Old Testament manuscripts previously in our possession (which dated to A.D. 980). Comparing the two sets of manuscripts shows that they are essentially the same, with very few changes. The fact that manuscripts separated by a thousand years are essentially the same indicates the incredible accuracy of the Old Testament's manuscript transmission.

The copy of the book of Isaiah discovered at Qumran illustrates this accuracy. Though the copy of Isaiah found at the Dead Sea in 1947 was a thousand years older than the oldest dated manuscript previously known, the manuscripts proved to be word-for-word identical with our standard Hebrew Bible in more than 95 percent of the text. The 5 percent of variation mainly involved minor slips of the pen and some variations in spelling. It is quite obvious that the biblical copyists took great care in their work.

Death and Dying

1. Defining Death ◆ 2. Biblical Descriptions of Death

1. Defining Death. The New Testament word for "death" carries the idea of *separation*. At the moment of physical death, man's spirit separates or departs from his body (2 Corinthians 5:8). This is why, when Stephen was being put to death by stoning, he prayed, "Lord Jesus, receive my spirit" (Acts

7:59). At the moment of death "the spirit returns to God who gave it" (Ecclesiastes 12:7). Verses such as these indicate that death for the believer involves his or her spirit departing from the physical body and immediately going into the presence of the Lord in heaven. Death for the believer is thus an event that leads to a supremely blissful existence (Philippians 1:21-23).

For the unbeliever, however, death holds grim prospects. At death the unbeliever's spirit departs from the body and goes not to heaven but to a place of great suffering (Luke 16:19-31).

Both believers and unbelievers remain as spirits, in a disembodied state, until the future day of resurrection. The resurrection bodies of believers will be specially suited to dwelling in heaven in the direct presence of God—the perishable will be made imperishable and the mortal will be made immortal (1 Corinthians 15:53). Unbelievers, too, will be resurrected, but they will spend eternity apart from God (John 5:28-29).

2. Biblical Descriptions of Death. Death is described in a rich variety of ways in the Bible, enabling us to understand a great deal about this mysterious event:

A. *The Way of All the Earth.* Sometimes death is described as "the way of all the earth," emphasizing the universality of the death experience. When David was about to die, he said to Solomon his son, "I am about to go the way of all the earth...so be strong, show yourself a man" (1 Kings 2:1-2).

B. *The Journey of No Return.* Job spoke of his eventual death by saying, "Only a few years will pass before I go on the journey of no return" (Job 16:22). Such words remind us of the permanence of passing from mortal life.

C. *Breathing One's Last.* Job reflected that "man dies and is laid low; he breathes his last and is no more" (Job 14:10). This description of death focuses solely on the cessation of life in the physical body.

D. *A Withering Away.* Scripture says that man "springs up like a flower and withers away; like a fleeting shadow, he does not endure" (Job 14:2). The flower fades. Its beauty quickly vanishes. So it is with human life.

E. *Departing.* The apostle Paul said, "If I am to go on living in the body, this will mean fruitful labor for me. Yet what shall I choose? I do not know! I am torn between the two: I desire to depart and be with Christ, which is better by far" (Philippians 1:22-23). Paul considered departure from earthly life and into the Lord's presence something to be desired.

F. *Dismissal from Earthly Life.* Recognizing that God alone is sovereign over the timing and circumstances of death, Simeon, after beholding the Christ child as God had promised, said, "Sovereign Lord, as you have promised, you now dismiss your servant in peace" (Luke 2:29).

G. *Earthly Tent Being Destroyed.* The apostle Paul graphically described death as an earthly tent being destroyed (2 Corinthians 5:1). Our present bodies are temporary and flimsy abodes. They are weak, frail, and vulnerable. But a time is coming when these "habitations" will be resurrected and our resurrection bodies will be permanent and indestructible.

H. *Paradise.* To one of the thieves being crucified with Him, Jesus said, "I tell you the truth, today you will be with me in paradise" (Luke 23:43). Paradise is a place of incredible bliss and serene rest in the very presence of God (2 Corinthians 12:2).

I. *The Physical Body "Sleeps."* Death is often described in the Bible as "sleep," for the body takes on the appearance of sleep. The soul, however, does not sleep. It is fully conscious. The believer's soul in the afterlife is fully awake and active in the presence of God (Revelation 6:9-11). The unbeliever's soul is fully conscious in a place of great suffering (Luke 16:19-31).

Demonology

1. Origin ◆ 2. Nature ◆ 3. Activities ◆
4. Classes ◆ 5. Ranks

1. *Origin.* Many scholars believe Revelation 12:4 refers to the fall of the angels who followed Satan's rebellion: "His [Satan's]

D

tail swept a third of the stars out of the sky and flung them to the earth." It has long been recognized that the word "stars" is sometimes used of angels in the Bible (see Job 38:7). If "stars" refers to angels in Revelation 12:4, it would appear that after Lucifer rebelled against God (Isaiah 14:12-15; Ezekiel 28:12-19), he was able to draw a third of the angelic realm after him in this rebellion. Lucifer apparently led a massive angelic revolt against God. These fallen angels are the demons of the New Testament (see Ephesians 3:10; 6:12; Revelation 12:7).

2. Nature. Demons are portrayed in Scripture as being evil and wicked. They are designated "unclean spirits" (Matthew 10:1 NASB), "evil spirits" (Luke 7:21), and "spiritual forces of wickedness" (Ephesians 6:12 NASB). All these terms point to the immoral nature of demons.

3. Activities. Demons, under Satan's lead, seek to disseminate false doctrine (1 Timothy 4:1). As well, they wield influence over false prophets (1 John 4:1-4) and seek to turn men to the worship of idols (see Leviticus 17:7 NASB; Deuteronomy 32:17; Psalm 106:36-38). Demons hinder answers to the prayers of believers (Daniel 10:12-13,20) and instigate jealousy and faction among believers (James 3:13-16). Scripture also portrays them as inflicting physical diseases on people (such as dumbness, Matthew 9:33; blindness, 12:22; and epilepsy, 17:14-18). They also afflict people with mental disorders (Mark 5:2-5; 9:17-27; Luke 8:27-29; 9:37-42). They cause people to be self-destructive (Mark 5:5; Luke 9:42). They are even responsible for the deaths of some people (Revelation 9:14-19).

4. Classes. Presently there are two classes or groups of demons. One group of demons is free and active in opposing God and His people (Ephesians 2:1-3). The other group is confined (2 Peter 2:4). These confined demons are apparently being punished for some sin other than the original rebellion

81

against God. Some theologians believe these angels are guilty of the unnatural sin mentioned in Genesis 6:2-4, and because of the gross depravity of this sin they are permanently confined to Tartarus.

D

5. Ranks. Just as God's holy angels are organized according to rank, so fallen angels are organized according to rank—including principalities, powers, rulers of the darkness of this world, and spiritual wickedness in high places (see Ephesians 6:12). All fallen angels, regardless of their individual ranks, follow the leadership of their malevolent commander in chief—Satan, the prince of demons.

Deuteronomy

The book of Deuteronomy, written by Moses in about 1410 B.C., contains the words Moses spoke to the Israelites as they were camped in the plains of Moab, preparing to enter into the Promised Land (Deuteronomy 1:1). This was Moses's farewell address, and he was passing the mantle on to Joshua.

Some scholars have argued that Moses could not have written Deuteronomy, for the last chapter in the book records his death. This is not an insurmountable problem, however, for it seems clear that Moses wrote every chapter in the book *except* the last chapter (see Deuteronomy 1:5; 31:9,22,24; 1 Kings 2:3; 8:53; 2 Kings 14:6; 18:12; Matthew 19:7-8; Acts 3:22-23), which may have been written by Joshua, his successor.

The word "Deuteronomy" literally means "second law," and accurately describes some of the book's contents. Indeed, the Ten Commandments recorded in Exodus 20 are repeated in Deuteronomy 5, with minor variations. Other laws recorded in Exodus are also repeated in Deuteronomy.

Further, the book contains a restatement and reaffirmation of the covenant God made with the Israelites at Sinai (Deuteronomy 1–30). The covenant is couched in the form of ancient Hittite suzerainty treaties made between a king and his subjects. In such treaties, there would always be a preamble naming the author of the treaty, a historical introduction depicting the relationship between the respective parties, a list of required stipulations explaining the responsibilities of each of the parties, a promise of either blessing or judgment invoked depending on faithfulness or unfaithfulness to the treaty, a solemn oath, and a ritual of ratification of the treaty. Such parallels between ancient treaties and God's covenant with Israel show that God communicated to His people in ways they were familiar with.

Devil—See *Satan.*

Disciples

The word "disciple" comes from the Greek word *mathetes,* which literally means "a learner." A disciple is hence a learner. He is one who learns about and learns from Jesus Christ.

The word seems to be used both specifically and generally in the New Testament. Specifically, Jesus chose 12 men to be His disciples and designated them "apostles" (Mark 3:13-19). They spent three years with Him, digesting His teachings and witnessing His mighty miracles among the people. The disciples included Peter, Andrew, James, John, Philip, Bartholomew, Thomas, Nathaniel, Matthew, and others.

More generally, the term is used to refer to Christians as learners or followers of Christ in the New Testament. The "following" aspect of the disciple is a heavy emphasis in the New Testament. The life of a disciple is portrayed in Scripture as a life of total commitment. Disciples of Christ are self-denying (Matthew 16:24) and live sacrificially (Luke 14:33). They make Christ their top priority (Luke 14:26). They are steadfast in their commitment to Him (John 8:31) and bear fruit in their lives (John 15:8).

Disease—See *Health and Healing.*

Divination and Sorcery

1. Pagan Practices ◆ 2. Biblical Condemnation

1. *Pagan Practices.* People of pagan nations often engaged in various forms of divination in order to determine the future or to determine the will of the gods. Sometimes these ancient occultists would seek communication with the dead through spiritists or mediums and try to obtain paranormal information (Deuteronomy 18:10-11; 1 Samuel 28:3,8-9). Others would engage in the practice of witchcraft, designed to extract information from a pagan god (Numbers 22:6-7; 23:23; Joshua 13:22).

Some in ancient times would conjure spells (Deuteronomy 18:11) or practice sorcery (Exodus 22:18; Deuteronomy 18:10). Others would interpret omens (Genesis 30:2-7; 44:5). Some in Babylon would observe and interpret the stars (astrology), since the stars were believed to be connected to the pagan gods (Daniel 1:20; 2:2,10,27; 4:7; 5:7,11,15 KJV). Still others might practice soothsaying by, for example, examining the liver of a dead animal that had been used for sacrifice. If there were any abnormalities in the liver, they would try to interpret those abnormalities as a possible indication of some aspect of the will of the gods.

2. *Biblical Condemnation.* The Bible condemns *all* forms of occultism, divination, and sorcery. Leviticus 19:26 commands, "Do not practice divination or sorcery." Leviticus 19:31 instructs, "Do not turn to mediums or seek out spiritists, for you will be defiled by them. I am the LORD your God." Exodus 22:18 instructs that sorceresses are to be put to death. We read in Leviticus 20:27, "A man or woman who is a medium or spiritist among you must be put to death. You are to stone them; their blood will be on their own heads."

In 1 Samuel 28:3 we are told that Saul rightly "expelled the mediums and spiritists from the land." Later, however, we read that "Saul died because he was unfaithful to the LORD; he did not keep the word of the LORD, and even consulted a medium for guidance" (1 Chronicles 10:13).

Acts 19:19 reveals that many who converted to Christ in Ephesus destroyed all their paraphernalia formerly used for occultism and divination: "A number who had practiced sorcery brought their scrolls together and burned them publicly. When they calculated the value of the scrolls, the total came to fifty thousand drachmas."

Divorce—See *Marriage.*

Ecclesiastes

"Ecclesiastes" comes from a Hebrew word *(qoheleth)* meaning "teacher" or "speaker." The author of Ecclesiastes is apparently Solomon, for he is identified as "son of David, king in Jerusalem" (Ecclesiastes 1:1). The book was probably written in 935 B.C.

Most Bible scholars believe the book of Ecclesiastes presents two contrasting ways of looking at man's plight in the world. One is the secular, humanistic, materialistic viewpoint that interprets all things from a limited earthly perspective (a perspective "under the sun")—not recognizing God or His involvement in man's affairs (see Ecclesiastes 1:14; 2:11,17,26; 4:4,16; 6:9). This earthly perspective is one completely unaided by divine revelation. It sees life as futile and meaningless, with no purpose in life. There is nothing new under the sun, but rather what is taking place now is what has already taken place many times in the past and what will take place in the future. Truly, there is nothing new. Life is meaningless. There is no ultimate satisfaction in anything we do, because we will end up with the same doomed fate as all other humans that preceded us.

The other perspective is a godly, spiritual perspective that interprets life and its problems from a God-honoring viewpoint (see Ecclesiastes 3:1-15; 5:18-20; 6:1-2; 9:1). This perspective takes divine revelation into account regarding how life and its problems are to be interpreted. This perspective recognizes God, and is one that finds meaning in life and enjoys life. God can be involved in all that we do (2:24-26; 3:13; 5:18-20; 9:7-10). Our ultimate meaning in life is not to be found in the things around us, which pass away, but in God alone (2:25). The conclusion of the writer of Ecclesiastes is that we should remember God while we are still young (12:1), fear Him, and keep His commandments (12:13).

Education

1. Significance ◆ 2. Role of Parents ◆ 3. Reading
and Writing ◆ 4. Trades and Homemaking Skills

E

1. *Significance.* Among the Jews, the child was considered
the most important person in the community. They believed
that out of all the people on earth, the child was most dear
to the heart of God. Understandably, then, educating children
was considered a monumentally important task.

2. *Role of Parents.* In fulfilling their task of educating children, the Jews did not simply send all their kids off to school
and leave everything in the hands of teachers. (In Old Testament times, there were no schools for children anyway.)
Rather, the parents played the critical role. In fact, the ancient
Jews believed that the home was the absolute center of education for children.

Certainly the Jews in New Testament times considered
schools important. A rabbi of good character would teach
such schools. Generally, students at varying levels of learning
would be in a single classroom, so there was much individual
instruction that took place. While one student was being
instructed, other students were busy with assignments. Most
students would go to such local schools from ages six through
twelve. If training beyond this was desired, they would go to
Jerusalem to study under one of the greater rabbis.

As important as school training was, however, schools
could not—and were not intended to—take the place of parents. This stress on parents educating children is not something the Jews just decided upon for themselves. Rather, God
commanded parents to educate their children in the ways of
the Lord. All Jewish parents' desire for their children's education is encapsulated in Proverbs 1:8, which portrays a

E

father speaking to his son: "Listen, my son, to your father's instruction and do not forsake your mother's teaching." By parental instruction, children were trained in the art of godly living. And then, as the children grew to adulthood, they themselves would be prepared to train *their* children just as they had been trained. This is God's ideal.

In Deuteronomy 6:6-9 we read God's instructions regarding the spiritual education of children. In this passage, we see just how high a priority this education is with God:

> These commandments that I give you today are to be upon your hearts. Impress them on your children. Talk about them when you sit at home and when you walk along the road, when you lie down and when you get up. Tie them as symbols on your hands and bind them on your foreheads. Write them on the doorframes of your houses and on your gates.

The word "impress" in this passage ("impress them on your children") literally means "to whet." The Jews sought to *whet their children's appetites* for the things of God. Their goal was to make the things of God palatable to their children so their appetite would grow.

The word "impress" is also a present-tense word. This means that the "impressing" is to be a continuous and ongoing activity. It is not a mere Sabbath activity. It is a seven-day-a-week activity.

Solomon, the wisest man who ever lived, once said, "Train a child in the way he should go, and when he is old he will not turn from it" (Proverbs 22:6). The word "train" comes from a word root that means "palate" or "roof of the mouth." The ancient Arabs used a form of this verb to denote the action of a midwife rubbing the palate of a newborn child with olive oil or crushed dates to give it a desire for food and take nourishment. The word connotes the idea of "creating a desire for" or "creating a taste for." The picture being portrayed by Solomon is that parents are to develop in their children a personal desire for the things of God—a hunger for His Word and a desire for fellowship with His people.

In Jewish thinking, if the child at a young age was given a desire for the Lord and His ways—if he "tasted" the reality of genuine godly experiences and the joy of following His Word—he would not want to turn aside from his spiritual heritage when he reached adulthood. It would ideally stick with him for his entire life.

3. *Reading and Writing.* Other things were taught to children besides religion. For example, it seems obvious that reading and writing were systematically taught during biblical days—certainly in New Testament times, and at least significantly in Old Testament times. We know this to be true because, among other things, Joshua expected written reports of the land of Canaan (Joshua 18:4,8). Further, archaeological discoveries show widespread use of reading and writing in biblical days.

4. *Trades and Homemaking Skills.* Additionally, boys would often learn some kind of a manual trade from their fathers. Jesus, for example, learned the trade of carpentry from His father, Joseph (Mark 6:3). Girls, on the other hand, were taught homemaking skills by their mothers. They were taught how to cook and how to make clothes. Education was quite practical.

Egypt

1. Geography ◆ 2. History ◆ 3. Religion

1. *Geography.* Egypt is a country found at the northeast corner of Africa. To the north is the Mediterranean Sea; to the east is Palestine and Arabia; to the south is Nubia; and to the west is a vast desert. Egypt naturally divides into two realms—Upper Egypt, which is the valley of the Nile, and Lower Egypt, which is the plain of the Delta. In the Bible,

Egypt is called Mizraim, which literally means "two Egypts." From north to south, Egypt is about 540 miles long.

Because of its close proximity to the Nile, the land is extremely fertile. This caused the ancients in Egypt to worship the Nile as a god.

E

2. History. Egyptian history can be summarized in terms of three periods of great strength: the Old Kingdom, the Middle Kingdom, and the New Kingdom. The Old Kingdom lasted from 2700 to 2200 B.C. During this time, the great pyramids of Egypt were built. The Middle Kingdom lasted from 2000 to 1800 B.C. This was roughly the time when Abraham made a journey into Egypt (see Genesis 12:10-20). The New Kingdom lasted from 1570 to 1100 B.C. This period roughly parallels the time prior to Moses's birth through the time of the prophet Samuel. Following each of these periods of strength came a period of weakness. Once the New Kingdom declined in strength, Egypt was dominated by various other nations, culminating in Roman rule during New Testament times.

3. Religion. Perhaps of greatest interest to Bible students is the religion of Egypt. Egypt was polytheistic (they believed in many gods). Even to the present day, scholars are unsure about the total number of gods the Egyptians worshiped. Most lists contain approximately 80 deities. The dedication of the Egyptians to their gods is evident even to the casual observer as he tours modern Egypt. Beautiful temples honoring various gods virtually fill the landscape. The ancient Egyptians truly paid homage to the many gods they worshiped.

In Egyptian religion, the god at the top of the totem pole was the sun god, Re. He was considered the creator, father, and king of the gods. He was considered the most excellent, most distinguished god in the pantheon. Next in line was the pharaoh of Egypt, who was considered to be the son of Re. Hence, the pharaoh of Egypt was himself considered a god in his own right. Inasmuch as Re was considered superior to all other gods, his son—the pharaoh—was also considered to possess unmatched power as a god. This adds a whole new dimension to the Exodus account. It is as if a contest occurs between the true God on the one side and Pharaoh and the false gods of Egypt on the other side (see Numbers 33:3-4).

As alluded to above, the Egyptians venerated the Nile and all that was associated with it. The river Nile was worshiped by the Egyptians under various names and symbols. It was considered the father of life. So revered was the Nile by the Egyptians that hymns were written in its honor.

History reveals that the Egyptians greatly venerated animals. Evidence for this is found in the necropolis of sacred bulls that was discovered near Memphis (in Egypt), an area well known for its worship of both Ptah and Apis bulls. The Apis bull was thought to be the sacred animal of the god Ptah; this explains the associated worship of the Apis bull at the site near Memphis. At any one given time, there was only one sacred Apis bull. As soon as one died, another was chosen to take its place. Such sacred bulls were supposed to have been recognized by 28 distinctive marks that identified them as divine and indicated that they were to become objects of worship.

The Egyptians also believed in numerous gods that were supposed to be able to help in various spheres of life. For example, Sekhmet, a lion-headed goddess, was considered to have had the power to bring infectious epidemics to an end. Osiris is believed to have functioned as a god of agriculture, while Shu was considered the Egyptian god of the atmosphere. Nut, the Egyptian sky goddess, had the task of ensuring the blessings of sun and warmth. Seth was an Egyptian god whose duty was to watch after the crops of the land. Serapis was a god believed to be able to protect the land from locust invasions. Atum was the god of the setting sun, and Thoth was a moon god of Hermopolis. Ptah was the god of life, Min was the god of procreation and reproduction, and Hathor was one of seven deities who was believed to attend the birth of children.

E

Egyptians were also heavily involved in magic—both black magic and white magic. White magic was supposed to ward off problems, while black magic was considered a means of bringing harm to people. Egyptians therefore wore lucky charms in order to protect themselves from such magic. All in all, Egyptians were thoroughly engulfed in paganism and occultism.

Election

1. Definition ◆ 2. Foreknowledge View ◆
3. Sovereignty View ◆ 4. Commonalities

1. *Definition.* Election is that sovereign act of God of choosing certain individuals to salvation before the foundation of the world.

2. *Foreknowledge View.* There are two primary views Christians have had regarding the issue of election. The first view is that God's election is based on His foreknowledge. This view says that God used His foreknowledge to look down the corridors of time to see who would respond favorably to His Gospel message, and on that basis He elected certain persons to salvation. Several arguments are offered in favor of this view:

- Scripture teaches that God's salvation has appeared to all men, not merely the elect (Titus 2:11).

- The Bible teaches that Christ died for all (1 Timothy 2:6; 4:10; Hebrews 2:9; 2 Peter 2:1; 1 John 2:2).

- There are numerous exhortations in Scripture to turn to God (Isaiah 31:6; Joel 2:13-14; Matthew 18:3; Acts 3:19), to repent (Matthew 3:2; Luke 13:3,5; Acts 2:38; 17:30), and to believe (John 6:29; Acts 16:31; 1 John 3:23).

- Scripture seems to indicate that election is based on God's foreknowledge of who would respond positively to such exhortations (Romans 8:28-30; 1 Peter 1:1-2).

Among the arguments offered against this view are statements in Scripture indicating that the Father gave certain ones to Christ (John 6:37; 17:2,6,9). Christ said, "No one can come to me unless the Father who sent me draws him" (John 6:44). Moreover, in Romans 9:10-16 God is said to have chosen Jacob rather than Esau, even before they were born and before they had done either good or bad.

E

We read in Acts 13:48 that "all who were appointed for eternal life believed." Ephesians 1:5-8 and 2:8-10 represent salvation as originating in the choice of God and as being all of grace (see also Acts 5:31; 11:18; Romans 12:3; 2 Timothy 2:25). Finally, many claim that if election is not unconditional and absolute, then God's whole plan is uncertain and liable to miscarriage.

3. Sovereignty View. The second view (my view) is that God's election is based on His sovereign choice. A number of arguments are offered in favor of this view:

- Biblical statements support election by choice (Acts 13:48).

- The whole process of salvation is a gift of God (Romans 12:3; Ephesians 2:8-10).

- Certain verses speak of human beings having been given to Christ (John 6:37; 17:2), and of the Father drawing men to Christ (John 6:44).

- There are examples in Scripture of the sovereign calling of God upon individuals, like Paul (Galatians 1:15) and Jeremiah (Jeremiah 1:5), even before they were born.

- Election is necessary in light of man's total depravity (Job 14:1; Jeremiah 13:11; Romans 3:10-20).

- Election is necessary in light of man's inability (Ephesians 2:1).

93

- Election is compatible with God's sovereignty (Proverbs 19:21; Jeremiah 10:23).

- Election is portrayed as being from all eternity (2 Timothy 1:9).

  - It is on the basis of election by choice that the appeal to a godly life is made (Colossians 3:12; 2 Thessalonians 2:13; 1 Peter 2:9).

E

Two primary arguments have been suggested against this view:

(1) It is argued that if election is limited by God, then surely the atonement must be limited as well (providing salvation only for the elect). However, this conclusion is clearly refuted by John 1:29, 3:16, 1 Timothy 2:6, Hebrews 2:9, and 1 John 2:2.

(2) It is argued that election by choice makes God responsible for "reprobation." However, those not included in election suffer only their due reward. God does not "elect" a person to hell. Those not elected to salvation are left to their own self-destructive ways.

4. Commonalities. Whichever view one concludes is the correct one, the following facts should be kept in mind: God's election is loving (Ephesians 1:4-11); election glorifies God (Ephesians 1:12-14); and the product of election is a people who do good works (Ephesians 2:10; see also Colossians 3:12; Romans 11:33-36).

Elijah and Elisha

1. Elijah ◆ 2. Elisha

1. Elijah. Elijah's name means "The Lord is my God." Elijah was an animated prophet who dressed strangely and lived an ascetic lifestyle (2 Kings 1:8). He ministered during the ninth century B.C. during Ahab's and Ahaziah's reigns in the northern kingdom of Israel. He is well known for his defense of the one true God of Israel.

Elijah is perhaps best known for standing against the worship of the Canaanite god, Baal, urging the people to commit themselves to the true God of Israel. Elijah challenged the 850 priests of Baal and Asherah to prove the existence of their god (1 Kings 18:21). A sacrifice was set up, and the priests of Baal were challenged to have Baal burn the sacrifice, which would prove his existence. However, if he was unable to do this, and Israel's God *was* able to burn up the sacrifice, this would prove that the God of Israel was the one true God. Baal's prophets did their best, calling on Baal all day long, dancing around the altar. But it was to no avail. Baal did not reply. Elijah then quickly called on the one true God of Israel, and the altar was immediately consumed by fire. The God of Israel was mightily vindicated on that day. Baal's impotence (nonexistence) was obvious to all. As a judgment, the prophets of Baal were then slaughtered at Elijah's command (1 Kings 18:40).

2. Elisha. Eventually Elijah trained a new prophet named Elisha to carry on the work he had begun. Elijah was swept up into heaven in a whirlwind by a chariot of fire, and his mantle fell on Elisha (see 2 Kings 2:1-11). The spirit of Elijah was recognized as having fallen on Elisha (see 2 Kings 2:15). Elisha's name means "My God saves."

Elisha served in the northern kingdom of Israel from 850 to 800 B.C. This would have been during the reigns of Jehoram, Jehu, Jehoahaz, and Joash. Elisha was quite versatile, not only speaking forth prophecies and performing miracles, but also advising kings and helping the disadvantaged. His miracles included parting the Jordan River so he could cross on dry land (2 Kings 2:14), purifying an unhealthy spring (2 Kings 2:19-21), miraculously multiplying a widow's oil in a jar such that she was able to use it to pay off her debts (2 Kings 4:1-7), and curing Naaman of leprosy (2 Kings 5:1-14).

A very famous story of Elisha is found in 2 Kings 6:15-17. In this story Elisha and his servant were utterly surrounded by a hostile pagan army. But they were not alone. Elisha's servant was paralyzed with fear until Elisha prayed, "O LORD, open his eyes so he may see." Then the servant was divinely enabled to see that they were surrounded and defended by a vast number of angels on every side.

E

End Times

1. Rapture ◆ 2. Daniel's 70 Weeks (Daniel 9:25-27)
◆ 3. Tribulation ◆ 4. Antichrist ◆
5. Armageddon ◆ 6. Millennial Kingdom ◆
7. New Heavens and a New Earth

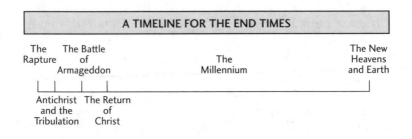

A TIMELINE FOR THE END TIMES

The Rapture — The Battle of Armageddon — The Millennium — The New Heavens and Earth

Antichrist and the Tribulation — The Return of Christ

1. *Rapture*. The Rapture is that glorious event in which the dead in Christ are raised from the dead and living Christians are instantly translated into their resurrection bodies—and *both* groups are caught up to meet Christ in the air (1 Thessalonians 4:13-17). There are four primary views regarding the timing of the Rapture. Partial Rapturism is the view that only spiritual Christians will be raptured when Christ returns. (Hardly anyone holds to this view anymore.) Pretribulationism is the view that Christ will rapture the entire church before any part of the Tribulation begins. Posttribulationism is the view that Christ will rapture the church after

the Tribulation at the Second Coming of Christ. Midtribula-
tionism is the view that Christ will rapture the church in the
middle of the Tribulation period.

Most Christians today are either "pretribs" or "posttribs."
Personally, I think the pretrib position is most consistent with
the biblical testimony. God has promised to keep the church
from the time of testing coming upon the entire earth (Revelation 3:10), and has promised to deliver the church from the
wrath to come (1 Thessalonians 5:9).

But it is not an issue worth fighting over. The different
views of the Rapture may disagree over the *timing* of end-time
events, but they all agree on the big picture: There *will* be a
Rapture and we *will* live forever with Jesus in heaven. In the
long haul (after we've been with Christ for billions of years in
heaven), the question of whether the Rapture happened
before or after the Tribulation period will truly seem significant.

2. *Daniel's 70 weeks (Daniel 9:25-27).* In Daniel 9, God provided a prophetic timetable for the nation of Israel. The
prophetic clock began ticking when the command went out
to restore and rebuild Jerusalem following its destruction by
Babylon (Daniel 9:25). According to this verse, Israel's
timetable was divided into 70 groups of seven years, totaling
490 years.

The first 69 groups of seven years—or 483 years—counted
the years "from the issuing of the decree to restore and
rebuild Jerusalem until the Anointed One, the ruler, comes"
(Daniel 9:25). The "Anointed One," of course, is Jesus Christ.
"Anointed One" means "Messiah." The day that Jesus rode
into Jerusalem to proclaim Himself Israel's Messiah was
exactly 483 years to the day after the command to restore and
rebuild Jerusalem had been given.

At that point God's prophetic clock stopped. Daniel
describes a gap between these 483 years and the final seven
years of Israel's prophetic timetable. Several events were to
take place during this "gap," according to Daniel 9:26:

E

1) The Messiah will be killed.

2) The city of Jerusalem and its temple would be destroyed (which occurred in A.D. 70).

3) The Jews would encounter difficulty and hardship from that time on.

The final "week" of seven years will begin for Israel when the Antichrist confirms a "covenant" for seven years (Daniel 9:27). When this peace pact is signed, this will signal the beginning of the Tribulation period. That signature marks the beginning of the seven-year countdown to the Second Coming of Christ (which follows the Tribulation period).

3. *Tribulation.* The Tribulation will be a definite period of time at the end of the age that will be characterized by great travail (Matthew 24:29-35). It will be of such severity that no period in history, past or future, will equal it (Matthew 24:21). It is called the time of Jacob's trouble, for it is a judgment on Messiah-rejecting Israel (Jeremiah 30:7 KJV; Daniel 12:1-4). The nations will also be judged for their sin and rejection of Christ (Isaiah 26:21; Revelation 6:15-17). The period will last seven years (Daniel 9:24,27).

Scripture indicates that this period will be characterized by wrath (1 Thessalonians 1:10; 5:9), judgment (Revelation 14:7), indignation (Isaiah 26:20-21 NASB), trial (Revelation 3:10), trouble (Jeremiah 30:7), destruction (Joel 1:15), darkness (Amos 5:18), desolation (Daniel 9:27), overturning (Isaiah 24:1-4), and punishment (Isaiah 24:20-21). The term "Tribulation" is quite appropriate.

4. *Antichrist.* The apostle Paul warned of a "man of law-lessness," which is the Antichrist (2 Thessalonians 2:3,8-9). This individual will perform counterfeit signs and wonders and deceive many during the future Tribulation period (2 Thessalonians 2:9-10). The apostle John describes this individual in the book of Revelation as "the Beast" (Revelation 13:1-10).

This demon-inspired individual will rise to prominence in the Tribulation period, seek to dominate the world during this time, attempt to destroy the Jews, persecute believers, and set up his own kingdom (Revelation 13). He will speak arrogant and boastful words in glorifying himself (2 Thessalonians 2:4). His assistant, the false prophet, will seek to make the world worship him (Revelation 13:11-12). People around the world will be forced to receive his mark, without which they cannot buy or sell (Revelation 13:16-17). But to receive this mark ensures one of being the recipient of God's wrath. This beast will be defeated and destroyed by Jesus at His Second Coming (Revelation 19:11-21).

5. Armageddon. "Armageddon" literally means "Mount of Megiddo," and is about 60 miles north of Jerusalem. This is the site for the final horrific battle of humankind just prior to the Second Coming (Revelation 16:16). Napoleon is reported to have once commented that this site is perhaps the greatest battlefield he had ever seen.

6. Millennial Kingdom. There are three theological views regarding what has been called the Millennial Kingdom. Premillennialism says that following the Second Coming, Christ will institute a kingdom of perfect peace and righteousness on earth that will last for 1000 years. After this reign of true peace, the eternal state begins (Revelation 20:1-7; see also Isaiah 65:17-25; Ezekiel 37:21-28; Zechariah 8:1-15). This is my personal view and is based on a literal interpretation of Scripture.

Amillennialism, a more spiritualized view, says that when Christ comes, eternity will begin with no prior thousand-year (millennial) reign on earth. Amillennialists generally interpret the "thousand-year" reign of Christ metaphorically and say it refers to Christ's present (spiritual) rule from heaven.

The postmillennial view (another spiritualized view) says that through the church's progressive influence, the world will be "Christianized" before Christ returns. Immediately following this return, eternity will begin. A practical problem for this viewpoint is that the world seems to be getting worse and worse instead of being "Christianized."

E

7. New Heavens and a New Earth. In the Garden of Eden where Adam and Eve sinned against God, a curse was placed upon the earth by God (Genesis 3:17-19). Hence, before the eternal kingdom can be made manifest, God must deal with this cursed earth. Indeed, the earth—along with the first and second heavens (the earth's atmosphere and the stellar universe)—must be renewed. The old must make room for the new.

The Scriptures often speak of the passing of the old heaven and earth. For example, in the book of Revelation we read, "Then I saw a new heaven and a new earth, for the first heaven and the first earth had passed away, and there was no longer any sea....He who was seated on the throne said, 'I am making everything new!'" (Revelation 21:1-5). The Greek word used to designate the newness of the cosmos is *kainos.* This word means "new in nature" or "new in quality." Hence, the phrase "new heavens and a new earth" refers not to a cosmos that is totally other than the present cosmos. Rather, the new cosmos will stand in continuity with the present cosmos, but it will be utterly renewed and renovated.

In keeping with this, Matthew 19:28 speaks of "the renewal of all things." Acts 3:21 (NASB) speaks of the "restoration of all things." The new earth, being a renewed and an eternal earth, will be adapted to the vast moral and physical changes which the eternal state necessitates. The new heavens and the new earth will be brought into blessed conformity with all that God is—in a state of fixed bliss and absolute perfection. The new earth will actually be a part of heaven itself.

100

Entertainment—See *Sports and Games.*

Ephesians

The epistle to the Ephesians was written by the apostle Paul in A.D. 61. Ephesus was a city characterized by luxurious homes, elegant buildings, and wide avenues. A hundred or so wealthy aristocrats owned most of the land around the city; these individuals also controlled the local government. Ephesus was a leading commercial and trade center of the ancient world, and was understandably one of the more prominent cities in the province of Asia.

Ephesus is well known for its temple of the Roman goddess Diana (Greek: *Artemis*), a structure that was considered one of the seven wonders of the world. It was a city where many pagans lived. It was a city that really needed the Gospel.

During his third missionary tour, the apostle Paul spent about three years in Ephesus building up the church there (Acts 19). When he left, his young associate Timothy pastored there for another year or so, seeking to establish them in sound doctrine (1 Timothy 1:3-4).

Paul later wrote his epistle to the Ephesians while a prisoner in Rome. However, he intended it to be a *circular* letter to be read not just at the church at Ephesus but at other churches as well. This conclusion is based on several factors. First, the phrase "To the saints in Ephesus" is missing from some ancient biblical manuscripts. Further, the letter does not aim to solve any specific problems of any specific church, but rather contains general truths relevant to all churches.

In this epistle, Paul speaks of God's eternal sovereign purpose for the church (Ephesians 1:3-14), as well as the spiritual blessing and spiritual endowment that are ours in Jesus Christ (see 2:4-10). Believers should therefore live a life worthy of the high calling with which they have been called (4:1; see also 2:10).

Paul also speaks of how all things in the universe find their ultimate unity in the person of Jesus Christ (Ephesians 4:1-16).

This especially includes the church, where both Jews and Gentiles—believers from every nation in the world—are united in Christ. In Christ there are no racial, religious, cultural, or social barriers. In view of this unity, believers should act with love toward one another, whether husbands and wives, masters and slaves, or parents and children (chapter 5:1–6:9).

The Epistles

Paul's General Epistles	Paul's Prison Epistles	Paul's Pastoral Epistles	Other General Epistles
Romans	Ephesians	1 and 2 Timothy	Hebrews
1 and 2 Corinthians	Philippians	Titus	James
Galatians	Colossians		1 and 2 Peter
1 and 2 Thessalonians	Philemon		1, 2, and 3 John
			Jude
			Revelation

Epistles

Approximately one-third of the New Testament is made up of epistles, or letters. Letters became a very important form of communication some 300 years prior to the time of Jesus in the Greek-speaking world. These letters typically included an introduction (the sender's name and some form of greeting), the body, and a conclusion. They were not delivered by a postal system, but rather were generally hand delivered by a messenger.

Many of the New Testament epistles or letters were written to brand-new churches that had just been formed and had certain problems and/or questions that needed to be addressed (1 and 2 Thessalonians are examples). The apostle Paul would often write letters to churches as follow-ups to his missionary work among them (as he did with the Ephesians). Hence, Paul's letters were very personal in nature. In some cases, Paul would give advice to the leader of a particular church (as is the case in 1 Timothy). Other times he would address the church as a whole (as he did with the Philippians).

Other New Testament epistles—the "general epistles"—were not directed at specific churches but were rather circulated to a number of churches and dealt with general concerns. These are primarily the non-Pauline epistles (such as 1 and 2 Peter, and 1, 2, and 3 John).

Though often addressed to specific churches or groups of churches, the letters also have tremendous relevance for Christians today. Indeed, the issues dealt with in the epistles are relevant to every generation.

Essenes—See *Jewish Sects* and *Dead Sea Scrolls.*

Esther, Book of

The book of Esther was written by an unknown author in about 465 B.C. Some have suggested that Mordecai, Ezra, or Nehemiah may have written the book, but there is no hard evidence for this. Whoever the author was, he was well aware of Persian culture and had a strong sense of Jewish nationalism.

Esther is distinguished from other Bible books in that God is never mentioned. Yet, God is seen working behind the scenes sovereignly and providentially all throughout the book. This short book describes how an insidious plot had been launched by the evil Haman to destroy the Jews. God not only thwarted the plot, but brought the plotter's evil back upon himself (Haman was executed instead of the Jews). In order to bring about this end, God had earlier providentially brought the beautiful (Jewish) Esther to become the queen of the Persian king, Xerxes I, who ruled Persia from 486 to 465 B.C. It would seem that God elevated Esther to this position of authority specifically to save the Jews from destruction (see Esther 4:14). Her cousin Mordecai was instrumental in helping Esther to understand this fact. This drama illustrates God's providential control of human history. Scholars have noted that this book provides the background for the institution of the festival of Purim (see *Festivals, Annual*).

E   Ethics and Behavior

While salvation is by faith in Christ alone (Acts 16:31), with no works in view (Romans 3:28), Scripture is abundantly clear that God calls the believer to a life of high ethics and good behavior. As Christians walk in dependence upon the Holy Spirit, they are enabled to live the kind of lives that are pleasing to God.

Scripture admonishes us to "live such good lives among the pagans that, though they accuse you of doing wrong, they may see your good deeds and glorify God on the day he visits us" (1 Peter 2:12). Our walk is to be blameless (Psalm 15:2), and our obedience to God should be obvious to all (Romans 16:19).

As Christians, we are to be "without fault in a crooked and depraved generation," in which we "shine like stars in the universe" (Philippians 2:15). We are to say "'no' to ungodliness and worldly passions, and to live self-controlled, upright and godly lives in this present age" (Titus 2:11-12).

God calls us to rid ourselves "of all such things as these: anger, rage, malice, slander, and filthy language from your lips" (Colossians 3:8). We are to rid ourselves of "all deceit, hypocrisy, envy, and slander of every kind" (1 Peter 2:1). And we must keep a clear conscience (1 Peter 3:16), ever keeping in mind that just as God is holy, so we are called to be holy in all we do (1 Peter 1:15).

Evangelism

The word "evangelism" comes from the Greek verb *evangelizomai,* which means "proclaim the good news." Hence, evangelism involves proclaiming to other people the Gospel (or good news) of salvation in Jesus Christ (Luke 15; John 3:16; Romans 5:8; 10:14-15; Ephesians 4:11; 2 Timothy 4:5; 2 Peter 3:9). Evangelism is not a task to be left in the hands of the professionals only (pastors and ministers), but rather all Christians are called to be ambassadors for Christ (2 Corinthians 5:17-21).

E

As for the content of the Gospel message, the apostle Paul in 1 Corinthians 15:3-4 said: "For what I received I passed on to you as of first importance: that Christ died for our sins according to the Scriptures, that he was buried, that he was raised on the third day according to the Scriptures." The "Gospel," according to this passage, has four components:

1) Man is a sinner.

2) Christ is the Savior.

3) Christ died as man's substitute.

4) Christ rose from the dead.

This is the Gospel Paul and the other apostles preached; it is the Gospel we too must preach. (See *Gospel.*)

Eve—See *Adam and Eve.*

Evil, Problem of

1. The Problem Defined ◆ 2. The Origin of Evil ◆
3. God Will Overcome Evil

1. *The Problem Defined.* The problem of evil may be viewed in simple form as a conflict involving three concepts: *God's power, God's goodness,* and *the presence of evil in the world.* Common sense seems to tell us that all three cannot be true at the same time. Solutions to the problem of evil typically involve modifying one or more of these three concepts: limit

God's power, limit God's goodness, or modify the existence of evil (such as calling it an illusion).

Certainly if God makes no claims to being good, then the existence of evil is easier explained. But God *does* claim to be good (1 Chronicles 16:34; Psalm 118:29). If God were limited in power and was simply not strong enough to withstand evil, then the existence of evil is easier explained. But God *does* claim to be all-powerful (2 Chronicles 20:6; Psalm 147:5; Ephesians 1:19-20). If evil were just an illusion that had no reality, then the problem does not really exist in the first place. But evil is *not* an illusion. It is real.

Today we face the reality of both *moral evil* (evil committed by free moral agents: war, crime, cruelty, class struggles, discrimination, slavery, and various injustices) and *natural evil* (hurricanes, floods, earthquakes, and the like). God is good, God is all-powerful, and yet evil exists. This is the problem of evil in its most basic form.

2. The Origin of Evil. The original creation was "very good" (Genesis 1:31). There was no sin, no evil, and no death. Yet today, the world is permeated with sin, evil, and death. What brought it about? Scripture indicates that the turn downward came the moment Adam and Eve used their God-given free wills and volitionally chose to disobey God (3:1-7).

Some people wonder why God could not have created man in such a way that he would never sin, thus avoiding evil altogether. Such a scenario would mean that man would no longer have the capacity to make choices and to freely love. It would require that God create robots that act only in programmed ways—like one of those chatty dolls where you pull a string on its back and it says, "I love you." But love cannot be programmed; it must be freely expressed. God wanted Adam and all humanity to show love by freely choosing obedience.

We may conclude, then, that God's plan had the *potential* for evil when He bestowed upon man the freedom of choice, but the actual *origin* of evil came as a result of man, who directed his will away from God and toward his own selfish

106

desires. Ever since Adam and Eve made evil *actual* on that first occasion in the Garden of Eden, a sin nature has been passed on to every man and woman (Romans 5:12; 1 Corinthians 15:22), and it is out of the sin nature that we continue to use our free wills to make evil actual (Mark 7:20-23).

Even natural evil—earthquakes, tornados, floods, and the like—is rooted in man's wrong use of free choice. We must not forget that we are living in a fallen world, and because of that, we are subject to disasters in the world of nature that would not have occurred had man not rebelled against God in the beginning (Romans 8:20-22). The Garden of Eden had no natural disasters or death until *after* the sin of Adam and Eve (see Genesis 1–3). There will be no natural disasters or death in the new heavens and new earth, when God puts an end to evil once and for all (see Revelation 21:4).

3. *God Will Overcome Evil.* Christian philosophers believe this may not be the best possible world as it now exists, but it is the best way *to* the best possible world (there will be a world of Christians in heaven who have freely chosen to follow Christ). Let us not forget that God is not finished yet. Too often people fall into the trap of thinking that because God has not dealt with evil *yet*, He is not dealing with it *at all*. Evil *will* one day be done away with. Just because evil is not destroyed right now does not mean that it never will be.

In view of the above facts, the existence of evil in the world is seen to be compatible with the existence of an all-good and all-powerful God. We can summarize the facts this way:

1) If God is all-good, He will defeat evil.

2) If God is all-powerful, He can defeat evil.

3) Evil is not *yet* defeated.

4) Therefore, God can and *will one day* defeat evil.

Evolution—See *Creation.*

Exile—See *Captivity and Exile.*

E

Exodus

1. Significance of the Book ◆ 2. Occasion ◆
3. Historicity

1. *Significance of the Book.* Exodus is one of the most-loved books in the Old Testament. One reason for this is that it has all the elements of a great story—strong personalities, powerful drama, great dialogue, and victorious underdogs. But more important, it is a true story about how God redeemed His people from bondage.

The book of Exodus is a continuation of the story that began in Genesis—particularly chapters 37–50. This is clear not only because the first seven verses of Exodus 1 repeat information from Genesis, but also because the first word of verse 1 in the Hebrew text of Exodus is the word "and."

In the Hebrew Bible, Exodus is entitled "And these are the names..." This title is based on the opening words of the book (Exodus 1:1). The ancients often entitled a book according to its first words.

When the Hebrew Bible was translated into the Greek language, this book was given a new title. It was called "Exodus" from the Greek word *exodos.* This is a compound word that joins two Greek words: *ek* (meaning "out of") and *odos* (meaning "a road"). Taken together, the word *exodos* means "a road out of" or "departure." This title describes the central event in the book: Israel's departure from Egypt as a result of the ten plagues God inflicted on Pharaoh and the Egyptians.

The book also deals with God's establishment of a theocratic (God-ruled) nation under Moses by means of a new "constitution" called the Sinai Covenant (chapters 16–40). In this covenant, God gave instructions for the ordering of life among the Hebrew people through the commandments given to Moses at Mount Sinai. Exodus also provides detailed information about the tabernacle and the ministry of the priests. The book was probably written around 1440 B.C.

E

2. Occasion. From the time of Joseph's death at the end of Genesis to the time of the book of Exodus, nearly 300 years had passed. The Israelites had once been favored and privileged guests of the pharaoh and Joseph, but now they had become a nation of slaves. The pharaoh who had been favorably disposed toward Joseph had died. Egypt had forgotten its indebtedness to Joseph.

The new pharaoh, unfamiliar with Joseph, departed from his predecessor's graciousness. He introduced a harsh policy against the Hebrews designed to guarantee the national security of Egypt and alleviate fears of a possible Israelite rebellion.

The backdrop of the pharaoh's fear was the Israelite's incredible growth—to about 2 million people. The pharaoh feared that if a foreign invader made war with Egypt, the Israelites might join forces with them and overrun Egypt (Exodus 1:10). The pharaoh thus decided to initiate a policy that would exploit their labor potential (by slavery) while at the same time check their growing population. He did this by consigning the Israelites to hard labor in building treasure cities.

The Israelites suffered cruel bondage in this way for many years. But God had not forgotten the promise He made to the patriarchs. He "remembered his covenant with Abraham, with Isaac and with Jacob" (Exodus 2:24). He would send a deliverer.

3. Historicity. Some scholars have raised concern about the historicity of Exodus in view of the fact that no Egyptian records mention the event. However, this should not cause undue concern. The Egyptians were *soundly defeated* in the Exodus event, and despite the efforts of the mighty pharaoh, the Israelites got away. Rulers of strong nations in ancient times sought to commemorate their victories, not humiliating defeats. In their own self-interest, the Egyptians likely chose not to record this event. It is understandable why the pharaoh would not want it to be recorded that Egypt lost a chariot brigade during the pursuit of some runaway slaves.

Ezekiel, Book of

The book of Ezekiel was written by the prophet Ezekiel, the son of Buzi, between 593 and 570 B.C., and his messages were for the Jews in exile. God had called him into service as a prophet when he was about 30 years of age. At the time, he was training to be a priest. Like all the other Jews, however, he soon found himself living in exile in Babylon, and this captivity would last 70 years.

Ezekiel's name literally means "God is strong" or "strengthened by God." To carry on his work of confronting the people regarding their sins and bringing comfort to them while in exile, Ezekiel would surely need God's strength.

As a prophet, Ezekiel was quite unique. He would often dramatize God's message by using signs, symbols, and parables. (For example, he said the dispersed Jews were like dry bones in the sun in chapter 37.) By using such techniques, Ezekiel graphically communicated that God's judgment falls as a result of human sin. This is the message he proclaimed during the first part of his ministry.

In 597 B.C., when he and some 3000 other Jews were exiled in Babylon by Nebuchadnezzar (the uncontested ruler of the world at that time), Ezekiel started to speak a new message—words of hope and comfort, teaching that God would regather His people from the ends of the earth, and a new temple would one day be built (Ezekiel 40). He tried to give the people something to look forward to.

Ezra, Book of

The book of Ezra was probably written by Ezra between 457 and 444 B.C. The Hebrew form of Ezra's name means "Jehovah helps." Ezra speaks about the return of the Jewish people from 70 years of captivity in Babylon. This return was allowed by the decree of King Cyrus of Persia. Actually, there were two "returns" from Babylon, one led by Zerubbabel (Ezra 1–6), and then nearly six decades later, one under Ezra (7–10). The first return had as its aim the rebuilding of the temple (1:1–2:70). The second return had as its aim Ezra's rebuilding (or reform) of his peoples' spiritual lives (7:1–8:36). Ezra was instrumental in teaching the Jews about God's law. He sought to revive his people according to this law (9:1–10:44).

E

Faith

1. *Perceiving Unseen Realities.* The apostle Paul defined faith as "being sure of what we hope for and certain of what we do not see" (Hebrews 11:1). The big problem for most people is that they tend to base everything on what the five senses reveal. And since the spiritual world is not subject to any of these, the faith of many people is often weak and impotent.

The eye of faith, however, perceives this unseen reality. The spiritual world lies all about us, enclosing us, embracing us, altogether within our reach. God Himself is here awaiting our response to His presence. He is here to comfort us. This spiritual world will come alive to us the moment we begin to reckon upon its reality.

This is illustrated in the story of Elisha in 2 Kings 6:8-17. Elisha found himself in a situation where he was completely surrounded by enemy troops, yet he remained calm and relaxed. His servant, however, must have been climbing the walls at the sight of this hostile army with vicious-looking warriors and innumerable battle chariots on every side. Undaunted, Elisha said to him: "Don't be afraid...Those who are with us are more than those who are with them" (6:16). Elisha then prayed to God, "'O LORD, open his eyes so he may see.' Then the LORD opened the servant's eyes, and he looked and saw the hills full of horses and chariots of fire all around Elisha" (6:17). God was protecting Elisha and his servant with a whole army of magnificent angelic beings!

The reason Elisha never got worried was because he was "sure of what he hoped for and certain of what he did not see" (Hebrews 11:1). The eye of faith recognizes that God acts on our behalf even when we do not perceive it with our physical senses.

2. Conditioning the Faith Muscle. Bible expositors have often commented that faith is like a muscle. A muscle has to be repeatedly stretched to its limit of endurance in order to build more strength. Without increased stress in training, the muscle will simply not grow.

In the same way, faith must be repeatedly tested to the limit of its endurance in order to expand and develop. Very often, God allows His children to go through trying experiences in order to develop their faith muscles (1 Peter 1:7).

This principle is illustrated in the book of Exodus. Following Israel's deliverance from Egypt, God first led them to Marah, a place where they would have to trust God to heal the water to make it drinkable. It is significant that God led them to Marah before leading them to Elim, a gorgeous oasis with plenty of good water (Exodus 15:22-27). God could have bypassed Marah altogether and brought them directly to Elim if He had wanted to. But, as is characteristic of God, He purposefully led them through the route that would yield maximum conditioning of their faith muscles. God does the same thing with us. He often governs our circumstances so as to yield maximum conditioning of our faith muscles.

3. Faith and the Word of God. There is no question that the Word of God can strengthen the faith of believers. John's Gospel tells us that "these things are written that you may believe" (John 20:31). Paul tells us that "faith comes from hearing the message, and the message is heard through the word of Christ" (Romans 10:17). If someone should ask, "How can I increase my faith?" the answer is this: Saturate your mind with God's Word.

113

4. *Hope That Fuels Faith.* Our hope in the future glory of the afterlife fuels our faith in the present. Hope and faith—these are closely tied to each other in the pages of Scripture. The apostle Paul tells us that faith involves "being sure of what we *hope* for" (Hebrews 11:1, emphasis added). Moses illustrates this fact for us:

> By faith Moses, when he had grown up, refused to be known as the son of Pharaoh's daughter. He chose to be mistreated along with the people of God rather than to enjoy the pleasures of sin for a short time. He regarded disgrace for the sake of Christ as of greater value than the treasures of Egypt, because *he was looking ahead to his reward.* By faith he left Egypt, not fearing the king's anger; he persevered because *he saw him who is invisible.* (Hebrews 11:24-27, emphasis added)

Moses could have had immeasurable power, authority, and riches if he had chosen to stay in Egypt. Yet he gave it all up because of his faith in God. He perceived another King, another kingdom. And his faith was nourished by his hope of a future reward, a hope of living in the eternal city with the living Lord of the universe, a hope that gave him an eternal perspective. May we follow Moses's lead!

Fall, The

"The Fall" is a theological term that refers to the sin of the first man and woman, Adam and Eve, and the subsequent plunging of the human race into a state of sin and corruption. Adam and Eve's sin did not just affect them in an isolated way. It affected the entire human race. Ever since then, every human being born into the world has been born in a state of sin (see Psalm 51:5; Romans 5:12,19; 1 Corinthians 15:21-22).

Theologians affirm that since the time of Adam and Eve, every human being is born into the world "totally depraved." This does not mean that every human being is as bad as they can be, or that they commit all the sins that are possible, or

114

that they are incapable of doing kind and benevolent things to others. What it does mean is that every human is contaminated in every part of his being by sin, and that there is nothing that any human being can do to earn merit before a just and holy God (see Galatians 2:16). Man is too entrenched in sin to be able to impress God by what he considers to be "good works."

Interestingly, before the Fall there were four levels of authority: God—man—woman—animals. In the Fall this is inverted into precisely the opposite: animal (serpent)—woman—man—God. Eve listened to the serpent instead of Adam; Adam listened to Eve instead of God.

F

False Prophets and Teachers

1. God's People Can Be Deceived ◆ 2. Criteria for Recognizing a False Prophet

1. *God's People Can Be Deceived.* Scripture contains many warnings against false prophets and false teachers for the simple reason that it is entirely possible for God's own people to be deceived. Ezekiel 34:1-6, for example, indicates that God's sheep can be abused and led astray by wicked shepherds. Jesus warned His followers: "Watch out for false prophets. They come to you in sheep's clothing, but inwardly they are ferocious wolves" (Matthew 7:15). Why would Jesus warn His followers to "watch out" if there was no possibility that they could be deceived (see also Matthew 24:4,11)? The apostle Paul likewise warned his Christian readers about the possibility of deception (2 Corinthians 11:2-3; see also Acts 20:28-30). It is in view of the possibility of such deception that the Bible exhorts believers to "test" those who claim to be prophets (see 1 John 4:1-2).

2. *Criteria for Recognizing a False Prophet.* How can believers recognize a false prophet? Deuteronomy 18:21-22

F

indicates that false prophets are those who give false prophecies that do not come true. Other verses in the Bible indicate that false prophets sometimes cause people to follow false gods or idols (Exodus 20:3-4; Deuteronomy 13:1-3); they often deny the deity of Jesus Christ (Colossians 2:8-9); they sometimes deny the humanity of Jesus Christ (1 John 4:1-2); they sometimes advocate abstaining from certain foods and/or meats for spiritual reasons (1 Timothy 4:3-4); they sometimes deprecate or deny the need for marriage (1 Timothy 4:3); they often promote immorality (Jude 4-7); and they often encourage legalistic self-denial (Colossians 2:16-23). A basic rule of thumb is that if a so-called prophet says anything that clearly contradicts *any part* of God's Word, his teachings should be rejected (Acts 17:11; 1 Thessalonians 5:21).

Family

1. Members ◆ 2. Instituted by God ◆
3. Authority of the Father ◆ 4. Inheritance

1. *Members.* In modern society the family unit typically consists of a father, mother, and their children. But this is not the way it was among the early Israelites. In biblical times the family unit included grandparents, aunts, uncles, grandchildren, and even slaves and servants. Moreover, families in those days were patriarchal in the sense that the father was the head of his immediate family (wife and children) and the grandfather was considered the head of the entire clan. (The word "patriarchy" means "rule of the father.") Some families were even larger due to polygamous relationships. This large size of families is illustrated with Jacob, whose family numbered 66 people when they moved to Egypt (Genesis 46:26).

2. *Instituted by God.* God Himself instituted the family unit for the good of all human beings. God designed the marriage

116

relationship involving one man and one woman (monogamy was always God's ideal, see Genesis 1–2). God told the first man and woman, Adam and Eve, to be fruitful and multiply (1:28), thus introducing children into the family unit.

In order to protect commitment to God and harmony within the family, God's law commanded that believers were not to marry among unbelievers (Exodus 34:13-16; Deuteronomy 7:3-4). This same truth is emphasized by the apostle Paul (2 Corinthians 6:14). A striking negative example of the importance of this principle is found in the person of Solomon, who, in his old age, was led astray by some of his foreign wives who worshiped other gods (1 Kings 11:4).

3. *Authority of the Father.* It was not until later in biblical history that Israelites began to settle into homes and the family unit became smaller. At that time, the father became the sole authority of his house. In fact, fathers had *so much* authority that modern people have a hard time understanding it. For example, the man as the head of the house could easily divorce his wife for any reason without having to go through a court of law. He could essentially say, "I divorce you," and that was the end of the matter. If the woman was a bad cook, he could divorce her. In a culture where women had few rights, such a divorce would be devastating to her. It was also within the father's rights to sell a child into slavery if he deemed it necessary. Of course, it should not be assumed that this happened often, but it was nevertheless within the rights of the father to do so.

4. *Inheritance.* Another area where women received less than a "fair shake" relates to inheritance rights. Generally speaking, sons would inherit their father's estate upon their father's death, with the firstborn son receiving a double portion of the inheritance. Daughters would receive an inheritance only if there were no sons in the family.

F

Farming

Farming was important in biblical times, for it was the major source of food. Different farming activities took place in different months. For example, in October and November, farmers planted seeds of wheat, barley, and flax, scattering them by hand and then using a plough to cover the seed with earth. Later, in January and February (perhaps even March), other seeds—millet, peas, lentils, melons, and cucumbers—were planted. During this time the winter rains fell.

In June, July, and August, the vines were pruned. These vines were planted in rows, and branches from the vines were raised to rest on support hedges. When these vines started to produce fruit, shelters would be erected to protect them.

Different crops were then harvested in different months. For example, flax was harvested in March and April. Wheat and barley were harvested in April, May, and June.

Wheat and barley were among the most important crops. Following harvesting, the stalks of the wheat and barley were cut, bundled, sliced into sheaves, and loaded for transportation to a threshing floor. This threshing floor was often a community property used by a number of farmers. When the threshing took place, the farmer would typically chop up the stalks and loosen the grain. Then the farmer would toss the stalks into the air with a shovel. The lighter straw was blown aside, while the heavier grain fell back to the floor. This made the process of separating the grain from the stalk relatively easy.

Later, in August and September, fruits such as figs, pomegranates, and grapes were harvested. The grapes were squeezed and the juice was used to make wine. This "squeezing" took place by putting the grapes into small vats with special floors that were angled toward container jars, and hired workers would literally stomp or tread upon the grapes with their bare feet, causing the juice to flow into the jars.

Farming was quite clearly central to Israel's survival.

Fasting

The word "fast" is rooted in a Hebrew word that means "cover the mouth"—thus indicating abstinence from food and/or drink. In the Old Testament, only one fast was commanded, and that was on the annual Day of Atonement (Leviticus 16:29-31). It was only after the fall of Jerusalem that additional "fast days" were instituted (see Zechariah 7:3-5; 8:19).

Ideally, fast days were to be a time of self-denial and repentance from sin. During fasts, the people were supposed to humble their souls before God while abstaining from food. They were also to reflect on their relationship with God and the need to fully obey His commandments.

Unfortunately, the Jews of New Testament times would often make a show of their fasts, tearing their clothes and putting dust and ashes on their heads, not bathing, and not combing their hair. They made sure everybody *knew* they were fasting. Jesus condemned such external theatrics and made it clear that the most important thing was the internal change in a person's heart (Matthew 6:16-18).

There are several very famous fasts recorded in the Bible. Moses abstained from bread and drink during his 40 days on Mount Sinai when he received the law from God (Exodus 34:28). Jesus also fasted for 40 days before His temptation (Matthew 4:2).

Festivals, Annual

1. The Passover and the Feast of Unleavened Bread ◆
2. Feast of Harvest ◆ 3. Feast of Ingathering ◆
4. Day of Atonement ◆ 5. Feast of Purim ◆
6. Hanukkah

1. *The Passover and the Feast of Unleavened Bread.* The Passover is the most significant event in Israel's religious history. This festival celebrates the escape of the Jews from Egypt under the leadership of Moses.

119

Jewish Festivals

JEWISH FESTIVALS	JEWISH MONTH	OUR MONTH
Passover and Unleavened Bread	Nisan	April
	Iyyar	May
Harvest (Weeks, First Fuits, or Pentecost)	Sivan	June
	Tammuz	July
	Ab	August
	Elul	September
Trumpets, Day of Atonement, and Ingathering	Tishri	October
	Marchesvan	November
Dedication (Hanakkuh)	Kislev	December
	Tebet	January
	Shebat	February
Purim	Adar	March

Passover was celebrated the evening before the fourteenth of Nissan (see Exodus 12:1-11). Each family sacrificed a lamb to commemorate the sacrifice that took place just prior to the Israelites' exodus from Egypt. On that occasion, God literally "passed over" each Israelite house that had the blood of a lamb sprinkled on the doorpost. The lives of the firstborn children of Israel were thereby spared (see Exodus 12).

During the Passover meal and throughout the following week, unleavened bread was eaten (see Exodus 23:15). This

F

type of bread was made without yeast and was prepared very quickly. Such bread served to remind those celebrating Passover of the hurried preparations that were made when Pharaoh finally allowed the Israelites to leave Egypt.

2. Feast of Harvest. The Feast of Harvest (Exodus 23:16) was held in the spring at the beginning of the wheat harvest (see Exodus 34:22). In this feast, two loaves made of new grain were to be presented to the Lord (Leviticus 23:15-21). In this way, the people gave thanks to God for the grain He provided them. This feast is also called the Feast of Weeks (Exodus 34:22) because it was held seven weeks (or 50 days) after the Feast of Unleavened Bread.

In later Judaism, the Feast of Harvest came to commemorate the giving of the law at Mount Sinai, though no Old Testament passages substantiate this. In New Testament times, the feast was called "Pentecost" (Acts 2:1), which means "50."

3. Feast of Ingathering. The Feast of Ingathering (Exodus 23:16) was held in early autumn (September–October) at the end of the agricultural year, after the harvest had been gathered in. The feast was a time of great gladness and thanksgiving for the final harvest, which God had provided the people. Elsewhere in Scripture, this feast is called the Feast of Tabernacles or Feast of Booths because the Israelites lived in temporary shelters after God brought them out of Egypt (Leviticus 23:33-36; Deuteronomy 16:13-15; 31:10). This feast, which lasted eight days, commemorated the desert wanderings following the Exodus. The people would make themselves a shelter of branches, and this served to remind them of how their ancestors had lived in tents in the desert.

4. Day of Atonement. On this day, all Israelites would confess their sins to God and ask His forgiveness and cleansing (see Leviticus 16; Numbers 29:7-11; 2 Chronicles 7:8-9). The high priest first offered a sacrifice for his own sins, and then he offered a sacrifice on behalf of the people. On this day alone the high priest was permitted to enter into the Holy of Holies in the temple to offer the sacrifice. Following this, the high priest would then lay hands on a scapegoat in a symbolic transference of the peoples' sins to the goat, and it was sent into the desert, representing the fact that the people's sins had been taken away.

F

5. *Feast of Purim.* "Purim" literally means "lots," and this day of celebration relates back to the lots that were cast by the chief minister of King Ahasuerus to decide which day he should massacre the Jews. As we read in the Old Testament book of Esther, the Lord saved the Israelites from the plot to massacre them. Hence, there is great cause for celebration (see Esther 3:7; 9:23-32).

6. *Hanukkah.* On this holy day, the Jews commemorated both the cleansing and rededication of the temple by Judas Maccabaeus in 164 B.C. This took place after Antiochus Epiphanes defiled the temple (see Daniel 8:9-12; John 10:22).

Flood, Noah's

The flood of Noah's time came upon humankind because the whole earth became filled with violence and corruption (Genesis 6). Noah stood out as the only one who honored and obeyed God during this time (verse 9). He was a just and righteous man.

Some scholars have questioned whether this flood was universal and have suggested that perhaps it was just a local phenomena in the general location of Noah. The biblical evidence, however, supports the idea that the flood was worldwide and universal. After all, the biblical text indicates that the waters climbed so high on the earth that "all the high mountains under the entire heavens were covered" (Genesis 7:19). They rose so greatly on the earth that they "covered the mountains to a depth of more than twenty feet" (verse 20). The flood lasted some 377 days (nearly 54 weeks), indicating more than just local flooding. The Bible also says that every living thing that moved on the earth perished, "all the creatures that swarm over the earth, and all mankind. Everything on dry land that had the breath of life in its nostrils died. Every living thing on the face of the earth was wiped out... Only Noah was left, and those with him in the ark" (verses 21-23). The language of Genesis 6–9 is surely that of a universal flood.

F

Further, the universal view best explains the fact that there is a worldwide distribution of diluvia deposits. A universal flood would also explain the sudden death of many woolly mammoths frozen in Alaskan and Siberian ice. Investigation shows that these animals died suddenly by choking or drowning and not by freezing.

Finally, there is supportive evidence in the fact that there are many universal flood legends (over 270) among people of various religions and cultural backgrounds all over the world. These people attribute the descent of all races to Noah.

Flowers and Plants

There are many different kinds of flowers mentioned in the Bible. Jesus, for example, makes reference to lilies of the field (Matthew 6:28; Luke 12:27). The hills of Galilee, during springtime in particular, are covered with brightly colored flowers such as the yellow chrysanthemum, crocus poppy, narcissus, cyclamen, and anemone, all of which were broadly categorized as lilies.

Jesus also made mention of the mustard seed, which is a very small seed that grows into a great plant. In fact, mustard plants can grow up to 15 feet high, though most grow to around four feet high. Jesus used this plant to illustrate that the kingdom of God starts small but grows mightily (see Matthew 13:31-32).

A spongelike plant mentioned in both the Old and New Testaments is the hyssop. A hyssop is a common plant—perhaps a species of origanum—that grows on rocky surfaces. This plant has a straight stalk, a mintlike flavor, and stiff branches with hairy leaves. It was widely used in biblical times in rites of purification and to sprinkle the blood of sacrifices (Exodus 12:21-22; Leviticus 14). In the New Testament, we find Jesus being given vinegar on the cross by a hyssop sponge (John 19:29).

Understandably, in view of the desert climate of much of Palestine, thistles, thorns, and tares are often mentioned in the New Testament. Recall, for example, that Jesus spoke of tares in His parable of the wheat and tares, where wheat represents believers and tares represent unbelievers (Matthew 13:24-30 NASB). Further, a crown of thorns was put on Jesus' head at His trial prior to His crucifixion (Mark 15:17).

Spikenard is a plant that was often used in ancient times to make perfume. Mary anointed Jesus' head with this sweet-smelling ointment to honor Him (Mark 14:3 KJV).

Cumin and dill were used as spices and seasoning herbs in biblical times. Dill seeds, for example, were a common ingredient in bread. In Matthew 23:23 we find Jesus speaking against the Pharisees who gave one-tenth of everything to God, including their seasoning herbs like cumin and dill. However, Jesus said they paid virtually no attention to the more important matters of honesty, justice, and mercy.

An important plant in the production of paper in ancient times was the papyrus, which grew in the Nile Delta. Stems of the papyrus were cut into strips, and one strip would be laid upon another at right angles and pressed on a flat surface. Later, a papyrus roll would be formed by placing sheets of the paper end to end and pasting them together.

Myrrh is referenced in both the Old and New Testaments. For example, in the New Testament we find the wise men bringing a gift of myrrh to the baby Jesus (Matthew 2:11; see also Genesis 37:25). Myrrh is essentially a yellow gum that comes from a shrub, and in Bible times it was used as a medicine, spice, and holy oil.

These and many other flowers and plants are featured throughout the pages of the Bible.

Food and Drink

1. Daily Task ◆ 2. Threats to Food Supply ◆
3. Common Foods ◆ 4. Provisions for Poor

F

1. *Daily Task.* Unlike some parts of the world today where there is plenty of food to buy in local supermarkets, in the ancient Near East there was not an abundance of food but generally only enough to meet daily needs. The production and preparation of food was a daily task, and there were no guarantees that everyone would have a full stomach.

2. *Threats to Food Supply.* In biblical times, there were always threats to the food supply—even in Palestine, the land of "milk and honey" (Exodus 13:5). An enemy might invade and destroy all the crops. Locusts might swoop in out of nowhere and consume the crops in less than an hour. If there was not enough rain, the crops would not grow. Because of such factors, famines often occurred in biblical times. So long as everything went well, however, people could generally produce enough food for daily needs.

3. *Common Foods.* Generally speaking, people in biblical times would eat such things as fruit, vegetables, bread, fish, and meat. They drank either water, goat's milk, wine, or perhaps water with enough wine in it to purify it. Common fruit of the day included figs, grapes, pomegranates, olives, and citrus fruit. Vegetables included melons, cucumbers, onions, leeks, beans, lentils, and peas. Many vegetables were eaten raw, though lentils and beans were generally boiled. Sometimes these vegetables were used to make a pot of soup or stew. (Read about Esau foolishly surrendering his birthright for a hearty serving of such soup in Genesis 25:29-34.)

125

Rich people often ate such meats as lamb, veal, and beef. The more common people generally ate cheaper meats, such as that of goats and birds, if they ate meat at all. (In many cases, common people ate meat only on special occasions, such as a guest's visit or perhaps a wedding feast.) The meat was most often boiled. According to Old Testament Law, certain kinds of animals could not be eaten (such as swine). The kinds of animals permissible for eating were those that chewed the cud and had divided hooves (see Leviticus 11:3). Animal fat was forbidden as food (Leviticus 3:17; 7:23). Only fish with fins and scales were permissible for food. Insects that had legs and could leap into the air (grasshoppers, for example) were also permitted.

Bread was a principle food in Bible times (see Isaiah 3:1 NASB). Bread was typically made from barley or wheat grains, though other grains were certainly available and used at times. The grain was ground by placing it on a large stone and then rubbing it with a smaller stone. Later in biblical history, a millstone was used. The ground grain was then used to make bread. During the process, a piece of fermented dough (leavening) from the previous day's baking of bread was mixed into the new dough, so the bread would rise properly when baked. A typical workingman's lunch might be a few loaves of barley bread.

For seasoning, the ancients used salt, cumin, and dill, which were widely available. If a person had a sweet tooth, honey from wild bees was used.

4. *Provisions for Poor.* The law stipulated that farmers should leave the corners of their fields unharvested. This way, poor people who walked by could pick some food to eat (see Leviticus 19:9-10; 23:22; Ruth 2:2).

Forgiveness

Forgiveness involves pardoning or excusing the sins, faults, and shortcomings of others. Because of the salvation Christ accomplished at the cross, those who place their faith in Him are completely forgiven of *all* their sins (Acts 2:38).

A popular passage in the Old Testament on the forgiveness of sins is Psalm 103:11-12: "For as high as the heavens are above the earth, so great is his love for those who fear him; as far as the east is from the west, so far has he removed our transgressions from us." There is a definite point that is "north" and another that is "south"—the North and South Poles. But there are no such points for "east" and "west." It does not matter how far one goes to the east; one will never arrive where east begins because by definition east is the opposite of west. The two never meet. They could never meet because they are opposites. To remove sins "as far as the east is from the west" is to put them where no one can ever find them. That is the forgiveness God grants believers.

One of the most potent illustrations of the forgiveness of sins in the New Testament relates to the apostle Paul's comments on the "certificate of debt" in Colossians 2:13-14. In ancient days, whenever someone was found guilty of a crime, the offender was put in jail and a certificate of debt was posted on the jail door. This certificate listed all the crimes the offender was found guilty of. Upon release, after serving the prescribed time in jail, the offender was given the certificate of debt, and on it was stamped "Paid in Full."

Scripture says that Christ took the certificate of debt of each of our lives and nailed it to the cross. His sacrifice "paid in full" the price for our sins. Interestingly, the phrase "It is finished," which Jesus uttered upon the cross in completing the work of salvation (John 19:30), comes from the same Greek word translated "paid in full." We are truly forgiven!

Scripture teaches that because God has forgiven us, we should also forgive others (Matthew 18:21-22, 35; Luke 17:4).

Fornication—See *Sex and Sexuality.*

Funerals

1. *A Fast Process.* Unlike modern funerals, the funerals in biblical times were performed quickly. This is for the practical reason that the hot climate would rapidly cause decay and stench. Traditionally, when a person died, he or she would immediately be bathed and then wrapped in strips of linen. Sometimes a gummy combination of spices was applied to the wrappings of the body. It was then carried by stretcher to the place of burial, either a grave or a cave. In some cases, entire families might be buried in a large cave. Eventually, in some areas, because of a lack of available cave space, bones would often later be removed from a cave and then stored in a wooden or stone chest.

2. *Occasional Cremations.* In the Bible, cremation is portrayed only as an exceptional method of disposing of bodies. Most often cremation took place in the midst of unusual circumstances. For example, in 1 Samuel 31:12 we read about the men of Jabesh-Gilead who burned the corpses of Saul and his sons in order to prevent desecration of their bodies at the hands of the Philistines. Cremation is not mentioned in the New Testament. Burial was the normal method, not only in New Testament times but also among the early church fathers.

3. *Period of Mourning.* Another distinction between modern times and biblical times is that today, most people prefer to mourn privately for their lost loved ones. By contrast, the ancient Israelites made a very big show of their grief. They would typically weep and wail loudly, put ashes on their heads, tear their clothing in grief, walk barefoot, shave their beards off, and much more. In many cases, professional mourners would be hired to add to the loud wailing. The traditional time of mourning was seven days, but an important person might be mourned for much longer. Joseph was mourned for 70 days.

F

G

Galatians

The apostle Paul wrote the epistle to the churches in the Roman province of Galatia in A.D. 50. The name "Galatia" was derived from a group of people known as the Gauls, who occupied the northern part of Asia Minor, an area formerly known as Cappadocia and Phrygia. In 25 B.C., the Romans incorporated this northern section into a larger division of land that was made into a province and given the name Galatia.

In his epistle to the Galatians, Paul sought to confirm his authority as a genuine apostle of Jesus Christ (Galatians 1:10–2:21). Apparently Judaizers who had infiltrated some of Paul's congregations had challenged Paul's credentials. They were unhappy with the way Paul freely invited Gentiles to come to God. They argued that in order to make the Gospel more appealing to Gentiles, Paul removed certain legal requirements (such as circumcision). Their purpose was therefore to "Judaize" these Gentile believers—that is, persuade them that, after believing in Christ, they must take an additional step and become Jews through circumcision, eat only the right kind of foods, and participate in certain Jewish feast days (see Acts 15:1-29; Galatians 2:15-16; 3:15;4:17-20; 5:1-12; 6:12-13).

All this effectively added works to grace, and Paul would not have it. Salvation, in Paul's theology, is a gift that is received by faith in Christ (Galatians 3:6-9). Paul went so far as to teach that if anyone delivers to the church any other gospel than the one he previously handed down (including a gospel from Judaizers), they were accursed before God (1:8). Salvation is by grace alone, Paul said, and there is no requirement for Gentiles to "become Jews" in order to be true Christians. Christians are to live according to the law of love, not the law of Moses.

Games—See *Sports and Games.*

Gehenna—See *Hell.*

Genealogies of Jesus

There are two different genealogies of Jesus in the Bible, one found in Matthew 1:1-17 and the other in Luke 3:23-38. Up to David, the two genealogies are very similar, practically the same. In fact, they share some 18 or 19 common names, depending on whether Matthan and Matthat are the same person. From David on, they are very different. Almost none of the names from David to Joseph coincide. (In fact, only two of the names—Shealtiel and Zerubbabel—coincide.) However, the genealogies are not irreconcilable.

Matthew's genealogy traces Joseph's line of descendants and deals with the passing of the *legal title* to the throne of David. As Joseph's adopted Son, Jesus became his *legal heir* so far as His inheritance was concerned. The "of whom was born Jesus" (Matthew 1:16) is a feminine relative pronoun, clearly indicating that Jesus was the physical child of Mary and that Joseph was not His physical father.

Matthew traced the line from Abraham and David in 41 links to Joseph. (Matthew obviously did not list every individual in the genealogy. Jewish reckoning did not require every name in order to satisfy a genealogy.) Abraham's and David's were the two unconditional covenants pertaining to the Messiah. Matthew's Gospel was written to Jews, so Matthew wanted to prove to Jews that Jesus was the promised Messiah. This would demand a fulfillment of the Abrahamic Covenant (Genesis 12:1-3) and the Davidic Covenant (2 Samuel 7:12-13). Matthew was calling attention to the fact that Jesus came to fulfill the covenants made with Israel's forefathers.

Luke's genealogy, by contrast, traces Mary's lineage all the way back beyond the time of Abraham to Adam and the commencement of the human race. Whereas Matthew's genealogy pointed to Jesus as the Messiah, Luke's genealogy points to Jesus as the Son of Man, a name often used of Jesus in Luke's Gospel. And whereas Matthew's genealogy presents the Messiah to the Jews, Luke's genealogy introduces the Son of Man to the entire human race.

Genesis

Genesis derives its name from the first three words of the book, "In the beginning." "Genesis" means "beginning." Genesis is the book of beginnings. It contains an account of the beginnings of the universe, the world, and humankind. Moses probably wrote the book between 1445 and 1405 B.C.

Besides speaking of God's creation of the universe (Genesis 1–2), the book also details the Fall of man and the consequences of that Fall (3), the lives of Adam and his family (4–5), Noah and the worldwide flood (6–10), the judgment that took place at the Tower of Babel, after which the nations were dispersed (11), descriptions of the lives of the patriarchs Abraham, Isaac, Esau, and Jacob (12–36), Joseph being betrayed and eventually reconciled with his brothers (37–45), and Jacob's move with his family to Egypt (46–50).

It is not too much to say that the book of Genesis constitutes the foundation for the rest of the Bible. Indeed, if there is a Creator, as the book of Genesis indicates, then human beings are creatures who are responsible to Him. If man is fallen in sin, as the book of Genesis indicates, then man is guilty and is in need of redemption. If one dismisses the book of Genesis as mere myth, then much of the rest of the Bible makes little sense.

Perhaps one of the most exciting things about Genesis is that a number of the people mentioned in the book are heroes of faith. For example, Abraham's faith was especially evident when he was being obedient to God's command to sacrifice his own son Isaac (Genesis 22:1-19). (God stopped him just in the nick of time.) Joseph, too, showed great faith, knowing that, despite how his brothers treated him cruelly, God was with him and was working in the situations he found himself in (50:20). In the end, God elevated Joseph to a supreme position in Egypt.

A major foundational covenant in the book of Genesis is the Abrahamic Covenant. God made this covenant with Abraham (Genesis 12:1-3; 15:1-21), and later reaffirmed it with Isaac (17:21) and Jacob (35:9-12). In this covenant, God promised Abraham:

1) I will make you a great nation.

2) I will bless you.

3) I will make your name great.

4) You will be a blessing.

5) I will bless those who bless you.

6) I will curse those who curse you.

7) All peoples on earth will be blessed through you.

Gentiles

"Gentile" is a Jewish term that refers to all people who are not Jews but foreigners (see Matthew 4:15; Romans 3:29; 11:11,13; 15:10; 16:4; Galatians 2:8,12,14; Ephesians 3:1). During the apostle Paul's day, "Gentile" was sometimes considered a term of scorn. The Jews even had a prayer that included the words, "I thank you, God, that I am not a Gentile or a dog." The Jews believed that even casual contact with a Gentile brought contamination, and so they made every effort to avoid them.

When Paul went from city to city preaching the Gospel, he generally appealed "to the Jew first" and then to the Gentiles (Romans 1:16 NASB). His greatest response in sharing the Gospel was always from the Gentiles (Acts 13:46; 18:6; 19:8-10; 21:19; 26:20,23; 28:28). This rejection by the Jews and reception by the Gentiles served as a confirmation of Paul's appointment as an apostle to the Gentiles (Romans 11:13).

Paul was uniquely qualified to preach the Gospel of God's grace to the Gentiles. He was formerly a Pharisee who had no doubt shared Pharisaical biases against Gentiles. But following his conversion, he came to see things from God's perspective. He saw that God loves *all* people equally and that His provision of salvation is for all. Hence, he began to preach that all who believe in Christ—Jew or Gentile—become a part of God's eternal family (see Galatians 3:28).

G

Geology of Palestine

Palestine was a desert, with sand and salt covering the landscape. Moreover, a large part of the land surface was limestone. The limestone made much of the ground surface quite rough and rocky, and cultivation of the soil was often difficult. (This makes some of Jesus' statements in Matthew 13 about planting seed in good soil instead of bad rocky soil more understandable.) Further, the hills of Palestine were sprinkled with many caves, which were often used as burial sites. Water wells were also scattered throughout the land.

Gifts of the Spirit

Spiritual gifts are special abilities bestowed sovereignly by the Holy Spirit upon individual believers for the purpose of edifying the church (body of Christ). These gifts include teaching, pastoring, evangelizing, the message of wisdom, the message of knowledge, faith, healing, miraculous powers, prophecy, distinguishing between spirits, speaking in different tongues, and the interpretation of tongues (Romans 12:3-8; 1 Corinthians 12:8-10; Ephesians 4:7-13; 1 Peter 4:10-11).

There is a difference between natural talents and spiritual gifts. Natural talents are from God but are transmitted through parents; spiritual gifts come directly from God the

Holy Spirit (Romans 12:3,6; 1 Corinthians 12:11; Ephesians 4:11). Natural talents are possessed from the moment of birth; spiritual gifts are received when one becomes a Christian. Natural talents are generally used to benefit human beings on the natural level; spiritual gifts bring spiritual blessing to people and edify believers (1 Corinthians 12:11; Ephesians 4:11-16).

There are similarities as well. Both talents and spiritual gifts must be developed and exercised. Otherwise one will not become proficient in their use. As well, both natural talents and spiritual gifts can be used for God's glory. For example, a Christian might have the spiritual gift of teaching. He might also have the natural talent of being able to play the guitar. It is feasible that this person could exercise his spiritual gift of teaching *and* his natural talent by writing and performing songs that teach about God.

Some Christians today—"cessationists"—believe that certain gifts, such as the gift of speaking in tongues and the gift of healing, passed away in the first century. Other Christians—"charismatics"—disagree and believe that all the spiritual gifts are for today.

God

1. One God ◆ 2. A Person ◆ 3. A Spirit ◆
4. Transcendent and Immanent ◆ 5. Attributes ◆
6. Names

1. *One God.* God is an eternal, all-powerful, all-knowing Spirit who is everywhere-present and who is the Creator and Sustainer of the universe. He has revealed Himself in the person of Jesus Christ and in the pages of Scripture.

There are no other gods besides the one true God of Scripture. During the time of Moses, God affirmed, "See now that I myself am He! There is no god besides me" (Deuteronomy 32:39). The God of the Bible is without rival. We find the same thing emphasized in Isaiah 44:6: "This is what the LORD says—Israel's King and Redeemer, the LORD Almighty: I am the first and I am the last; apart from me there is no God" (see also Isaiah 46:9).

2. A Person. A person is a conscious being—one who thinks, feels, purposes, and carries those purposes into action. A person engages in active relationships with others. You can talk to a person and get a response. You can share feelings and ideas with him. You can argue with him, love him, and even hate him. Surely by this definition God must be understood as a person. After all, God is a conscious being who thinks, feels, and purposes—and He carries those purposes into action. He engages in relationships with others. You can talk to God, and He will respond.

The biblical picture of God is that of a loving personal Father to whom believers may cry, "Abba" (Romans 8:15). "Abba" is an Aramaic term of great intimacy, loosely meaning "daddy." In keeping with this, Jesus often spoke of God as a loving Father. Indeed, God is the "Father of compassion" of all believers (2 Corinthians 1:3). He is often portrayed in Scripture as compassionately responding to the personal requests of His people. (A few good examples may be found in Exodus 3:7-8; Job 34:28, Psalm 81:10; 91:14-15; Philippians 4:6-7.)

3. A Spirit. The Scriptures tell us that God is Spirit (John 4:24). A spirit does not have flesh and bones (Luke 24:39 NASB). Hence, it is wrong to think of God as sort of an exalted man in the great beyond. Because God is a spirit, He is invisible. First Timothy 1:17 refers to God as "the King eternal, immortal, invisible, the only God." Colossians 1:15 speaks of "the invisible God" (see also John 1:18).

4. Transcendent and Immanent. The theological phrase "transcendence of God" refers to God's otherness or separateness from the created universe and from humanity. The phrase "immanence of God" refers to God's active presence within the creation and in human history (though all the while remaining distinct from the creation). God's transcendence and immanence are evident in numerous verses. In Deuteronomy 4:39, for example, we read, "Acknowledge and take to heart this day that the LORD is God in heaven above and on the earth below." In Isaiah 57:15 God states: "I live in a high and holy place, but also with him who is contrite and lowly in spirit." In Jeremiah 23:23-24 we read, "'Am I only a God nearby,' declares the LORD, 'and not a God far away? Can anyone hide in secret places so that I cannot see him?' declares the LORD."

5. *Attributes*. One great way to learn about God is to study His attributes. An attribute is a characteristic. The Bible speaks of many of God's characteristics, and the more we learn of these characteristics, the better we understand who God is.

- *God Is Self-Existent.* He is the uncaused First Cause, the self-existent One who brought the universe into being (John 1:3; Colossians 1:16).

- *God Is Eternal.* He has always existed and is beyond time altogether. He is the King eternal (1 Timothy 1:17) who alone is immortal (6:16).

- *God Is Love.* He is not just characterized by love; He is the very personification of love (1 John 4:8). Love virtually permeates His being.

- *God Is Everywhere-Present.* He is omnipresent. This does not mean that God in His divine nature is diffused throughout space as if part of Him is here and part of Him is there. Rather, God in His whole being is in every place. There is nowhere one can go where God is not (Psalm 139:7-8; Jeremiah 23:23-24; Acts 17:27-28; Hebrews 1:3).

- *God Is All-Knowing.* He knows all things, both actual and possible (Matthew 11:21-23). He knows all things past (Isaiah 41:22), present (Hebrews 4:13), and future (Isaiah 46:10). Because He knows all things, there can be no increase or decrease in His knowledge (Psalm 33:13-15; 139:11-12; 147:5; Proverbs 15:3; Isaiah 40:14; 46:10).

G

- *God Is All-Powerful.* He has the power to do all that He desires and wills. He is almighty (Revelation 19:6) and is abundant in strength (Psalm 147:5). No one can hold back His hand (Daniel 4:35), no one can reverse Him (Isaiah 43:13), and no one can thwart Him (Isaiah 14:27). Nothing is impossible with Him (Matthew 19:26), and nothing is too difficult for Him (Genesis 18:14).

- *God Is Sovereign.* He rules the universe, controls all things, and is Lord over all (Ephesians 1). There is nothing that can happen in this universe that is beyond the reach of His control. All forms of existence are within the scope of His absolute dominion (Psalm 50:1; 66:7; 93:1; Isaiah 40:15,17; 1 Timothy 6:15).

- *God Is Unchanging.* He is not subject to change in His being, nature, or attributes. Theologians call this "immutability." God Himself affirmed, "I the LORD do not change" (Malachi 3:6; James 1:17; see also Psalm 102:27; Isaiah 46:10-11; Hebrews 6:17).

- *God Is Holy.* He is entirely separate from all evil and is absolutely righteous (Leviticus 19:2). He is pure in every way (Exodus 15:11; Psalm 71:22; Isaiah 6:3; Revelation 15:4).

- *God Is Just.* He carries out His righteous standards justly and with equity. There is never any partiality or unfairness in God's dealings with people (Zephaniah 3:5; Romans 3:26).

6. Names. We also learn much about God from the names ascribed to Him in the Bible. These names are not man-made; God Himself used these names to describe Himself. They are *characteristic* names, each one making known something new about Him.

- *God Is Yahweh.* This name means that God is eternally self-existent (see Exodus 3:14-15). He never came into being at a point in time. He has always existed.

G

- *God Is Yahweh-Nissi.* This translates to mean "the Lord Our Banner." Israel could not defeat her enemies in her own strength. But the battles were to be the Lord's because He was Israel's banner—her source of victory (Exodus 17:15).

- *God Is Elohim.* This name means "Strong One," and it indicates fullness of power (Genesis 1:1). It pictures God as the powerful and sovereign Governor of the universe, ruling over the affairs of humanity.

- *God Is El Shaddai.* "El" in Hebrew refers to "Mighty God," but "Shaddai" qualifies this meaning and adds something to it (Genesis 17:1-20). Many scholars believe "Shaddai" is derived from a root word that refers to a mother's breast. This name, then, indicates not only that God is a Mighty God, but that He is full of compassion, grace, and mercy, just like a mother.

- *God Is Adonai.* This name means "Lord" or "Master," and conveys God's absolute authority over man (Genesis 18:27).

- *God Is the Lord of Hosts.* This title pictures God as the sovereign Commander of a great heavenly army of angels (Psalm 89:6-8 NASB; 91:11-12).

Gospel (Good News)

1. Definition ◆ 2. Faulty Concepts

1. *Definition.* The word "Gospel" refers to the good news of salvation in Jesus Christ. Perhaps the best single definition of the Gospel is found in 1 Corinthians 15:3-4: "For what I received I passed on to you as of first importance: that Christ died for our sins according to the Scriptures, that he was buried, that he was raised on the third day according to the Scriptures." The "Gospel," according to this passage, has four components:

1. Man is a sinner.
2. Christ is the Savior.
3. Christ died as man's substitute.
4. Christ rose from the dead.

This is the Gospel Paul and the other apostles preached; it is the Gospel we too must preach.

Of course, when explaining the Gospel to someone, this "skeleton" outline from 1 Corinthians 15:3-4 should be "fleshed out" with many other Scripture verses. Scripture says quite a bit about man's sin, Christ's role as Savior, Christ's death on the cross, and Christ's resurrection from the dead. An effective presentation of the Gospel should be rich in Scripture quotations on these issues. (See *Sin and Guilt, Salvation, Jesus Christ,* and *Resurrection.*) Scripture emphasizes that this Gospel message must be received by faith (see Romans 1:16-17).

2. *Faulty Concepts.* There are a number of misconceptions people have had about the Gospel. Following are three examples:

1. Some have taught that one must plead for mercy before one can be saved. However, this idea is never found in Scripture. Salvation comes by faith in Christ

140

(John 3:16; Acts 16:31). God provides pardon for anyone who believes; no one has to plead for it.

2. Some have taught that we must follow Christ's example and seek to live as He lived in order to be a Christian. *The Imitation of Christ,* a book by Thomas à Kempis, has been understood by many to teach that we become Christians by living as Christ did and obeying His teachings, seeking to behave as He behaved. From a scriptural perspective, however, we simply do not have it in us to live as Christ lived. We are fallen human beings (Romans 3:23). Only the Holy Spirit working in us can imitate Christ in our lives (Galatians 5:16-23).

G

3. Some have inadvertently communicated that prayer is a necessary component in becoming saved. In other words, one must pray the "prayer of repentance." The scriptural perspective is that even though prayer may be a vehicle for the expression of one's faith, it is the faith that brings about salvation (Acts 16:31), not the prayer through which that faith is communicated. In fact, one can bypass prayer altogether by simply exercising faith in one's heart, and one becomes saved at that moment.

We must always remember that salvation is a free gift that we receive by faith in Christ (Ephesians 2:8-9). This truly is good news!

Gospels, Four

1. *Selective Accounts.* The Gospels are selective accounts of the life of Jesus that communicate His identity and His message. That they are selective seems clear from statements we find in the Gospels themselves (see Luke 1:1-4; John 20:30; 21:25). They are also selective in the sense that they focus primarily on His three-year ministry, with the exception of a short discussion of His birth and infancy (Matthew 1–2; Luke 1–2). Since God the Holy Spirit inspired these Gospels (2 Timothy 3:16; 2 Peter 1:21), we can assume that *everything* God wanted us to know about the life of Jesus and His ministry is there.

G

The Gospels

	Recipients	Date Written	Depiction of Jesus
Matthew	Jews	Shortly after Mark	Messiah
Mark	Romans	A.D. 50–60	Man of action
Luke	Greeks	Shortly after Mark	Perfect man
John	Christians	A.D. 90	God

2. Distinctions Between the Gospels. Each of the four Gospel writers sought to reach a different audience and therefore included different emphases. Matthew wrote his Gospel to prove to Jews that Jesus was the promised Jewish Messiah. Mark's Gospel, by contrast, had no such Jewish motivation, but rather sought to portray to the Roman culture Jesus *in action* rather than as a teacher. Luke's Gospel is written in the New Testament's finest Greek. It stresses the wonderful blessings of salvation for all people and heavily emphasizes that God's grace is for the undeserving. John's Gospel, written much later than the other three and directed to Christians, focuses heavily on the identity of Jesus and thoroughly demonstrates His divine origin and deity. Such factors account for the differences among the Gospels.

3. No Genuine Contradictions. While the Gospels may seem to have some *apparent* contradictions, I do not believe they have *genuine* contradictions. There are differences, yes, but no actual contradictions. Certainly if all four Gospels were the same, with no differences, critics would be screaming "collusion" all over the place. The fact that the Gospels have differences shows there was no collusion but rather that they represent four different (but inspired) accounts of the same events.

One should not assume that a *partial* account in a Gospel is a *faulty* account. In Matthew 27:5, for example, we are told that Judas died by hanging himself. In Acts 1:18 we are told that Judas burst open in the middle and all his entrails gushed out. These are both partial accounts. Neither account gives us the full picture. But taken together we can easily reconstruct how Judas died. He hanged himself, and sometime later the rope loosened and Judas fell to the rocks below, thereby causing his intestines to gush out.

As one probes into alleged contradictions in the Gospel accounts, one consistently sees that they are all explainable in a reasonable way.

4. Jesus' Primary Teaching. In all four Gospels, it is clear that the very heart of Jesus' teaching is the kingdom of God. This refers to God's reign as King over all the earth—even in the hearts of people today. The kingdom of God arrived in New Testament times because the King (Jesus) had arrived. The kingdom was present because the King was present (see Matthew 5:3; 12:28; 19:24; 21:31,43; 25:34; Luke 12:32; John 3:3,5; 18:36; Romans 14:17; Colossians 1:13; James 2:5; 2 Peter 1:11; Revelation 12:10). There is also a future aspect of the kingdom involving a thousand-year reign of Christ on earth following the Second Coming (Revelation 20:1-6).

5. Timing of the Gospels. The Gospels were not actually composed until at least 30 years following the death of Jesus.

143

G

Prior to this time, the material that eventually made its way into the Gospels was passed down orally or preserved in various written documents that no longer exist. This should not lead one to conclude, however, that such material was (or became) inaccurate. The evidence indicates that oral tradition in biblical times was *extremely* accurate. Even from an early age, Jewish children were taught to remember oral material accurately. Further, we must not forget that the Holy Spirit inspired these Gospels (2 Timothy 3:16; 2 Peter 1:21), thereby guaranteeing their accuracy.

Government—See *Kingship*.

Grace

The word "grace" literally means "unmerited favor." "Unmerited" means this favor cannot be worked for. Grace, theologically speaking, refers to the *undeserved, unearned* favor of God. In regard to salvation, Romans 5:1-11 tells us that God gives His incredible grace to those who actually deserve the opposite—that is, condemnation.

Eternal life, according to Scripture, cannot be earned. Verse after verse in Scripture indicates that eternal life is a gift of grace that comes as a result of believing in the Savior, Jesus Christ. Jesus said: "I tell you the truth, he who believes *has* everlasting life" (John 6:47, emphasis added). "The *gift of God* is eternal life in Christ Jesus our Lord" (Romans 6:23, emphasis added; see also Revelation 21:6).

True grace is sometimes hard for people to grasp. After all, our society is performance-oriented. Good grades in school depend on how well we perform. Climbing up the corporate ladder at work depends on how well we produce. Nothing of any real worth is a "free ticket" in our society. But God's gift of salvation is a grace-gift. *It is free!* We cannot attain it by a good performance. Ephesians 2:8-9 (NASB) affirms, "By grace you have been saved through faith; and that not of yourselves, it is the gift of God; not as a result of works, that no one may boast." Titus 3:5 tells us that God "saved us, not on the basis of deeds which we have done in righteousness, but according to His mercy."

This does not mean, however, that this gift was free *for God.* The price God paid to provide us a grace-salvation was the very death of His Son. Jesus died on the cross for us. He ransomed us from death by His own death on the cross (2 Corinthians 5:21). Such is the wonder of God's grace.

G

Greece

1. Significance ◆ 2. Location ◆ 3. Religion ◆ 4. Games ◆ 5. Athens ◆ 6. Alexander the Great ◆ 7. Language

1. Significance. There are a number of references to the Greeks in the Old and New Testaments, including Ezekiel 27:19; Joel 3:6; John 7:35; 12:20; Acts 11:20; 17:4,12,17. Bible scholars agree that, depending on the context, such references can refer either to Greek-speaking people (Acts 17:22-34) or, more broadly, to Gentiles (non-Jews) (Galatians 3:28).

2. Location. Greece's location is easiest described by pointing to the three bodies of water that surround it. To the east of Greece was the Aegean Sea. To the south was the Mediterranean Sea. To the west was the Adriatic Sea. And to the north was a mountain of great significance to Greek religion: Mount Olympus (see below).

3. Religion. The Greeks believed in a variety of gods, including their supreme god named Zeus. They believed that Zeus ruled over all the other gods that lived on Mount Olympus. The gods of Greece were often pictured as human beings with human vices, such as jealousy, vengeance, and immorality, but what made them particularly dangerous was their power. Obviously, a vengeful and immoral deity with great power was something to be feared. The Greeks also believed in a form of astrology, holding that the planets governed the fates of human beings.

4. *Games.* The Greeks were well known for their Olympic games, held every four years. Athletes from various cities would meet at Olympia and participate in these games. In the beginning, the games were instituted as a means of honoring Zeus, but this passed with time.

5. *Athens.* Perhaps the most famous of Greek cities was Athens, with its many beautiful temples and buildings. These temples and buildings were surely visited by such well-known Athenian citizens as Socrates and Plato, whose writings on philosophy are still studied by students today. The New Testament tells us that the apostle Paul, during his second missionary tour, delivered a powerful sermon to the Greek-speaking Athenian intellectuals (see Acts 17:22-34).

6. *Alexander the Great.* The most famous king of Greece was Alexander the Great (336–323 B.C.), who conquered many lands and brought unity to the country. Because of his military conquests, Greek ideas (Hellenism) spread widely throughout the world. When Alexander died in Babylon, he left no clear successor to the throne, and by 275 B.C. the Greek empire was divided among three dynasties of Alexander's generals: Ptolemy, Antigones, and Seleucus.

7. *Language.* The Greek language is extremely important in view of the fact that Koine Greek is the language of the New Testament. It is a rich and precise language, ideally suited for such a purpose. It is interesting to observe that most of the New Testament authors were Jews, but they wrote their biblical books in Greek.

Guilt Offering—See *Offerings.*

H

Habakkuk, Book of

The book of Habakkuk was written by a prophet of the same name about 606 B.C. Aside from the fact that he was a prophet, little is known about the man.

A contemporary of Jeremiah in the seventh century B.C., Habakkuk wrestled with the suffering of good and innocent people and the prosperity of the wicked. Habakkuk, like many people today, asked, "Why do you let this happen, O God?" More specifically, he asked why God allowed the Babylonians (hardcore pagans) to successfully invade and injure the people of God (chapter 1). It seemed that wicked nations were being allowed to prosper, while God's people were getting squashed. The answer Habakkuk received from God was that, in the end, the wicked Babylonians and all like them would be destroyed, but those who trust in God will remain and be blessed (chapter 2). The bottom line is that we must live by total faith in God (2:4).

Hades—See *Hell.*

Haggai, Book of

The book of Haggai was written by a prophet of the same name around 520 B.C. Aside from the fact that he was a prophet, we know little of the man. His name literally means "festival," perhaps because he was born on the day of a major festival. His book is the second shortest in the Old Testament, so he was definitely a concise writer. He ministered during the reign of King Darius I (522–486 B.C.), and was probably about 80 years old when he wrote this book.

Haggai addressed his words to the people in Judah and Jerusalem who had returned from exile. He urged them to get their act together, to set their priorities straight, and to rebuild the temple (see Haggai 1:1-11). Then, he said, God would bring true blessing back upon them.

The problem was that when the people first returned from exile in 538 B.C. as a result of King Cyrus's decree, they made a good start in beginning to rebuild the temple, but now apathy had set in and the whole project had stagnated (Ezra 4:4-5). The people were too busy building their own homes to pay much attention to the temple. Haggai was one of the prophets chosen by God to get the people on their feet again and finish the task. Toward this end, Haggai preached a series of short fiery sermonettes.

The people needed encouragement because they felt defeated. They were excited to be home again, but they were also despondent over the ruined condition of their city. They were especially despondent over the fact that it was their own unfaithfulness that had brought about that ruin. Haggai sought to help them overcome this defeated state of mind and move on to obedience and service to God.

The rebuilding of the temple was important not only because it was the religious center of Jewish life, but also because it represented the presence of the one true God among the Israelites before a watching pagan world. For the temple *not* to be rebuilt might give the impression to pagan nations that God was no longer interested in Israel and no longer paying attention to the covenants He had made with His people.

The temple was finally rebuilt from 520 to 515 B.C.

Handwriting—See *Archaeology.*

Health and Healing

1. Disease in Biblical Days ◆ 2. Attaining Health in Biblical Days ◆ 3. Medical Specialists in Biblical Days ◆ 4. God Does Not Heal Everyone

1. *Disease in Biblical Days.* There are plenty of diseases and health problems mentioned in the Bible. We read of the deaf, the blind, the lame, lepers, those who were "bent double," high fevers, and various other diseases and health problems (see, for example, Mark 14:3; Luke 4:38-39; 7:22). Combine the fact that there were no penicillins and antibiotics in biblical days with the realities of water shortages, food shortages, oppressive heat, and cramped living conditions, and this is an ideal mixing pot for the spread of disease.

2. Attaining Health in Biblical Days. In the Jewish mentality, health came from pleasing God; sickness and disease came from displeasing Him. In view of this, the Israelites generally did not place medical skills as a high priority. Still, the historical record indicates that there were medicines that were used in biblical times, as well as medical professionals who were consulted.

Recall, for example, that Paul once told Timothy to take a little wine for his stomach ailment (1 Timothy 5:23). Further, wine mixed with myrrh was apparently considered a pain-killing drug that dulls the senses (it was offered to Jesus at the cross, Mark 15:23). Olive oil was considered to have medicinal values, as was the balm of Gilead (Jeremiah 8:22). Other medicines were made from such things as herbs, fruit, minerals, and parts of plants.

We can also deduce from Scripture that some of the laws God gave to the Israelites were for the purpose of maximizing health among the people. For example, God commanded the people to rest one day each week (Exodus 20:8-11). Modern experts can attest that such rest is a key to prolonged health of the body. Further, the law forbade certain foods from being eaten, including pork (which, being easily liable to becoming infected with parasites, could cause food poisoning in a subtropical climate) and contaminated water (see Leviticus 11 for a summary of dietary laws). The law also instructed that a person must pay attention to personal cleanliness, a key factor in maintaining health. If a person came into contact with a dead body, the person and his clothes had to be thoroughly washed (Numbers 19). Further, the people were instructed to go outside of camp to dispose of human excrement, putting it in a hole and covering it with dirt (see Deuteronomy 23:12-13). Such laws went a long way in keeping the people healthy in biblical days.

3. Medical Specialists in Biblical Days. Some people specialized in medical issues in biblical times. For example, we know there were midwives during the time of the Exodus (they were instructed by Pharaoh to kill Hebrew boys upon birth, a command they did not obey—Exodus 1:15-21). In New Testament times, we read that Luke was a physician (Colossians 4:14). Jesus certainly gave credence to the work of doctors when He affirmed that people who are well do not need a doctor, but the sick do (Matthew 9:12).

The historical record indicates that it was the Greeks who had the most highly developed skill in medicine in biblical days. Today, modern doctors continue to recite the Hippocratic Oath, derived from the ancient Greek Hippocrates, who emphasized that the doctor's first priority was to seek the life, health, and welfare of the patient. There is also evidence of developed medical skills in Rome, where various kinds of surgical instruments have been discovered.

4. God Does Not Heal Everyone. It is clear from Scripture that God does not promise to heal everyone. The apostle Paul was not healed, even though he prayed earnestly and faithfully (2 Corinthians 12:7-9). Despite Paul's divine ability to heal others (Acts 28:8-9), later he apparently could not heal either Epaphroditus (Philippians 2:25-26) or Trophimus (2 Timothy 4:20). Healing is always subject to the will of God. Sometimes God says yes to requests for healing. At other times He says no because He has a greater purpose in mind (see Job 1–2). Either way, all Christians can look forward to their future resurrection bodies in which any need for "healing" will be a thing of the distant past (1 Corinthians 15:53-54; Revelation 21:4).

Heaven

1. *Three Heavens.* The Bible makes reference to three different heavens. The first heaven is that of the earth's atmosphere (Job 35:5). The second heaven is that of the interstellar universe (Genesis 1:17 NASB; Deuteronomy 17:3 NASB). The third heaven is the ineffable and glorious dwelling place of God in all His glory (2 Corinthians 12:2). It is elsewhere called the "heaven of heavens" and the "highest heaven" (1 Kings 8:27; 2 Chronicles 2:6).

2. *Descriptions of Heaven.* There are a number of ways the "highest" heaven is described in the Bible. Each of the descriptions reveals something new, something exciting, about our future abode.

A. *The City of Glory.* In Revelation 21 we find a description of a city of great glory which, I believe, is what Jesus was referring to during His earthly ministry when He told the disciples: "In my Father's house are many rooms; if it were not so, I would have told you. I am going there to prepare a place for you. And if I go and prepare a place for you, I will come back and take you to be with me that you also may be where I am" (John 14:2-3). Christ has personally prepared this glorious abode for His followers.

Presented to our amazed gaze in Revelation 21 is a scene of such transcendent splendor that the human mind can scarcely take it in. This is a scene of ecstatic joy and fellowship of sinless angels and redeemed glorified human beings. The voice of the One identified as the Alpha and the Omega, the beginning and the end, utters a climactic declaration: "Behold, I am making all things new" (Revelation 21:5 NASB). Certainly the actual splendor of heaven far exceeds anything that we have yet experienced. As the apostle Paul said, "No

151

eye has seen, no ear has heard, no mind has conceived what God has prepared for those who love him" (1 Corinthians 2:9).

B. *The Heavenly Country.* Hebrews 11 is the Faith Hall of Fame in the Bible. In this pivotal chapter we read of the eternal perspective of many of the great faith warriors in biblical times. All of them were looking forward to living in the heavenly country (Hebrews 11:13-15). These great warriors of the faith were not satisfied with mere earthly things. They looked forward to "a better country"—heaven.

C. *The Holy City.* In Revelation 21:1-2 we find heaven described as "the holy city." This is a fitting description. Indeed, in this city there will be no sin or unrighteousness of any kind.

D. *The Home of Righteousness.* Second Peter 3:13 tells us that "in keeping with his promise we are looking forward to a new heaven and a new earth, the home of righteousness." What a perfect environment this will be to live in.

E. *The Kingdom of Light.* Colossians 1:12 refers to heaven as "the kingdom of light." Christ, of course, is the Light of the world (John 8:12). The eternal kingdom thus takes on the character of the King. Christ, the Light of the world, rules over the "kingdom of light."

F. *The Paradise of God.* The word "paradise" literally means "garden of pleasure" or "garden of delight." Revelation 2:7 makes reference to heaven as the "paradise of God." The apostle Paul said he was "caught up to paradise" and "heard inexpressible things, things that man is not permitted to tell" (2 Corinthians 12:4). Apparently this paradise of God is so resplendently glorious, so ineffable, so wondrous, that Paul was forbidden to say anything about it to those still in the earthly realm.

G. *The New Jerusalem.* The New Jerusalem, the eternal city, is said to measure approximately 1500 miles by 1500 miles by 1500 miles. The eternal city is so huge that it would measure approximately the distance between the Mississippi River and the Atlantic Ocean. It is tall enough that from the earth's surface it would reach about one-twentieth of the way to the moon.

The eternal city could either be cube-shaped or pyramid-shaped. It may be preferable to consider it shaped as a pyramid, for this would explain how the river of the water of life can flow down its sides as pictured in Revelation 22:1-2.

Hebrews

H

1. Word of Exhortation ◆ 2. Christological Emphasis ◆ 3. Authorship Unknown ◆ 4. Recipients ◆ 5. Occasion

1. *Word of Exhortation.* The book of Hebrews describes itself as a "word of exhortation," not as a letter (Hebrews 13:22). The exhortation draws heavily on the Old Testament and urges Hebrew Christians to remain steadfast in their commitment to Christ and His cause. It was probably written about A.D. 68.

2. *Christological Emphasis.* This book is, in one way, a New Testament commentary on the Old Testament and its relationship to Jesus Christ. It teaches that the offering of sacrifices and the various priestly activities were mere types that pointed to Christ, the once-for-all sacrifice for sin, the true Priest, the one Mediator between God and man (see Hebrews 7–9). Hebrews may be considered a grand portrait of Christ with the Old Testament as its background.

3. *Authorship Unknown.* Bible scholars are not sure who wrote this theological book. Though a number of hypotheses have been suggested through the centuries, perhaps only three are worthy of mention: the apostle Paul, Apollos, and Barnabas. Regardless of who actually wrote the epistle, at least four things are certain:

1. The author and his readers were known to each other (Hebrews 6:9; 13:18-19,23-24).

2. Timothy was known to both (13:23).

3. The writer was quite familiar with the Old Testament, including the Levitical system of sacrifices.

4. He writes in polished Greek, indicating a high level of education.

Whether Paul, Apollos, or Barnabas (or anyone else) is the author, we can be thankful for this book which speaks about the superiority of Jesus with incomparable skill and beauty.

4. Recipients. Whatever is known today of the original readers of Hebrews is derived from the epistle itself. The earliest manuscripts have the simple title, "to the Hebrews." This group was apparently a single congregation of Hebrew Christians living somewhere in the Roman world (Hebrews 2:3; 5:11-12; 6:9-10; see also 13:23-24). Scholars have suggested various hypotheses as to where they may have lived, including Jerusalem, Alexandria, Caesarea, Ephesus, the city of Rome, and Antioch in Syria. But there is no hard proof for any of these localities. As was true with the question of who wrote the epistle, scholars are equally unsure about the precise location of this community of Hebrew Christians.

5. Occasion. The author of Hebrews makes it clear that this group of Jewish believers was going through a severe period of persecution (Hebrews 10:32-34). The general tenor and content of the epistle indicate that this persecution was likely religious in nature.

For a Jew to become a believer in Jesus Christ in the first century required a great sacrifice. Such a believer was immediately branded as an apostate and a blemish to the Jewish nation. He was considered "unclean" in the strongest possible sense. Defecting Jews were immediately expelled from the synagogue; their children were denied the privilege of attending school at the synagogue; they lost their jobs in any geographical areas controlled by the Jews; in short, they lost everything of earthly value to them. Furthermore, the high priest of the Jewish nation had the authority to throw such troublesome Jews into jail (see Hebrews 10:33-34). It was circumstances such as these that apparently caused many of these Hebrew believers to wane in their commitment to Christ.

At first, these Jewish Christians joyfully accepted persecution (Hebrews 10:34). But after a while, it apparently became too much for them to bear and their endurance weakened (10:35-36). The warning passages in this epistle seem to indicate that these believers had degenerated in their faith and had become settled in a state of spiritual retrogression.

While they certainly never entertained thoughts of actually renouncing Jesus Christ, they nevertheless expressed the desire to drift back into the outward observances of Judaism (including rituals, ceremonies, and sacrifices; see Hebrews 6:1-2). They apparently reasoned that if they took part in such Jewish rituals, the Jewish leaders might be satisfied and leave them alone.

However, the book makes clear that Jesus is the ultimate fulfillment of the Old Testament, and Jesus is greater than all Old Testament institutions (Hebrews 1–7). Hence, to step back into Judaism in whatever form is unacceptable. The author of Hebrews calls his readers to move on to maturity in the Christian faith (6:1).

Hell

1. *A Real Place.* The Scriptures assure us that hell is a real place. But hell was not part of God's original creation, which

He called "very good" (Genesis 1:31). Hell was created later to accommodate the banishment of Satan and his fallen angels who rebelled against God (Matthew 25:41). Human beings who reject Christ will join Satan and his fallen angels in this infernal place of suffering.

2. Biblical Words for Hell. There are a variety of words in the Bible that either refer to or relate to the doctrine of hell:

A. *Sheol.* In the Old Testament, the Hebrew word *Sheol* is translated "hell." Sheol can have different meanings in different contexts. Sometimes the word means "grave" (Psalm 49:15 NASB). Other times it refers simply to the place of departed people. The Old Testament often characterizes this place as being full of horror (Psalm 30:9), weeping (Isaiah 38:3), and punishment (Job 24:19).

B. *Hades.* Hades is the New Testament counterpart to Sheol. The rich man, during the intermediate state, endured great suffering in Hades (Luke 16:19-31). Hades, however, is a temporary abode and will one day be cast into the Lake of Fire (hell). In the future, the wicked evildoers in Hades will be raised from the dead and judged at the Great White Throne judgment. They will then be cast into the Lake of Fire, which will be their permanent place of suffering throughout all eternity (Revelation 20:14-15).

C. *Gehenna.* Another word related to the concept of hell is Gehenna (Matthew 10:28). This word has an interesting history. For several generations in ancient Israel, atrocities were committed in the Valley of Ben Hinnom—atrocities that included human sacrifices, even the sacrifice of children to the false Moabite god Molech (2 Kings 23:10; 2 Chronicles 28:3; 33:6; Jeremiah 32:35). Eventually the valley came to be used as a public rubbish dump into which all the filth in Jerusalem was poured. Not only garbage but also the bodies of dead animals and the corpses of criminals were thrown on the heap where they—like everything else in the dump— would perpetually burn. The valley was a place where the fires never stopped burning.

This place was originally called (in the Hebrew) *Ge[gen]hinnom* (the valley of the son[s] of Hinnom). It was eventually shortened to the name *Ge-Hinnom*. The Greek translation of this Hebrew phrase is *Gehenna*. It became an appropriate and graphic term for the reality of hell.

3. Biblical Descriptions of Hell. The Scriptures use a variety of words to describe the horrors of hell:

A. *The Lake of Burning Sulfur/The Lake of Fire.* As noted above, one day the occupants of Hades will be resurrected from the dead, face the Great White Throne judgment, and then be tossed into the Lake of Fire. Those who end up there will be tormented day and night forever (Revelation 19:20; 20:10,14-15).

B. *Eternal Fire.* Jesus often referred to the eternal destiny of the wicked as "eternal fire." Following His Second Coming when He separates the sheep (believers) from the goats (unbelievers), Jesus will say to the goats: "Depart from me, you who are cursed, into the eternal fire prepared for the devil and his angels" (Matthew 25:41).

What precisely is the "fire" of hell? Some believe it is literal. And, indeed, that may very well be the case. Others believe "fire" is a metaphorical way of expressing the great wrath of God. Scripture tells us: "The LORD your God is a consuming fire, a jealous God" (Deuteronomy 4:24). "God is a consuming fire" (Hebrews 12:29). "His wrath is poured out like fire" (Nahum 1:6). "Who can stand when he appears? For he will be like a refiner's fire..." (Malachi 3:2). God said, "My wrath will break out and burn like fire because of the evil you have done—burn with no one to quench it" (Jeremiah 4:4). How awful is the fiery wrath of God!

C. *Fiery Furnace.* Scripture sometimes refers to the destiny of the wicked as the "fiery furnace." Jesus said that at the end of the age the holy angels will gather all evildoers and "throw them into the fiery furnace, where there will be weeping and gnashing of teeth" (Matthew 13:42,50). "Weeping" carries the idea of wailing as an outward expression of deep grief. This weeping will be caused by the environment, the company, the remorse and guilt, and the shame that is part and parcel of hell.

D. *Destruction.* Second Thessalonians 1:8-9 tells us that unbelievers "will be punished with everlasting destruction and shut out from the presence of the Lord and from the majesty of his power." The Greek word translated "destruction" in this verse carries the meaning "sudden ruin," or "loss of all that gives worth to existence." The word refers not to annihilation but rather indicates separation from God and a loss of everything worthwhile in life.

E. *Eternal Punishment.* Jesus affirmed that the wicked "will go away to eternal punishment, but the righteous to eternal life" (Matthew 25:46). Notice that the punishment of the wicked is just as eternal as the blessing of the righteous. One is just as long as the other.

F. *Exclusion from God's Presence.* The greatest pain suffered by those in hell is that they are forever excluded from the presence of God. If ecstatic joy is found in the presence of God (Psalm 16:11), then utter dismay is found in the eternal absence of His presence.

Holiness

The word "holy" comes from the Greek word *hagios,* which means "set apart" or "separated." It carries the idea of being set apart from sin and all that is unclean.

God is portrayed as the absolutely holy One of the universe. His holiness means not just that He is entirely separate from all evil but also that He is absolutely righteous (Leviticus 19:2). He is pure in every way. He is separate from all that is morally imperfect (see Exodus 15:11; 1 Samuel 2:2; Psalm 99:9; 111:9; Isaiah 6:3; Revelation 15:4).

God desires His children, who are adopted into His family by faith in Christ, to take on the family likeness of holiness. We read in 1 Peter 1:15, "Just as he who called you is holy, so be holy in all you do." In 1 Thessalonians 3:13, Paul exhorts: "May he strengthen your hearts so that you will be blameless and holy in the presence of our God and Father when our Lord Jesus comes with all his holy ones."

Holy City

Through the ages, the city of Jerusalem has been referred to as the Holy City. The city is famous worldwide in view of the fact that it was the scene of Jesus' arrest, trial, crucifixion, and resurrection.

The city itself rests in the Judean hills at about 2640 feet above sea level. During the time of Jesus, the city was probably home to about a quarter of a million people.

In Jewish thinking in biblical times, no city could possibly compare with Jerusalem. People from all around would go to Jerusalem for the three major festivals and to pay the annual temple tax. Jerusalem was the geographical heart of the Jewish religion. Jesus Himself made a number of visits to Jerusalem (Luke 2:22,41-42; John 2:13; 5:1; 10:22-23; 12:12).

Historically, King David of Israel captured the city in the tenth century B.C. During the reign of his son Solomon, Jerusalem became the center of religious life with the magnificent temple that was built there. As prophesied by Jesus, Jerusalem was utterly destroyed in A.D. 70 by Rome (Matthew 24:2).

Holy Spirit

1. Third Person of the Trinity ◆ 2. God ◆
3. A Person ◆ 4. Ministries

1. *Third Person of the Trinity.* There is one God, and in the unity of the Godhead, there are three co-equal and co-eternal persons: the Father, the Son, and the Holy Spirit, equal in divine nature, but distinct in personhood (see Matthew 28:19;

159

2 Corinthians 13:14). The Holy Spirit is the third person of the divine Trinity.

2. God. In Acts 5:3-4, we are told that lying to the Holy Spirit is equivalent to lying to God; this shows the divine nature of the Spirit. Scripture also reveals that the Holy Spirit has the attributes of deity, including omnipresence (Psalm 139:7), omniscience (1 Corinthians 2:10), omnipotence (Romans 15:19), holiness (John 16:7-11), and eternity (Hebrews 9:14). Such attributes can belong to God alone.

3. A Person. The Holy Spirit is a person, not a force. It has long been recognized that the three primary attributes of personality are mind, emotions, and will, and the Holy Spirit has each of these attributes.

A. *The Holy Spirit Has a Mind.* The Holy Spirit's intellect is seen in 1 Corinthians 2:10 where we are told that "the Spirit searches all things" (see also Isaiah 11:2; Ephesians 1:17). The Greek word for "search" means "to thoroughly investigate a matter." In keeping with this, Romans 8:27 (NASB) tells us that just as the Holy Spirit knows the things of God, so God the Father knows "what the mind of the Spirit is."

B. *The Holy Spirit Has Emotions.* In Ephesians 4:30 we are admonished, "Do not grieve the Holy Spirit of God." Grief is an emotion; it is something one feels. The Holy Spirit feels the emotion of grief when believers sin (see verses 25-29).

C. *The Holy Spirit Has a Will.* We are told in 1 Corinthians 12:11 (NASB) that the Holy Spirit distributes spiritual gifts "to each one individually just as He wills." The phrase "He wills" translates the Greek word *bouletai,* which refers to decisions of the will after previous deliberation. Only a person engages in such deliberation.

D. *The Holy Spirit's Works Confirm His Personality.* The Holy Spirit is seen doing many things in Scripture that only a person can do. For example, the Holy Spirit teaches believers (John 14:26), He testifies (John 15:26), He guides (Romans 8:14), He commissions people to service (Acts

13:2-4), He issues commands (Acts 8:29), He restrains sin (Genesis 6:3), He intercedes (prays) for believers (Romans 8:26), and He speaks to people (John 15:26; 2 Peter 1:21).

E. *The Holy Spirit Is Treated as a Person.* The Holy Spirit can be grieved (Ephesians 4:30), blasphemed (Matthew 12:32; Mark 3:29-30), lied to (Acts 5:3), obeyed (Acts 13:2-3), and He is sent by the Father (John 14:26). Such things can only be said of a person.

4. Ministries. The Holy Spirit is involved in many wonderful ministries. He was involved in the miraculous human conception of Jesus (Matthew 1:18-20). He came upon Jesus at His baptism (Matthew 3:16). He inspired Scripture (2 Timothy 3:16; 2 Peter 1:21). He is the agent of regeneration and brings about the new birth (John 3:1-6; Titus 3:5). He gives Christians spiritual gifts (1 Corinthians 12; 14). He is our divine comforter or helper (John 14; 15:26; 16:7). He bears witness to and glorifies Jesus Christ (John 15:26). He guides the church (John 14:25-26). He convicts people of sin (John 16:7-11). And He produces wonderful spiritual fruit in believers (Galatians 5:16-26). The Holy Spirit's ministry is pivotal to the spiritual life of believers.

Hosea, Book of

This touching book, written by Hosea during the closing days of Jeroboam II in about 710 B.C., depicts the heartfelt pain that Hosea suffered at the unfaithfulness of his own wife. This, in turn, gave the prophet a deep insight to the way God feels when His own people are unfaithful to Him.

Hosea was married to a woman named Gomer (Hosea 1:2-3), who eventually left him to go live with another man. She soon became a prostitute and offered her services to any who were interested. Hosea then found her, and, in compassion, paid for her freedom and took her back to live with him (chapter 3).

Just as Gomer had been unfaithful to the marriage covenant, so the Israelites—presently at political peace and enjoying material prosperity—had been unfaithful to the covenant God made with them (Hosea 2:2-5; 6:4-11; 8:1-14). They committed spiritual adultery and turned away from God, just as Gomer had committed physical adultery and turned away from Hosea. In their unfaithfulness, the Israelites engaged in an adulterous relationship with Canaanite deities (like Baal). Yet, just as Hosea loved Gomer, God still loved the Israelites, despite their unfaithfulness (11:1-12).

From the vantage point of the book, there was still time for the Israelites to repent and turn back to God. If they did not, then judgment would soon fall at the hands of the Assyrians (see Hosea 9:1–10:15).

Houses and Tents

1. Tents ◆ 2. Caves ◆ 3. Houses ◆ 4. Towns

1. *Tents.* Tents were popular "homes" in biblical times, particularly among shepherds who had to move sheep and goats around and among farmers who needed to be near their crops for part of the year. Abraham and his descendants lived in tents for hundreds of years (see Genesis 12:8). These tents were generally made from goat hair. The material of the tent was supported by poles that were about six feet high in the middle and shorter on the perimeter. Such tents were generally divided into two rooms. The exposed entrance area was where visitors could chat, while the rest of the tent was curtained off for private use. Sometimes the ground under the tent was bare earth; at other times a mat was laid down. Tents were often erected close together for the purpose of protection.

2. *Caves.* Other people in Bible times lived in caves. Though the idea of living in a cave might initially sound unattractive, the reality is that they did not have to be built (like houses), and so one could move right in; they involved very low maintenance; and they were relatively cool in the summer and warm during the winter. Caves were not bad homes!

3. *Houses*. As more and more Israelites settled in walled villages and communities, houses became more practical. These houses were generally constructed by using mud bricks and featured both windows and doors. The windows were strategically placed for maximum practicality. For example, since there was no glass at that time, the windows could not be sealed shut, and too many windows would make the house extremely cold in the winter. In view of this, most houses had only a few windows, and they were often placed high on a wall so there would be no direct drafts of air on those living within. These high windows also served to keep the house cooler during the hot summer months. Sometimes curtains of thick wool were placed over the windows during the cold months. The doors of the houses were made originally from woven twigs and eventually from wood and metal.

The floors of such houses were generally quite simple. Often floors were made of packed clay. Other floors might involve small stones or stone chippings being stomped into the earthen floor. Generally only wealthier people had mosaic floors, made by setting stone cubes in wet plaster. Wealthy people also had rugs on the floor.

Roofs were designed by laying beams across the top of the walls. Other beams were then laid across the top of these initial beams at right angles, thus reinforcing the roof. Following this, either earth or clay was laid across the top of these beams and smoothened.

In biblical times, the roof was more than just a "roof over your head." Sometimes the roof was actually part of the living quarters. If it was a hot night, members of the family might sleep on the roof where it was cooler. At other times, the roof could be used as a threshing floor. Or it might be used as a

H

163

place to dry fruit and grains. Women might sometimes wash clothes on the roof.

Of course, such houses were not nearly as efficient as modern houses. If there was a heavy rain, a leaky roof could be expected. During winter months, there would be plenty of smoke inside the house as a result of a fire built in a hole in the ground of the earthen floor (there were no fireplaces in those days). Also during the winter, animals would be brought inside the house to survive the harsh weather. This meant the house could stink. During the summer, there would be plenty of bugs flying around inside the house, especially if there was an oil lamp in the house that attracted bugs.

There was not much furniture in ancient times. Most often there was a bed, a table, a few stools to sit on, and perhaps a storage chest and some jars to hold food. The bed was generally just a mattress filled with wool that was laid out during the night and then stored away during the day to make more room.

4. Towns. Towns in ancient Israel generally had between 150 and 250 houses and a population of about 1000 people. In such towns, the houses were built very close to each other, and there were no real streets (there were only spaces between houses for people to maneuver around). The Romans began to build a road system between major population centers in the third century B.C.

Humanity

1. Creatures ◆ 2. Equality ◆ 3. Nature ◆
4. Fallen

1. Creatures. Human beings are creatures, created a little lower than the angels (Psalm 8:3-6; Hebrews 2:7-8) by God's own hands (Job 10:8-12; Isaiah 64:8). They are wonderfully complex (Psalm 139:14). They were created to live upon the

164

earth (Isaiah 45:12) and were made male and female (Genesis 5:2; Mark 10:6; see also Genesis 2:21-23). Ultimately, all human beings are descended from one man (Acts 17:26).

Man was created in the "image of God" (Genesis 1:26-27). This means that man is a finite reflection of God in his rational nature (Colossians 3:10), in his moral nature (Ephesians 4:24), and in his dominion over creation (Genesis 1:27-28). In the same way that the moon reflects the brilliant light of the sun, so finite man (as created in God's image) is a reflection of God in these aspects. As such, man is the noblest part of God's creation.

2. Equality. All human beings are equal in their nature and in their value to God. Not only have all human beings descended from a single man (Acts 17:26), but Scripture affirms that in Christ there is no Jew and Gentile, no slave and free, and no male and female (Galatians 3:28). We are all equal; there is no room for any kind of discrimination.

3. Nature. Scholars have debated whether man is composed of two aspects (body and soul/spirit) or three aspects (body, soul, and spirit). The dichotomist view is that man is composed of two parts—material (body) and immaterial (soul/spirit). In this view, "soul" and "spirit" are seen as essentially interchangeable. Man's entire immaterial part is called "soul" in 1 Peter 2:11 and "spirit" in James 2:26. Hence they must be equal.

In the trichotomist view, the soul and spirit are viewed as separate substantive entities. Hence, man is viewed as consisting of three realities—body, soul, and spirit. Trichotomists generally say the body involves world-consciousness, the soul involves self-consciousness, and the spirit involves God-consciousness. Support for this view is found in Hebrews 4:12 and 1 Thessalonians 5:23.

Perhaps a few distinctions would be helpful. If we are talking about mere *substance,* then we must conclude that man has only a material and an immaterial aspect. However, if we are talking about *function*, then we may say that within the sphere of man's immaterial aspect there are a number of functions—including that of soul and spirit. Other components of man's immaterial nature include the heart (Matthew 22:37; Hebrews 4:12), the conscience (Hebrews 10:22; 1 Peter 2:19), and the mind (Romans 12:2).

4. Fallen. Scripture reveals that human beings—since the Fall (Genesis 3)—have a radical propensity for evil. Romans 3:23 says, "All have sinned and fall short of the glory of God." Jeremiah 17:9 reveals that the human heart is "deceitful above all things and beyond cure." In Romans 7:18 the apostle Paul says: "I know that nothing good lives in me, that is, in my sinful nature. For I have the desire to do what is good, but I cannot carry it out." Christ became a human being to redeem us from our sin (Galatians 4:4-5).

Hymns and Songs

There is a very close relationship between praise and singing in the Old Testament. Moses and the Israelites sang praise to God in response to His deliverance of the Israelites from Egyptian bondage (Exodus 15:1-21). Deborah and Barak sang praise to God in response to being delivered from the Canaanites (Judges 5). Many of the Psalms were originally accompanied by music. In Isaiah, songs of praise most often focus on God's deliverance of Israel from exile and His future blessings on the nation (Isaiah 12:5-6; 27:2; 30:29; 42:10-11; 44:23). Believers are exhorted to sing new songs of praise (see Psalm 33:3; 40:3; Revelation 5:9; 14:3). They are exhorted to sing psalms, hymns, and spiritual songs (Ephesians 5:19; Colossians 3:16). Hymns and songs are hence a crucial part of the believer's life. (See *Music, Musicians, Instruments.*)

Idolatry

Pagan nations typically believed in a plethora of gods, and these gods were often represented as statues in the form of human beings or animals. People would then worship these images. Such idolatry was common to nations such as the Babylonians, the Assyrians, the Philistines, and the Egyptians.

Often these pagan nations believed the different gods were behind various aspects of the world of nature. For example, there might be one god in charge of crops. Another god might be related to the light provided by the sun or the moon. Other gods were related to the stars. Still other gods might be related to health and healing. And still other gods might be related to protecting the animals of the land. Many ancient idolaters believed that in order to be successful in life, one must please the gods and avoid their cruel treatment.

This is illustrated in the idolatry of Egypt. Osiris functioned as a god of agriculture, and Shu was considered the Egyptian god of the atmosphere. Nut, the Egyptian sky goddess, had the task of ensuring the blessings of sun and warmth. Seth was an Egyptian god whose duty was to watch after the crops of the land. Serapis was a god believed to be able to protect the land from locust invasions. Atum was the god of the setting sun, and Thoth was a moon god of Hermopolis. Ptah was the god of life, Min was the god of procreation and reproduction, and Hathor was one of seven deities who was believed to attend the birth of children.

Unlike the God of the Bible who is just, holy, and righteous in all His dealings, the pagan deities of the Babylonians, Assyrians, Philistines, and Egyptians, often represented as human beings, are typically portrayed as *acting* like human beings. They could love or hate; they could be merciful or cruel; they could be peaceful or violent. In short, these gods could be just as fickle as human beings are. God consistently condemns idolatry in all its forms (Exodus 20:4; Leviticus 26:1; 2 Kings 9:22).

Incarnation (of Jesus Christ)

1. Significance ◆ 2. Humanity ◆ 3. Normal Birth ◆
4. Normal Development ◆ 5. Two Natures ◆
6. One Person ◆ 7. Inscrutable Mystery ◆
8. Lasts Forever

1. Significance. In the Incarnation, the incomprehensible came to pass. The glorious Son of God forsook the splendor of heaven and became as genuinely human as we ourselves are. Surrendering His glorious estate, He voluntarily entered into human relationships in the world of time and space. Jesus became a man, was crucified on a cross, rose from the dead as the glorified God-man, and ascended back into His original glory. All of this, He did for our sake.

2. Humanity. To deny either the undiminished deity or the perfect humanity of Christ in the Incarnation is to put one-self outside the pale of orthodoxy (1 John 4:2-3). Innumerable passages in the New Testament confirm Christ's full humanity in the Incarnation. Hebrews 2:14 tells us, for example, that since His children "have flesh and blood, he too shared in their humanity so that by his death he might destroy him who holds the power of death—that is, the devil" (see also Romans 8:3; Galatians 4:4-5; 1 Timothy 3:16).

3. Normal Birth. While remaining fully God within the womb, as a human being Jesus experienced a normal fetal state, had an umbilical cord through which He received sustenance to His human body from His mother Mary, developed for nine months in the womb, and experienced a natural human birth. It is important to grasp that it was the *conception* of Jesus in Mary's womb that was supernatural, not His *birth* (see Isaiah 7:14; Luke 1:35; 2:6-7). The miraculous conception that resulted from the overshadowing ministry of the Holy Spirit made it possible for the eternal Son to take on a human nature through Mary.

4. *Normal Development.* Even though Jesus never for a moment surrendered any aspect of His deity, He experienced normal human development through infancy, childhood, adolescence, and into adulthood. According to Luke 2:40, Jesus "grew," "became strong," and was "filled with wisdom." These are things that could never be said of Jesus' divine nature. It was in His humanity that He grew, became strong, and became filled with wisdom. Likewise, Luke 2:52 tells us that "Jesus grew in wisdom and stature." Again, Jesus' growth in wisdom and stature is something that can only be said of His humanity.

Christ's development as a human was normal in every respect, with two major exceptions: 1) Christ always did the will of God, and 2) He never sinned. As Hebrews 4:15 tells us, in Christ "we do not have a high priest who is unable to sympathize with our weaknesses, but we have one who has been tempted in every way, just as we are—yet was without sin." Indeed, Christ is "holy," "blameless," and "pure" (Hebrews 7:26). Hence, though Christ was utterly sinless, His human nature was exactly the same as ours in every other respect.

Jesus' full humanity is plainly evident in the fact that He consistently displayed human characteristics. Besides growing as a normal child (Luke 2:40,52), Jesus had a physical body of flesh and bones (Luke 24:39), experienced weariness (John 4:6), knew hunger (Luke 4:2), felt sorrow (Matthew 26:37), wept (John 11:35), and needed sleep (Luke 8:23).

5. *Two Natures.* Crucial to a proper understanding of the Incarnation is grasping what is meant by the word "nature." This word is commonly used to designate the divine or human elements in the person of the incarnate Christ. In other words, "nature," when used of Christ's divinity, refers to all that belongs to deity, including all the attributes of deity. "Nature," when used of Christ's humanity, refers to all that belongs to humanity, including all the attributes of humanity. Christ in the Incarnation was fully God and fully man.

6. One Person. Though the incarnate Christ had both a human and a divine nature, He was only one person—as indicated by His consistent use of "I," "me," and "mine" in reference to Himself. Jesus never used the words "us," "we," or "ours" in reference to His human-divine person. Nor did the divine nature of Christ ever carry on a verbal conversation with His human nature.

Hence, the eternal Son of God—who, prior to the Incarnation, was one in person and nature (wholly divine)—became, in the miraculous Incarnation, two in nature (divine and human) while remaining one person. The Son, who had already been a person for all eternity past, joined Himself not with a human person but with a human nature at the Incarnation.

7. Inscrutable Mystery. One of the most complex aspects of the relationship of Christ's two natures is that, while the attributes of one nature are never attributed to the other, the attributes of both natures are properly attributed to His one person. Thus Christ at the same moment in time had what seem to be contradictory qualities. He was finite and yet infinite, weak and yet omnipotent, increasing in knowledge and yet omniscient, limited to being in one place at one time and yet omnipresent. In the Incarnation, the person of Christ is the partaker of the attributes of both natures, so that whatever may be affirmed of either nature—human or divine—may be affirmed of the one person.

Though Christ sometimes operated in the sphere of His humanity and in other cases in the sphere of His deity, in all cases what He did and what He was could be attributed to His one person. Thus, though Christ in His human nature knew hunger (Luke 4:2), weariness (John 4:6), and the need for sleep (Luke 8:23); just as Christ in His divine nature was omniscient

(John 2:24), omnipresent (John 1:48), and omnipotent (John 11); all of this was experienced by the one person of Jesus Christ.

8. *Lasts Forever.* When Christ became a man in the Incarnation, He did not enter into a temporary union of the human and divine natures that ended at His death. Rather, Scripture is clear that Christ's human nature continues forever. The miracle of the Incarnation will continue to be a miracle forever.

Christ was raised immortal in the very same human body in which He died (Luke 24:37-39; Acts 2:31; 1 John 4:2; 2 John 7). When Christ ascended into heaven, He ascended in the same physical human body, as witnessed by several of His disciples (Acts 1:11). When Christ returns, He will return as the "Son of Man"—a messianic title that points to His humanity (Matthew 26:64). At the same time, even though Jesus has fully retained His humanity and will return as the glorified God-man, the glory that He now has in heaven is no less than the resplendent glory that has been His as God for all eternity past (see John 17:5).

Inspiration of Scripture—See *Bible.*

Interpretation

1. *Spiritualization.* Some individuals in the past have taken a spiritualized approach to interpreting the Bible. Philo of Alexandria (died A.D. 50) believed the Old Testament was an allegory of divine things. In an allegory, one thing represents or stands for another thing. So, for example, the Song of Solomon was interpreted as an allegory of the relationship between Christ and His church (the bride of Christ). The allegorical approach was popular during the Middle Ages but began to wane after the Reformation. Most scholars today believe the proper approach to interpreting the Bible is the literal method, which is discussed below.

2. *The Author's Intended Meaning.* Instead of superimposing a meaning on the biblical text, the objective interpreter seeks to discover the author's intended meaning (the only true meaning). What a passage means is fixed by the author and is not subject to alteration by readers. Our goal must be *exegesis* (drawing the meaning out of the text) and not *eisogesis* (superimposing a meaning onto the text).

3. *Context.* In seeking the biblical author's intended meaning, it is critical to interpret Bible verses in context— both the immediate context and the broader context. The immediate context of a verse is the paragraph (or paragraphs) of the biblical book in question. The broader context is the whole of Scripture. We must keep in mind that the interpretation of a specific passage must not contradict the total teaching of Scripture. Individual verses do not exist as isolated fragments but as parts of a whole. The exposition of these verses, therefore, must involve exhibiting them in right relation both to the whole and to each other. Scripture interprets Scripture.

4. *Historical Considerations.* The Christian faith is based on historical fact. Indeed, Christianity rests on the foundation of the historical Jesus whose earthly life represents God's full and objective self-communication to humankind (John 1:18). Jesus was *seen and heard* by human beings as God's ultimate revelation (1 John 1:1-3). This is why He could forcefully claim, "If you really knew me, you would know my Father as well" (John 14:7).

The apostle Paul, when speaking with the religious men of Athens, affirmed that the reality of the future judgment of all humanity rests on the objective, historical evidence for the resurrection of Jesus (Acts 17:16-17,31). This evidence is recorded for us in the New Testament Gospels, documents that are based on eyewitness testimony and written very close in time to the events they report on. Based on how people respond to God's objective, historical revelation contained in Scripture, they will spend eternity in a real heaven or a real hell.

5. *Genre.* A literal approach to Scripture recognizes that the Bible contains a variety of literary genres, each of which has certain peculiar characteristics that must be recognized in order to interpret the text properly. Biblical genres include history (for example, Acts), drama (Job), poetry (Psalms), wise sayings (Proverbs), letters (Paul's writings), and apocalyptic writings (Revelation).

An incorrect genre judgment will lead one far astray in interpreting Scripture. A parable should not be treated as history, nor should poetry or apocalyptic literature (both of which contain many symbols) be treated as straightforward narrative. The wise interpreter allows his knowledge of genres to control how he approaches each individual biblical text. In this way, he can accurately determine what the biblical author was intending to communicate to the reader.

6. *Interpreting the Old Testament.* God gave revelation to humankind progressively throughout Old and New Testament times. He did not just give His entire revelation for all time to our first parents, Adam and Eve, or to Moses, the lawgiver. Rather, as time went on—as the centuries slowly passed—God provided more and more revelation that became progressively full so that by the time the New Testament was complete, God had told us everything He wanted us to know.

In view of this, a key interpretive principle is that one should always interpret the Old Testament in view of the greater light of the New Testament. The Old Testament is much clearer when viewed through the lens of the New Testament.

7. Descriptive or Prescriptive? When reading the Bible, a key question to ask is this: Is the Bible verse in question merely descriptive, or is it prescriptive? In other words, is the verse merely *describing* something that took place in biblical times, or is it *prescribing* something that Christians should be doing for all time? This principle might be illustrated with the tongues of fire that initially fell on those who were baptized on the Day of Pentecost (Acts 2:3-4). Scholars believe this is descriptive, not prescriptive.

8. Dependence on the Holy Spirit. Scripture tells us that we are to rely on the Holy Spirit's illumination to gain insights into the meaning and application of Scripture (John 16:12-15; 1 Corinthians 2:9-11). The Holy Spirit, as the "Spirit of truth" (John 16:13), guides us so that "we may understand what God has freely given us" (1 Corinthians 2:12). This is logical: Full comprehension of the Word of God is impossible without prayerful dependence on the Spirit of God, for He who inspired the Word (2 Peter 1:21) is also its supreme interpreter.

Isaac—See *Patriarchs.*

Isaiah, Book of

1. Significance ◆ 2. Historical Backdrop ◆
3. Message

1. Significance. Isaiah is considered the greatest of the Old Testament prophets. Some have even called him the "prince" of Old Testament prophets. Certainly his book is a prince-sized book; it's the third longest in the Bible. Only Jeremiah and the Psalms exceed it in length.

The New Testament authors quote from Isaiah quite often (21 times). This shows they thought it was a very important book. Jesus thought it was important too. He even inaugurated His public ministry with a quotation from Isaiah (Luke 4:17-21).

2. Historical Backdrop. Isaiah's name means "The Lord saves." His name is appropriate, for salvation was an important part of his message to the people of Judah. Of course, salvation and judgment often go together in the Bible. If a person refuses to be saved and turns away from God, then he must suffer the consequences in judgment. Isaiah combines these themes in his book.

Isaiah was born and reared in Jerusalem in days of great prosperity. It would seem his family was an affluent one. He was also apparently highly educated and very intelligent.

According to Jewish tradition, Isaiah's father, Amoz, was a brother of King Amaziah. This would make Isaiah a first cousin to King Uzziah and a grandson of King Joash. Isaiah had many opportunities to fellowship with royalty. He even gave advice on foreign affairs to King Hezekiah.

Isaiah received his call from God in the year of King Uzziah's death (740 B.C.). His ministry continued through the reign of Hezekiah, who died in 687 B.C. This means Isaiah's ministry spanned about half a century. He wrote his book between 740 and 680 B.C.

3. Message. The book of Isaiah is one of the best-loved prophetic books in the Old Testament. The primary reason for this is that it contains more references to the person and work of Jesus Christ than any other book in the Old Testament. John 12:41 says that Isaiah "saw Jesus' glory and spoke about him."

Isaiah is often referred to as "the messianic prophet." He predicted the Messiah's virgin birth (7:14), His deity and kingdom (9:1-7), His righteous reign (11:2-5), His vicarious suffering and death (52:13–53:12), and much more. No wonder the great composer Handel based so much of his musical masterpiece the *Messiah* on the book of Isaiah.

Aside from speaking about Christ, Isaiah preached about God's righteousness (Isaiah 5:16; 11:4; 42:6,21; 51:6), warned about judgment for sin (chapters 13–23), and proclaimed God's love and forgiveness (54:10; 55:3; 63:9). He also prophesied the glory that awaits those who remain faithful to God (chapters 2–4; 62–63). One thing that stands out in this book is God's tremendous power, majesty, glory, and sovereignty (44–45). Despite the greatness of the nations on the earth, they are as nothing before God Almighty (40:15).

According to tradition, Isaiah was martyred during King Manasseh's reign (696–642 B.C.) by being sawed in half inside a hollow log. Some believe Hebrews 11:37 may be referring to this event.

Jacob—See *Patriarchs.*

James, Book of

This book was written by James, the oldest half-brother of Jesus and leader of the Jerusalem church (Acts 12:17), between A.D. 44 and 49. James was one of the "pillars" of the early church (Galatians 2:9).

In his epistle, James stresses the importance of righteous conduct. Perhaps the most important point he makes is that it is not enough to be a *hearer* of God's Word; one must be a *doer* of God's Word (James 1:22-25). He stresses that faith without works is dead (2:14-26), meaning that one's faith in Christ must show itself in the way one lives—in all areas of life, including not showing partiality, controlling the tongue, having a right attitude toward money, and being humble, patient, and prayerful. One who merely claims to have faith, but does not show that faith in the way one lives, has a spurious faith.

James was writing to Jewish Christians ("to the twelve tribes"—James 1:1) who were in danger of giving nothing but lip service to Jesus. This situation may have arisen as a result of the persecution of Herod Agrippa I (Acts 12). Perhaps some of these Jewish Christians had become a little "gun-shy" about living the Christian life. James's intent, therefore, is to distinguish *true faith* from *false faith.* He shows that true faith results in outward works, which become visible evidences of faith's invisible presence. The lifestyle James expects of the true believer includes control of the tongue (James 3), submission to God (4), a right attitude toward money (5:1-6), and patience in the midst of suffering (5:7-12).

Jeremiah, Book of

The book of Jeremiah was written by a prophet of the same name between 627 and 570 B.C. His name literally means

"Jehovah throws," a term referring to the laying of a foundation. Certainly Jeremiah's words, like any prophet's words, were foundational for the people. He was born into a priestly family and was called from birth to be a spokesman for God (Jeremiah 1:5). He was from the small village of Anathoth (1:1).

Jeremiah began his ministry in Judah during the reign of Josiah (640–609 B.C.) and continued through the reigns of four other kings: Johoahaz (609 B.C.), Johoiakim (609–598 B.C.), Jehoiachin (598–597 B.C.), and Zedekiah (597–586 B.C.). He prophesied during the same general time as the prophets Habakkuk, Zephaniah, and Ezekiel.

Jeremiah was given a harsh message to deliver to the people, and he expressed inadequacy in fulfilling the prophetic task to which he was called (Jeremiah 1:6-10). For decades he warned the Israelites of an impending judgment that was coming, but he was virtually ignored (chapters 2–35). Nobody would listen. They remained in such horrible sins as flagrant idol worship, adultery, injustice, tyranny against the helpless, dishonesty, and more. Such sins were causing Jeremiah's people to rush toward judgment. And because Jeremiah pointed toward a coming judgment, his life was often endangered by political and religious leaders (36–38).

The judgment that finally came upon the people of God was the Babylonian exile (Jeremiah 39–45). Jerusalem and its temple were destroyed in 587 B.C., and the Babylonians took all the people captive. Though Jeremiah as a prophet had to speak forth about this coming judgment, he was nevertheless mournful and grieved at what he saw coming upon his nation.

Jesus Christ

1. Significance of Name ◆ 2. Deity ◆ 3. Eternal Son of God ◆ 4. Works (Miracles) ◆ 5. Words ◆ 6. Offices

1. *Significance of Name.* The angel Gabriel's pronouncement to Mary that her child would be called *Jesus* (Luke 1:31)

is full of meaning. "Jesus" means "the Lord saves" or "the Lord is salvation" (or, more literally, "Yahweh saves" or "Yahweh is salvation"). It is the counterpart of the Old Testament name "Joshua," the name of the one who led Israel out of the wilderness experience into a new land and a new life. Jesus the Savior leads us out of our spiritual wilderness experience into a new kind of existence and a new life of fellowship with God.

2. Deity. There are numerous evidences for the deity of Christ. For example, His deity is proved by the names ascribed to Him in the Bible, including God (Hebrews 1:8), Lord (Matthew 22:43-44), and King of kings and Lord of lords (Revelation 19:16). He also has all the attributes of deity, including omnipotence (Matthew 28:18), omniscience (John 1:48), omnipresence (Matthew 18:20), and immutability (Hebrews 13:8). Beyond this, a comparison of the Old and New Testaments provides powerful testimony to Jesus' identity as Yahweh. Support for this is found, for example, in Christ's crucifixion. In Zechariah 12:10, Yahweh is speaking prophetically: "They will look on me, the one they have pierced." Though Yahweh is speaking, this is obviously a reference to Christ's future crucifixion. We know that "the one they have pierced" is Jesus, for He is described this same way by the apostle John in Revelation 1:7.

Another illustration is Isaiah 6:1-5, where Isaiah recounts his vision of Yahweh "seated on a throne, high and exalted" (verse 1). He said, "Holy, holy, holy is the LORD [Yahweh] Almighty; the whole earth is full of his glory" (verse 3). Isaiah also quotes Yahweh as saying: "I am the LORD; that is my name! I will not give my glory to another" (42:8). Later, the apostle John—under the inspiration of the Holy Spirit—wrote that Isaiah "saw Jesus' glory" (John 12:41). Yahweh's glory and Jesus' glory are equated.

It is also highly revealing that Old Testament passages about Yahweh were directly applied to Jesus in the New Testament. For instance, Isaiah 40:3 says: "In the desert prepare the way for the LORD [Yahweh]; make straight in the wilderness

179

a highway for our God [Elohim]." Mark's Gospel tells us that Isaiah's words were fulfilled in the ministry of John the Baptist preparing the way for Jesus Christ (Mark 1:2-4).

Certainly Jesus was worshiped as God many times according to the Gospel accounts. He accepted worship from Thomas (John 20:28), the angels (Hebrews 1:6), some wise men (Matthew 2:11), a leper (Matthew 8:2), a ruler (Matthew 9:18), a blind man (John 9:38), an anonymous woman (Matthew 15:25), Mary Magdalene (Matthew 28:9), and the disciples (Matthew 28:17). The fact that Jesus willingly received (and condoned) worship on various occasions says a lot about His true identity, for it is the consistent testimony of Scripture that only God can be worshiped (Exodus 34:14).

3. Eternal Son of God. Perhaps no name or title of Christ has been so misunderstood as "Son of God." Some have taken the term to mean that Christ came into existence at a point in time and that He is in some way inferior to the Father. Some believe that since Christ is the Son of God, He cannot possibly be God in the same sense as the Father.

Such an understanding is based on a faulty conception of what "Son of..." meant among the ancients. Though the term can refer to "offspring of," it carries the more important meaning, "of the order of." The phrase is often used this way in the Old Testament. For example, "sons of the prophets" meant "of the order of prophets" (1 Kings 20:35). "Sons of the singers" meant "of the order of singers" (Nehemiah 12:28 NASB). Likewise, the phrase "Son of God" means "of the order of God," and represents a claim to undiminished deity.

Ancient Semitics and Orientals used the phrase "son of..." to indicate likeness or sameness of nature and equality of being. Hence, when Jesus claimed to be the Son of God, His Jewish contemporaries fully understood that He was making an unqualified claim to be God. Indeed, the Jews insisted, "We have a law, and according to that law he [Christ] must die, because he claimed to be the Son of God" (John 19:7; see also

5:18). Recognizing that Jesus was identifying Himself as God, the Jews wanted to kill Him for committing blasphemy.

Scripture indicates that Christ's Sonship is an *eternal* Sonship. It is one thing to say that Jesus became the Son of God; it is another thing altogether to say that He was always the Son of God. We must recognize that if there was a time when the Son was not the Son, then—to be consistent— there was also a time when the Father was not the Father. If the First Person's designation as "Father" is an eternal title, then the Second Person's designation as "Son" must be so regarded.

Clear evidence for Christ's eternal Sonship is found in the fact that Christ is represented as already being the Son of God before His birth in Bethlehem. For instance, Hebrews 1:2 says God created the universe *through* His "Son"—implying that Christ was the Son of God prior to the Creation. Moreover, Christ *as the Son* is explicitly said to have existed "before all things" (Colossians 1:17; see verses 13-14). As well, Jesus, speaking as the Son of God (John 8:54-56), asserts His eternal preexistence before Abraham (verse 58).

4. Works (Miracles). The miracles of Jesus provide further evidence about His divine identity. Jesus' miracles are often called "signs" in the New Testament, for signs always signify something—in this case, that Jesus is the divine Messiah. Some of Jesus' more notable miracles include turning water into wine (John 2:7-9), walking on the sea (Matthew 14:25; Mark 6:48; John 6:19), calming a stormy sea (Matthew 8:26; Mark 4:39; Luke 8:24), feeding 5000 men and their families (Matthew 14:19; Mark 6:41; Luke 9:16; John 6:11), raising Lazarus from the dead (John 11:43-44), and causing the disciples to catch a great number of fish (Luke 5:5-6).

5. Words. Jesus' teachings were always presented as being ultimate and final. He never wavered in this. He unflinchingly placed His teachings above those of Moses and the prophets— and in a Jewish culture at that! He always spoke in His own authority. He never said, "Thus saith the Lord..." as did the prophets; He always said, "I tell you the truth..." He never retracted anything He said, never guessed or spoke with uncertainty, never made revisions, never contradicted Himself, and never apologized for what He said. He even asserted that "heaven and earth will pass away, but my words will never pass away" (Mark 13:31), elevating His words directly to the realm of heaven.

Jesus' teachings had a profound effect on people. His listeners always seemed to surmise that these were not the words of an ordinary man. When Jesus taught in Capernaum on the Sabbath, the people "were amazed at his teaching, because his message had authority" (Luke 4:32). After the Sermon on the Mount, "the crowds were amazed at his teaching, because he taught as one who had authority, and not as their teachers of the law" (Matthew 7:28-29). When some Jewish leaders asked the temple guards why they had not arrested Jesus when He spoke, they responded: "No one ever spoke the way this man does" (John 7:46).

One cannot read the Gospels long before recognizing that Jesus regarded Himself and His message as inseparable. The reason Jesus' teachings had ultimate authority was because He was (is) God. The words of Jesus were the very words of God!

6. Offices. Jesus, the divine Messiah, fulfilled the three primary offices of Prophet, Priest, and King. As Prophet, Jesus gave major discourses such as the Upper Room Discourse (John 14–16), the Olivet Discourse (Matthew 24–25), and the Sermon on the Mount (Matthew 5–7). He also spoke as a prophet on many occasions on the subject of the kingdom of God.

As our divine High Priest, Jesus represents God the Father to us and represents us to God the Father. He is our mediator (1 Timothy 2:5). As the ultimate High Priest, Jesus performed the ultimate sacrifice—He shed His own blood on our behalf (Hebrews 7:27). Jesus also prays on our behalf (Hebrews 7:25), just as Old Testament high priests prayed for the people.

Jesus' Kingship is addressed throughout Scripture—from Genesis to Revelation. Genesis 49:10 prophesied that the Messiah would come from the tribe of Judah and reign as King. The Davidic Covenant in 2 Samuel 7:16 promised a Messiah who would have a dynasty, a people over whom He would rule, and an eternal throne. In Psalm 2:6, God the Father is portrayed announcing the installation of God the Son as King in Jerusalem. Psalm 110 affirms that the Messiah will subjugate His enemies and rule over them. Daniel 7:13-14 tells us that the Messiah-King will have an everlasting dominion. These and many other Old Testament passages point to Christ's role as sovereign King.

When we get to the New Testament, we find that before Jesus was even born, an angel appeared to Mary and informed her that her son would "reign over the house of Jacob forever; his kingdom will never end" (Luke 1:32-33). After Jesus was born in Bethlehem, some Magi from the east came to Jerusalem and asked, "Where is the one who has been born king of the Jews? We saw his star in the east and have come to worship him" (Matthew 2:1-2). When Jesus comes again, He will come as the King of kings and Lord of lords (Revelation 19:16). Christ will truly rule forever.

Jewelry and Cosmetics

1. Jewelry ◆ 2. Perfume ◆ 3. Cosmetics

1. Jewelry. Women in Palestine wore jewelry for special occasions. This jewelry would include such items as rings (Hosea 2:13), earrings (Exodus 32:2-3; Numbers 31:50), necklaces (Judges 8:25-26), bracelets (Genesis 24:22), and anklets (see Isaiah 3:18-21). Sometimes the anklets made tinkling sounds, thereby drawing attention to them. Rings worn by men in ancient times were typically signet rings that were engraved with the owner's name and/or symbol to show ownership.

These various pieces of jewelry were made from different kinds of metal, including gold and silver. Some of them were adorned with precious stones or colored glass. It is believed that the Hebrews learned the art of making jewelry from the Egyptians (see Exodus 32:2-3).

In the New Testament, the admonition to modest dress served to minimize the use of such jewelry. In fact, the apostle Paul wrote: "I also want women to dress modestly, with decency and propriety, not with braided hair or gold or pearls or expensive clothes" (1 Timothy 2:9). The biblical emphasis is on inner beauty, not outer adornments.

2. Perfume. Perfume in Bible times was made from sweet smelling extracts taken from herbs, flowers, and resins. Such perfumes were often added to oil and then rubbed on the skin. It was often only the rich who could afford to purchase perfumes. These perfumes were typically used to cover the natural body odor of a person living in a hot climate. Perfumes were also applied to dead bodies (2 Chronicles 16:14), beds (Proverbs 7:17), and clothing (Psalm 45:8).

3. Cosmetics. Like modern days, women in Bible times often wore makeup to enhance their appearance (Esther 2:3). They would sometimes paint their toenails and fingernails with a colored dye derived from crushing the leaves of a plant. They would also wear eye shadow made from ground-up minerals in an oil base. Excessive use of such cosmetics is frowned upon in the Bible (Jeremiah 4:30; Ezekiel 23:40).

Jewish Sects

1. Pharisees ◆ 2. Sadducees ◆ 3. Scribes ◆
4. Zealots ◆ 5. Samaritans

1. Pharisees. The Pharisees were a religious and political party in Palestine during New Testament times. The word

"Pharisee" comes from an Aramaic word meaning "separated"; they were "the separated ones." Scholars are not sure from what or whom Pharisees separated, but suggestions include non-Pharisaic Jews, common people, and Gentiles.

The Pharisees of New Testament times might be considered religious purists. They sought to preserve and obey the law and encouraged other people to do the same. They placed heavy emphasis especially on the Sabbath, tithing, and ritual purity (Matthew 23:23-26; Mark 7:1-13; 2:24; Luke 11:37-42).

There were about 6000 Pharisees during the time of Jesus. We know from the Gospel accounts that Jesus experienced much Pharisaic opposition to His ministry (see Matthew 15:1-12). We also know that Jesus often spoke against the Pharisees for being more committed to external observance of the law than to a true inward relationship with God. Jesus believed them to be hypocrites, with hearts that were far from God (Matthew 6:2,5,16; 23:5-7).

2. Sadducees. The Sadducees were fewer in number than the Pharisees, but they were nevertheless the more influential group. The name "Sadducees" derives from Zadok, the high priest of the Jews during the reigns of David and Solomon (2 Samuel 15:24; 1 Kings 1:34).

The Sadducees typically came from wealthy families, and many of them were landowners and aristocrats. Most of the chief priests in New Testament times were Sadducees. The high priest would be chosen from among them. They were clearly dominant in the Sanhedrin, the supreme court and legislative body of the Jews.

The Sadducees believed only in the Torah, the first five books of Moses (Genesis, Exodus, Leviticus, Numbers, and Deuteronomy). They denied the existence of angels, the resurrection, and the immortality of the soul because these doctrines were not taught in the Torah (so they thought).

The New Testament witness is clear that the Sadducees opposed both Jesus (Matthew 22:23-33) and the early church

J

(Acts 4:1-3; 5:17-18). Jesus sternly warned His followers about the "leaven" of the Sadducees (Matthew 16:1-12 NASB).

3. Scribes. Early in biblical history, the scribes served as copyists, editors, and teachers. Because many people in biblical times could not read or write, they would often go to a scribe to fulfill these functions. For example, if a person needed to draw up a legal document, people would visit a scribe who, for a fee, would complete the task. For people who could not read, the scribe would both read and interpret the document for them.

The scribes were also involved in copying and recopying portions of Scripture for some 1500 years of biblical history. They were specially trained for this task, and they paid a great deal of attention to accuracy.

Eventually the nature of the scribe took on a more exalted status and they became those who officially interpreted the law of God. In New Testament times they were often called "lawyers" (NASB) or "teachers of the law," which points to their role as experts in the Mosaic Law (see Matthew 22:35; Luke 7:30). The time came when their official interpretation of the Law of Moses became more important to Jews than the Mosaic Law itself.

During New Testament times, the scribes had become a distinct political party made up of highly educated people—the upper class of society—and often closely associated with the Pharisees (Matthew 12:38; Mark 7:5; Luke 6:7 NASB). Many were members of the Sanhedrin. Prominent examples would include Gamaliel and Nicodemus (John 3:1; Acts 5:34).

Jesus sternly warned His followers about the religious hypocrisy of the scribes (Matthew 23).

4. Zealots. In biblical times, the Zealots were a group of fanatical Jewish patriots who believed that the Jews should not be subject to any foreign power, such as the Romans (Matthew 10:4). They did not believe the Romans had the authority or the right to impose taxes on the Jewish people.

Indeed, they considered it to be treason against God to pay taxes to the Roman emperor, for God was their true King. They were willing to fight to the death for their cause. They seized control of Jerusalem in A.D. 66, and this ultimately led to Rome's siege and destruction of the city in A.D. 70. Soon after, the Romans overcame the Zealot stronghold of Masada in A.D. 73.

5. Samaritans. The Samaritans of New Testament times were considered half-breeds by mainstream Jews. In Jewish history, some Israelites from the tribes of Ephraim and Manasseh intermarried with Assyrians following the fall of Samaria in 722 B.C. Hence, mainstream Jews considered the Samaritans to be racially unclean. While Samaritans claimed to worship the same God as the Jews, they constructed a rival temple on Mount Gerizim, claiming that theirs was the true Bethel ("house of God").

Jews and Judaism

The term "Jew" comes from the Hebrew word, *Yehudi*, which originally referred to a descendant of Judah (2 Kings 16:6 KJV). Sometime following the Babylonian captivity, however, the word came to refer to *all* Hebrews, the descendants of Abraham, all those of the country of Judah (2 Chronicles 32:18 KJV; Jeremiah 32:12; 34:9; 38:19). In New Testament times, the term likewise referred to Israelites in general (as opposed to Gentiles—Galatians 2:14; Titus 1:14).

Judaism, which derives from the Greek word *Ioudaismos*, refers to the religion of the Jews (Galatians 1:13-14). Jews believe that the entirety of God's Word is communicated in the Old Testament, and they give special attention to the Torah, God's Law, found in the first five books of the Old Testament. Their primary confession of faith is the Shema, which affirms that Yahweh is the one true God (Deuteronomy 6:4). (See *Shema*.)

187

Job, Book of

The book of Job, written by an unknown author probably prior to 1445 B.C., has become famous because it deals with a problem that many human beings have struggled with: If there is a good God, and if God is just, then why do good people suffer? Job is an upright man who has done nothing wrong, and yet catastrophe overwhelms him at every side. He loses his possessions as well as his family, and he finds himself engulfed in heinous physical suffering (Job 1:13-22).

Job's friends visited him and offered him the common wisdom of the day, which said that God blesses obedience but brings about calamity for disobedience. The implication is clear: Job's own wickedness must have brought about this calamity. However, Job knew he had lived righteously before God and his friends were misguided in their opinions (see Job 3–27). All the while, neither Job nor his friends were aware that behind the scenes, Satan had approached God and requested permission to bring about these calamities.

Later in the story, God intervened, and though He did not answer all the questions raised by Job, Job nevertheless seemed satisfied at the mere sight of God (Job 38:1–42:6). In the end, Job was restored in his health and his possessions, and all was well. His faith in God, even in the midst of suffering, is the key lesson of the book.

Joel, Book of

This book was written by Joel, son of Pethuel, in about 835 B.C. (Joel 1:1). Joel's name means "the Lord is God."

A devastating swarm of locusts had just ripped through the land of Judah, resulting in famine. This black cloud of devouring insects struck like a firestorm. As these consuming locusts ate up the agricultural produce and caused the light of the sun to be hidden and darkened, Joel saw in this catastrophe a little foretaste of the day of judgment that was surely coming upon God's people (Joel 1:15–2:11). In fact,

Joel indicated that as bad as the locust plague was, it would pale by comparison to God's day of judgment. He therefore called the people to repentance (2:12-17). The reality is, Joel said, that *God cannot ignore sin.* Blessing can only follow obedience.

John, 1, 2, and 3

By the time the aging apostle John wrote these epistles in about A.D. 90, Christianity had already been around for some 50 years. By now, plenty of time had passed for spiritual and doctrinal errors to develop. The primary heretical system John seems to be dealing with is an early strain of Gnosticism. Apparently some Gnostic teachers were conducting an itinerant ministry in John's congregations, seeking converts. John wrote his epistles to warn true followers of Jesus Christ against such heresies.

J

Of great concern to John were the Gnostic errors about Jesus. The primary error related to whether Jesus was *both* human *and* divine. The root of the problem was the Greek idea that the spiritual and material realms are entirely separate and have nothing to do with each other. It was argued by some false teachers that the spiritual Christ did not actually become human but rather entered into the human Jesus at the time of the baptism, and left the human Jesus before the crucifixion. This scenario avoids the idea that the spiritual became material when Jesus came into the world. John responded:

> This is how you can recognize the Spirit of God: Every spirit that acknowledges that Jesus Christ has come in the flesh is from God, but every spirit that does not acknowledge Jesus is not from God. This is the spirit of the antichrist, which you have heard is coming and even now is already in the world (1 John 4:2-3).

Another aspect of this error related to the idea that whatever was done in the physical body could not in any way tarnish the spirit. This opened the door to gross immorality and libertinism. John thus emphasized that God is light, and those who follow Him are to walk in the light and obey His commands (see 1 John 1:5-10; 3:8-10). Instead of buying into such absurd doctrines, John said the thing we really ought to be focusing on is genuine fellowship with God through Jesus Christ (1 John 1:3-4; 2:28; 5:11-13). He emphasized that our fellowship with God entails a certain kind of behavior on our part. We cannot claim to be in fellowship with God while at the same time engaging in sin—the gross kinds of sin these false teachers were espousing. Rather, true fellowship with God will affect the way we live on a day-to-day basis.

J

John, Gospel of

John was a fisherman by trade. He was sometimes called a "son of thunder" by Jesus—perhaps because of a feisty nature (Mark 3:17). John was very close to Jesus, and is identified as the "disciple whom Jesus loved" (John 13:23). So close was John to Jesus that John was with Mary at the foot of the cross when Jesus was crucified, and Jesus entrusted the care of his mother to John before He died (John 19:26-27). Besides his Gospel, John also wrote 1, 2, and 3 John and the book of Revelation.

John's Gospel was likely written around A.D. 90. Its purpose was to set forth Jesus as the Savior and Redeemer of the world by presenting convincing proofs of His deity, humanity, and messiahship. The Gospel has the evangelistic aim of persuading men to trust in Christ, the divine Messiah (see John 20:31). It is interesting to observe that the word "believe" occurs about 100 times in this Gospel (more than any other Gospel).

A large portion of John's Gospel deals with the doctrine of God. In fact, over half the Gospel deals with truths relating to the Father, Son, and Holy Spirit. This is significant in light of John's evangelistic aim. In a cultural atmosphere where there were many cults, false religions, and divergent philosophical schools of thought, it is easy to see why John went to such extremes to prove the existence of the one *true* God.

An important concept in John's Gospel is that Jesus reveals the Father to the world. Jesus was the supreme revelation of God. For instance, John 1:18 says, "No one has ever seen God, but God the One and Only, who is at the Father's side, has made him known." In John 14:9, Jesus said, "He who has seen me has seen the Father."

In demonstrating the true identity of Jesus as the divine Messiah, John used a number of revealing titles of Christ. Jesus is called "the Lord" (4:3; 6:23; 11:2; 20:20; 21:12), "Son of God" (1:49; 5:25; 11:4,27), "Son of Man" (3:14-15; 5:27; 6:27,62), "Teacher" or "Rabbi" (1:38,49; 3:2; 4:31; 6:25; 9:2; 11:8; 20:16), "King" (1:49; 12:13; 18:33,37), "Christ" (1:20; 3:28), and "Messiah" or "Christ" (1:41; 4:25-26; 11:27). Most of these titles clearly point to the deity of Christ. John also demonstrated that Jesus has the attributes of deity, including omniscience (4:29), omnipresence (14:23), and preexistence (1:1; 8:58; 17:5). The miracles He performed further demonstrate His divine identity (for example, John 2:23; 5:1-15).

While John fully established Jesus' deity, he also demonstrated that in the Incarnation, Jesus was fully human (John 1:14). Indeed, He had a human body (19:40), a human soul (12:27), and a human spirit (11:33; 13:21). Jesus also manifested human characteristics, such as becoming thirsty (19:28-30) and getting tired (4:6).

In sum, Jesus in the Incarnation was fully God *and* fully man. Such is the perfect redeemer of humankind that John speaks of in his Gospel. Jesus came "down out of heaven" (6:41-42), and was born of Mary, who was "Jesus' mother" (2:1). This is crucial to John's message of salvation, for in order for God to *save* man, He Himself must *become* a man and die as a substitutionary sacrifice for the sins of man (John 1:29,36).

John the Baptist

1. Unusual Person ◆ 2. Prepared the Way ◆
3. Spirit and Power of Elijah

1. *Unusual Person.* John was a cousin of Jesus and was miraculously born to Zechariah and Elizabeth in their old age (Luke 1:5-25,57-66). He was an unusual character, for he lived in the desert, his clothing consisted of camel's hair (not too comfortable), and he ate locusts and wild honey for breakfast, lunch, and dinner.

2. *Prepared the Way.* The Old Testament prophet Isaiah spoke of an individual who would prepare the way for the coming of the Messiah (Isaiah 40:3), and this prophecy was fulfilled 700 years later in the ministry of John the Baptist. John, who was born six months before Jesus was born, proclaimed "I am the voice of one calling in the desert, 'Make straight the way for the Lord'" (John 1:23).

John the Baptist came to testify concerning Jesus who would bring salvation to humankind. John cried out, saying, "This was he of whom I said, 'He who comes after me has surpassed me because he was before me'" (John 1:15,30). This is an extremely significant statement by John, for it indicates that even though Christ in His human manifestation was born *after* John, as the eternal Son of God He *preceded* John, and John knew this.

3. *Spirit and Power of Elijah.* Jesus began His public ministry by being baptized in the Jordan River by John the Baptist (Matthew 3:13). Later in His ministry, Jesus said that John was "the Elijah who was to come" (Matthew 11:13-14). Luke 1:17 clarifies what Jesus meant by pointing out that the ministry of John the Baptist was carried out "in the spirit and power of Elijah." Christ is clearly portraying John as a mighty prophet. Indeed, Jesus asserted that "no one has arisen greater than John the Baptist" (Matthew 11:11).

John was eventually executed for publicly speaking out against Herod's marriage to his sister-in-law (Matthew 14:1-12).

Jonah, Book of

This book was written by Jonah, son of Amittai, in about 760 B.C., during the reign of Jeroboam II. It records how Jonah, a prophet of the northern kingdom, was commanded by God to witness to the inhabitants of Nineveh, the capital of Assyria (a pagan nation). Since the Assyrians had previously destroyed Israel in 722 B.C., Jonah resisted the idea of preaching to them, and he tried to run from God to get out of this assignment (he took off in the opposite direction, Jonah 1:1-3).

God providentially brought Jonah back by having him swallowed by a big fish, which vomited him up on the beach where he was supposed to be (Jonah 1:17). Giving heed to God's providential actions, Jonah did as he was told and communicated the message to the Ninevites given to him by God. The Ninevites listened to Jonah's message and promptly repented, thereby averting a terrible judgment (3:6-10). This upset Jonah, for he did not want God to bless these pagans (4:1-3).

This Old Testament story serves to illustrate that God is not the sole possession of the Jews. Indeed, this brings to mind the fact that God's blessing is ultimately intended for all the people of the earth (see the Abrahamic Covenant in Genesis 12:1-3).

Joseph—See Patriarchs.

Joshua, Book of

This book was written by Joshua between 1405 and 1385 B.C. Joshua was Moses's assistant leader during the Exodus and the desert wanderings (Numbers 11:28). He was an extremely effective military commander and leader, and for this reason, he was a natural successor to Moses (see Deuteronomy 34; Joshua 1). This would have been when Joshua was about 90 years old.

Joshua was one of the only two original Israelites who left Egypt to have the faith and courage to enter into the Promised Land (Caleb was the other, Numbers 14:38). Joshua would certainly need this kind of faith and courage in leading the Israelites in conquering Canaan. His name is a shortened form of *Yehoshua*, which literally means "the Lord is salvation." The Lord's "salvation" would be evident in bringing victory over the inhabitants of Canaan.

J

The book of Joshua focuses on Israel's *entering* the land of Canaan (Joshua 1–5), Israel's *conquering* of the land of Canaan (6–12), and the *dividing* of the land of Canaan among the 12 tribes of Israel (13–24), all under the effective leadership of Joshua. This was all a fulfillment of promises given to Abraham and his descendants (Genesis 15:7; 26:2-3).

A key theme of the book of Joshua is the necessity of faith in God and obedience to Him. At the end of the book, Joshua reminded the people of God's covenant promises and urged them to continue obeying Him. Without such faith and obedience, God's blessing could not remain on the people. The people should have learned this lesson well, for they witnessed time and time again how God gave them military victory over their enemies, even though their enemies were more powerful than they were (see Joshua 6–8).

Joshua died at age 110.

Jude, Book of

Jude, a younger brother of Jesus and James, wrote this powerful little apologetic letter between A.D. 70 and 80. Earlier in his life, Jude had rejected Jesus as the divine Messiah (see John 7:1-5). But following Jesus' resurrection from the dead, he converted along with his other brothers (Acts 1:14). Jude went on to become a church leader in Jerusalem. He refers to himself as "a servant of Jesus Christ and a brother of James" (Jude 1).

Jude's letter is apologetic in the sense that it vigorously defends Christianity against false Gnostic-like teaching (Jude 5-16). The particular false teachers Jude was refuting were heretics who denied that Jesus was the Son of God and turned Christian liberty into a license to sin. They were teaching that being saved by grace opens the door for Christians to freely sin, since these sins will no longer be held against them.

Jude thus urged Christians to hold fast to the truth and stand fast against false teachers seeking to infiltrate the church. He urged them to contend earnestly for the faith once for all entrusted to the saints (Jude 3). He affirmed that God would punish and destroy false teachers. He also reminded his readers of God's past dealings with those who felt free to sin—including the unbelieving Israelites, the wicked people of Sodom and Gomorrah, and even the wicked angels (verses 5-7). Woe unto those who think they can so easily get away with sin!

Judges, Book of

The book of Judges was written by an unidentified author between 1043 and 1000 B.C. Jewish tradition in the Talmud says the author was the prophet Samuel. The book covers the time beginning with Joshua's death and ending with the rise of the prophet Samuel (Judges 2:6-9).

Primary attention is placed on the judges of Israel at that time. While the book is called "Judges," the Hebrew term for the title *(Shophet)* can mean "Deliverers" or "Saviors." This points to the intended role of these judges. As Judges 2:16 puts it, "Then the LORD raised up judges, who saved them out of the hands of these raiders."

The backdrop is that Joshua's conquest, while effective, still left pockets of resistance that continued to cause trouble for the Israelites. The "judges" were raised up specifically as military champions to lead the tribes of Israel against these culprits and to bring about final and complete conquest. These judges were needed, for at that time the 12 tribes of Israel had no central leadership. Four of the judges are listed in the faith Hall of Fame in Hebrews 11: Gideon, Barak, Samson, and Jephthah (see Judges 6–8; 4; 10:6–12:7; 13–16).

Unfortunately, Israel was anything but faithful to God during this time, even giving allegiance to some of the false local gods of paganism. Despite the fact that God had repeatedly blessed them, they always seemed to revert to going their own way instead of God's way (Judges 3:7; 6:1; 10:6; 13:1).

To many modern people the book of Judges is disturbing. One reads of treachery, violence, assassinations, people being burned to death, rape, and other such things. This was truly a time of political, social, and religious upheaval. Many theologians have noted that the primary problem of the people during this time was that they did what they considered to be right in their own eyes (Judges 21:25 NASB).

Judgment

1. God of Judgment ◆ 2. According to the Light
Given ◆ 3. Believers ◆ 4. Unbelievers

1. *God of Judgment.* The God of the Bible is a God of judgment. In the Old Testament we find God's judgment evidenced in expelling Adam and Eve from the Garden of Eden (Genesis 3), judging the corrupt world of Noah's day by sending a flood (Genesis 6–8), and judging Sodom and Gomorrah by a volcanic catastrophe (Genesis 18–19). Likewise, in the New Testament we find that judgment falls on Ananias and Sapphira for lying to God (Acts 5), on Herod for his self-exalting pride (Acts 12:21-25), and on Christians in Corinth who were afflicted with illness because they participated in the Lord's Supper unworthily (1 Corinthians 11:29-32). God holds people accountable for the things they do.

2. *According to the Light Given.* Scripture teaches that both Christians and non-Christians will one day face a judgment. This judgment will be based upon each particular person's exposure and response to the revealed will of God (Luke 12:48; see also Matthew 11:21-24). We may rest assured that God's judgment is utterly fair.

3. *Believers.* All Christians will one day stand before the Judgment Seat of Christ (Romans 14:8-10; 2 Corinthians 5:10). At that time each Christian's life will be examined in regard to deeds done while in the body (Psalm 62:12; Ephesians 6:7-8). Personal motives, intents of the heart, and the words we have spoken will also be weighed (Jeremiah 17:10; 1 Corinthians 4:5; see also Matthew 12:35-37).

The idea of a "judgment seat" relates to the athletic games of Paul's day. When races and games concluded, a dignitary would take his seat on an elevated throne in the arena, and one by one the winning athletes would come forward to receive a reward—usually a wreath of leaves, a victor's crown. In the case of Christians, each of us will stand before Christ the Judge and receive (or lose) rewards (called "crowns" in Scripture, 2 Timothy 4:8; James 1:12; 1 Peter 5:4; Revelation 2:10).

This judgment has nothing to do with whether or not the Christian will remain saved. Those who have truly placed faith in Christ are saved, and nothing threatens that. Believers are eternally secure in their salvation. This judgment rather has to do with the reception or loss of rewards.

It seems to be the testimony of Scripture that some Christians at the Judgment may have a sense of deprivation and suffer some degree of forfeiture and shame. Indeed, certain rewards may be forfeited that otherwise might have been received, and this will involve a sense of loss. The fact is, Christians differ radically in holiness of conduct and faithfulness in service. God in His justice and holiness takes all this into account. Some believers will be without shame and others with shame at the Judgment Seat of Christ (1 John 2:28). Second John 8 warns us, "Watch out that you do not lose what you have worked for, but that you may be rewarded fully."

4. Unbelievers. Unlike Christians, whose judgment deals only with rewards and loss of rewards, unbelievers face a horrific judgment that leads to their being cast into the Lake of Fire. The judgment that unbelievers face is called the Great White Throne Judgment (Revelation 20:11-15). Christ is the divine Judge, and those that are judged are the unsaved dead of all time. The Judgment takes place at the end of the Millennial Kingdom, Christ's 1000-year reign on planet earth.

Those who face Christ at this judgment will be judged on the basis of their works (Revelation 20:12-13). It is critical to understand that they actually get to this judgment because they are *already unsaved.* This judgment will not separate believers from unbelievers, for all who will experience it will have already made the choice during their lifetimes to reject the God of the Bible. Once they are before the divine Judge, they are judged according to their works not only to justify their condemnation but also to determine the degree to which each person should be punished throughout eternity (see Luke 12:47-48).

Justice and Righteousness

Righteousness and justice are among the most important attributes of God. The Scriptures portray God as *singularly* righteous, with no hint of unrighteousness (unlike the concept of God in some other world religions). We read: "Lord, God of Israel, you are righteous!" (Ezra 9:15). "You are always righteous, O Lord" (Jeremiah 12:1). "For the Lord is righteous, he loves justice" (Psalm 11:7). "The Lord loves righteousness and justice" (Psalm 33:5). "Righteousness and justice are the foundation of your throne" (Psalm 89:14).

That God is *just* means He carries out His righteous standards justly and with equity. There is never any partiality or unfairness in God's dealings with people (Zephaniah 3:5; Romans 3:26). His justness is proclaimed emphatically in both the Old and New Testaments (see, for example, Genesis 18:25; John 17:25; Hebrews 6:10).

As God is righteous and just, so God desires all of His children to be righteous and just (John 7:24; 1 Peter 3:12; 1 John 3:7). As children of God (1 John 3:2), we are to take on the family likeness.

Justification

1. Justification Defined ◆ 2. Roman Catholic Versus Protestant View

1. *Justification Defined.* Humankind's dilemma of "falling short" of God pointed to the need for a solution, and that solution is found in justification (Romans 3:24). The word "justified" is a legal term and involves being "declared righteous" or "acquitted." Negatively, the word means that one is once-for-all pronounced not guilty before God. Positively, the word means that man is once-for-all pronounced righteous. When a person trusts in Christ for salvation, he is pronounced "not guilty" and is pronounced once-for-all righteous (Romans 3:25,28,30).

Though the Jews previously tried to earn right standing with God by works, Paul indicated that God's declaration of righteousness (justification) is given "freely by his grace" (Romans 3:24). The word "grace" means "unmerited favor." It is because of God's unmerited favor that human beings can freely be declared righteous before God.

This does not mean God's declaration of righteousness has no objective basis. Quite the opposite. The word "redemption" literally means "ransom payment." This is a word adapted from the slave market. We were formerly enslaved to sin and

Satan, but Jesus ransomed us by His death on the cross. His shed blood was the ransom payment (Romans 3:25). This makes justification possible.

2. Roman Catholic Versus Protestant View. Justification in the Roman Catholic view involves a transformation whereby the individual actually *becomes* righteous. It is viewed as a *process* in which God gradually perfects us. Good works and participation in the sacraments further this process.

By contrast, Protestants view justification as a singular and instantaneous event in which God *declares* the believing sinner to be righteous. Justification viewed in this way is a judicial term. God makes a legal declaration. It is not based on performance or good works. It involves God's pardoning of sinners and restoring them to a state of righteousness. This declaration of righteousness takes place the moment a person trusts in Christ for salvation (Psalm 32:1-5; 130; Luke 7:47-50; 18:9-14; Acts 10:43; Romans 3:25,28,30; 8:33-34; Galatians 4:21–5:12; 1 John 1:7–2:2). Good works do not contribute to justification at all but are rather viewed as the *result* of justification. Salvation comes about through faith (Romans 4:1-25; Galatians 3:6-14). Good works, however, are a by-product of salvation (Matthew 7:15-23; 1 Timothy 5:10,25).

The Protestant view is often referred to as "forensic justification." "Forensic" comes from a Latin word meaning "forum." This word has its roots in the fact that in the ancient Roman forum, a court could meet and make judicial or legal declarations. Forensic justification, then, involves God's judicial declaration of the believer's righteousness before Him. The believer is legally acquitted of all guilt and the very righteousness of Christ is imputed to his account. Henceforth, when God sees the believer, He sees him in all the righteousness of Christ.

K

Kingdom of God, Kingdom of Heaven

The terms "kingdom of God" and "kingdom of heaven" are essentially interchangeable terms in the Bible. The Gospels Mark, Luke, and John use the term "kingdom of God" (for example, Mark 1:15; Luke 9:2). Matthew, however, uses "kingdom of heaven" some 34 times but "kingdom of God" only four times. Why is this so? The apparent reason Matthew predominantly used "kingdom of heaven" is that he was a Jew writing to Jews and was showing sensitivity to the Jewish preference of avoiding using God's name when possible to make sure one was not using this name in vain (since the third of the Ten Commandments prohibits this, Exodus 20:7 NASB). The other Gospel writers were not writing to a Jewish audience and used the term "kingdom of God."

There are two primary senses in which "kingdom of God" and "kingdom of heaven" are used in Scripture: a *present* sense and a *future* sense. The present sense involves the idea that God spiritually rules over His people who have been delivered from the kingdom of darkness and transferred to the kingdom of Jesus Christ (Colossians 1:13). The kingdom exists wherever Christians are submitting to the kingship and rule of God (Romans 14:17; 1 Corinthians 4:20).

The future aspect of the kingdom relates to the future millennial reign of Jesus Christ on earth. Following the Second Coming, Christ will institute a kingdom of perfect peace and righteousness on earth that will last for 1000 years. After this reign of true peace, eternity begins (see Revelation 21–22). This kingdom is prophesied many times in the Old Testament (for example, Isaiah 65:17–66:24; Jeremiah 32:36-44; Zechariah 14:9-17).

Kings, 1 and 2

These books were written by an unknown author around 550 B.C. They were originally a single book but were divided into two books by the translators of the Septuagint (the Greek translation of the Hebrew Old Testament that predates Christ).

These books focus heavy attention on how Israel divided into two kingdoms. Early in 1 Kings, we find a stable kingdom under the leadership of King Solomon (1 Kings 1–9). During this time the kingdom was united, and it was characterized by glory and splendor. As an outworking of the covenant promises God had made to Israel in the book of Deuteronomy, the nation was truly blessed by God so long as the nation continued to obey God's laws.

When the nation turned from God, however, it weakened religiously, morally, economically, and politically (see 1 Kings 11–12). As the nation strayed further and further from the worship of the one true God, things went from bad to worse. Internal strife weakened the kingdom, and it eventually split into two kingdoms—the northern kingdom (retaining the name Israel) and the southern kingdom (called Judah).

The two sets of kings and their kingdoms remained indifferent to God's laws and His prophets. They were thoroughly disobedient, and this ultimately led to Israel's fall in 722 B.C. and the crushing Babylonian captivity for Judah in 587 B.C. The author clearly communicates that this dire situation was a direct result of the people's long-term disobedience to God (see 1 Kings 9:3-9). Even so, God's mercy was always still available if there was repentance.

Kingship, Human and Divine

1. God, the Source of Authority ◆ 2. Government in Israel ◆ 3. Roman Emperors ◆ 4. Jesus as King

1. *God, the Source of Authority.* God is a God of order. This order is evident in the authority structures He set up among human beings. For example, in the family unit, God has instituted an ordered structure with the man as the head of the house and then both parents over the children (1 Corinthians 11:3; Ephesians 6:1). In the church, God has assigned elders to bring order to the church (1 Timothy 5:17). In the same way, God is clearly the author of human government and kingship (Romans 13:1-6). Below are two (brief) representative examples of human governments.

2. Government in Israel. Patriarchal rule was common in biblical times. Indeed, Israel's history begins with the person of Abraham, who ruled his family and whose family developed into a nation by the time of the Exodus. At this time, Moses, as a representative of God, was the leader over the 12 family clans of Israel, and all of Israel submitted to God as their King and Lawmaker. Israel was a theocracy, a God-ruled nation (see Exodus 19–20). Following Moses's death, Joshua took over the leadership role. And when he died, elders in various cities took over leadership roles (Joshua 24:31; Judges 11:5), as did judges (Judges 2:16-19).

Eventually, there came a time when Israel wanted a human king, just as the other nations around them had a king (see Genesis 17:6; 35:11). Saul was to become the first king of Israel (1 Samuel 9). Unfortunately, he did not prove to be nearly as effective as later kings, such as David and Solomon. The reigns of the various kings of Israel and Judah are described in 1 Kings 12–2 Kings 25 and 2 Chronicles 10–36.

3. Roman Emperors. Other nations in Bible times had rather sophisticated governments. The Roman Empire was a good example. The emperor was the head ruler, and he exercised general authority over all of Rome. The Roman troops served to enforce his orders. There was a time in Rome's history when the emperor was worshiped as a god. Those who refused to worship him were executed.

There was also a Roman senate that governed over the peaceful provinces of Rome. Governors, called "proconsuls," were appointed by the senate to govern in these areas. The emperor sent troops to keep order in nonpeaceful provinces and assigned deputies to enforce his rule.

Other nations had exalted kings like Rome did. For example, in Egypt, the pharaoh was considered to be a god as the son of Re, the sun god. Likewise, in Assyria the king was spoken of in divine terms.

4. *Jesus as King.* The ultimate "king" mentioned in both the Old and New Testaments is Jesus Christ. Genesis 49:10 prophesied that the Messiah would come from the tribe of Judah and reign as a King. The Davidic Covenant in 2 Samuel 7:16 promised a Messiah who would have a dynasty, a people over whom He would rule, and an eternal throne. In Psalm 2:6, God the Father is portrayed announcing the installation of God the Son as King in Jerusalem. Psalm 110 affirms that the Messiah will subjugate His enemies and rule over them. Daniel 7:13-14 tells us that the Messiah-King will have an everlasting dominion. These and many other Old Testament passages point to Christ's role as sovereign King.

The New Testament tells us that before Jesus was born, an angel appeared to Mary and informed her that she would give birth to a Son who would "reign over the house of Jacob forever; his kingdom will never end" (Luke 1:32-33). After Jesus was born in Bethlehem, some Magi from the east came to Jerusalem and asked, "Where is the one who has been born king of the Jews? We saw his star in the east and have come to worship him" (Matthew 2:1-2). When they found Jesus, they bowed down and worshiped Him—even though He was just a babe (verse 11).

At the close of His ministry, Christ was arrested and tried before Pilate, and His kingship was treated with utter scorn. The governor's soldiers took Jesus into the Praetorium and ridiculed Him:

> They stripped him and put a scarlet robe on him, and then twisted together a crown of thorns and set it on his head. They put a staff in his right hand and knelt in front of him and mocked him. "Hail, king of the Jews!" they said. They

204

spit on him, and took the staff and struck him on the head again and again. After they had mocked him, they took off the robe and put his own clothes on him. Then they led him away to crucify him (Matthew 27:28-31).

After Jesus had been crucified, a sign—in rank mockery—was put above His head on the cross that read, "This Is Jesus, the King of the Jews" (verse 37). At the Second Coming, Christ will be vindicated as the King of kings and Lord of lords (Revelation 19:16). Woe to those who took part in this mockery of Christ!

K

Lake of Fire—See *Hell.*

Lamentations

The mournful prophet Jeremiah wrote the book of Lamentations in about 586 B.C. The title of the book, which literally
means "funeral songs," is descriptive of its contents. It
expresses the deep anguish of the Israelites over the destruction of Jerusalem—the very city of God—by the Babylonians
in 587 B.C. Jeremiah seems to have witnessed the destruction firsthand. The temple was destroyed, and the people were
deported to live in Babylon in exile. This book literally depicts
the funeral of a city. It is the only book in the Bible that consists solely of laments.

Worse comes to worst when the Israelites come to realize
that the reason this horror has fallen on them is their utter
unfaithfulness to and rebellion against God (Lamentations
1:20-22). This realization was surely good cause for
lamenting. Jeremiah, of course, was not surprised at the
destruction of Jerusalem, for he had been prophesying of this
judgment for some 40 years (see Jeremiah 1–29). But the
people had not listened.

In the end, Jeremiah also emphasized that God is characterized by love and mercy. His compassions never fail (see
Lamentations 3:23). Hence, there is yet hope for the nation
(5:19-22).

Land and Property

During Bible times, each family owned a little chunk of land
(1 Kings 4:25; Micah 4:4), and everyone in the family was
responsible for contributing to its care and upkeep. The men

in the family would often work their trade and perhaps do some farming, while the children took care of the family animals, looked after the vines, and performed other small tasks.

In Jewish thinking, the land each person possessed was a gift from God and must be treated as such. Though land could be bought and sold, Old Testament law stipulated that every fiftieth year was a year of Jubilee in which land that had been mortgaged to pay off a debt had to be returned to the family that owned it. Unfortunately, there is no record that the Jubilee was ever observed.

Canaan, the land flowing with milk and honey, was viewed as a land owned by God but given to His people (Joshua 24:11-13). When the Israelites finally possessed Canaan, a plot of land was given to each of the 12 tribes. Reuben, Gad, and half of the tribe of Manasseh settled in the east, while Asher, Naphtali, Zebulon, Issachar, Ephraim, and the other half-tribe of Manasseh settled in the northwest. Benjamin, Judah, Simeon, and Dan settled in the southwest. The Israelites were viewed as tenants of God's land (Leviticus 25:23).

Language and Communication

God created human language for a purpose. A plain reading of Genesis indicates that when God created Adam in His own rational image, He gave Adam the gift of intelligible speech. This enabled him to communicate objectively with his Creator and with other human beings (Genesis 1:26; see also 11:1,7). Scripture shows that God sovereignly chose to use human language as a medium of revelational communication, often through the "Thus saith the LORD" pronouncements of the prophets (see the KJV at Isaiah 7:7; 10:24; 22:15; 28:16; 30:15; 49:22; 51:22; 52:4; 65:13).

The most famous languages of the Bible are Hebrew (a Semitic dialect, akin to Phoenician and Ugaritic, in which the Old Testament was written) and Greek (that is, Koine Greek, the common everyday language of the Graeco-Roman world, in which the New Testament was written). But there are other languages that were common in Bible times. Indeed, Aramaic (another Semitic language akin to Hebrew) was a common language, and New Testament evidence indicates that Jesus even spoke Aramaic (see Mark 5:41; 7:34). As well, some small portions of the Old Testament were written in Aramaic (see Ezra 4:8–6:18; 7:12-26; Daniel 2:46–7:28).

Latin was another common language of the day. When the Romans nailed a sign above Jesus' head on the cross that said "Jesus of Nazareth, the King of the Jews," it was written in Aramaic, Latin, and Greek (John 19:19-20; see also Luke 23:38).

Other languages of relevance to the Bible include Akkadian (a Semitic language spoken in ancient Mesopotamia), Ugaritic (a northwest Semitic dialect that was the language of the Canaanites), Egyptian (a language of mixed origin, drawing from languages on the north coast of Africa and mixed with a Semitic language), and Syriac (a northwest dialect of Aramaic).

Law

A summation of the most important laws in the Old Testament is found in the Ten Commandments, which were not just religious rules but rules intended to govern the whole of life. After all, these commandments deal with such things as murder, adultery, stealing, accusing someone falsely, and coveting, as well as religious stipulations involving complete faithfulness to the one true God. Clearly, the Ten Commandments were intended to guide God's people not only in a proper relationship with Him but also in their relationships with other people as well.

One must not forget that Israel was in a covenant relationship with God (the Sinai Covenant, Exodus 19:3-25). As a covenant nation, there were stipulations that Israel was obligated to obey. The Bible indicates that these stipulations—the Ten Commandments—were recorded on two stone tablets. Though many modern movies have portrayed these tablets as containing five commandments each, it is more likely that these were two entire copies of the Ten Commandments. Among the ancients, when a covenant was made between two parties, it was traditional for each party to have a copy of the covenant stipulations. Since Israel was in a covenant with God, it was understandable that there be two copies made. These copies were kept in the Ark of the Covenant.

Of course, the broader "Mosaic Law" includes not just the Ten Commandments but the laws contained in Exodus 19–40, the book of Leviticus, and the first ten chapters of the book of Numbers. In the book of Exodus we find a listing of moral, civil, and religious laws. These laws deal with such issues as the rights of slaves, social duties, human rights, and damage to someone else's property. There were also instructions that governed the great religious festivals held in Israel. The laws contained in the book of Leviticus deal with the important issue of how God's people were to worship God, including the rituals connected with the tabernacle and the temple. In the book of Deuteronomy, we find a repetition of some of the same laws found in Exodus and Leviticus, but we also find warnings of what will happen if God's people disobey (see Deuteronomy 27–30).

The law was given to Israel not to place a burden on the people but to set them apart and distinguish them from surrounding pagan nations. The law was provided to make the Israelites wise, great, and pleasing to a holy God. Those who obeyed the law reaped great blessing. Those who disobeyed the law brought discipline upon themselves. This is one of the primary emphases of the Sinai Covenant (Exodus 19:3-25).

Scholars have noted that the Israelites were not the only ancient people to have a law code. Other ancient law codes that have been discovered include those of Ur Nammu (Sumerian, about 2050 B.C.), Lipit-Ishtar (Sumerian, about 1900 B.C.), Eshnunna (Akkadian, about 1875 B.C.), and Hammurabi (Babylonian, about 1690 B.C.). No law code has been discovered in Egypt, but this is to be expected since the pharaoh was considered "the law" in Egypt. The purpose of ancient law codes was to govern and regulate interpersonal relationships and maintain stability in the community.

Laziness—See *Work Versus Laziness.*

Leviticus

Leviticus was written by Moses between 1445 and 1405 B.C. and contains multiple ceremonial and ritual rules and regulations designed to govern every imaginable aspect of life among the ancient Israelites. Following the exodus of the Israelites from Egypt, Israel was called to a new way of life, involving priests, tabernacle worship, sacrifices, and the like, so such rules and regulations became necessary. Leviticus contains laws about offerings and sacrifices (Leviticus 1–7), laws on the appointment and conduct of priests (8–10), laws about ritual cleansing, personal hygiene, and food (11–15), instructions regarding the Day of Atonement (16), and information and laws regarding Israel's festivals (17–27).

This book takes its name from the Levites, the priestly tribe in ancient Israel. It was written essentially for the priests, who were then to instruct God's people on the laws contained in it.

Perhaps the most pivotal statement in the book of Leviticus is this: "Be holy, because I, the LORD your God, am holy" (Leviticus 19:2). All the laws, rules, and regulations contained in this book are merely an outgrowth of the call to be holy. The Israelites were to be holy or separate from the pagan nations around them. And since God, as the divine ruler, had made a covenant with the Israelites, the Israelites were obligated to obey the holiness stipulations of the covenant.

The rules and regulations regarding the Tabernacle and the sacrificial system are no longer binding on us today, for Christ's sacrifice was once-for-all, rendering the entire Old

210

Testament sacrificial system obsolete (Hebrews 9:13–10:18). Nor are the food laws and rules about hygiene binding on us today (Colossians 2:16-17). But what *does* remain is God's holiness and His call on His followers to live in holiness (1 Peter 1:15-16).

Lord's Day—See *Sabbath.*

Lord's Supper—See *Sacraments.*

Lucifer —See *Satan.*

Luke, Gospel of

L

The Gospel of Luke was written by Luke in A.D. 60. Luke was a doctor (Colossians 4:14), and the compassion he expresses throughout his Gospel is typical of a family doctor. An examination of his writing shows him to be a well-educated and cultured man. His is the longest of the four Gospels.

Modern archaeologists who have studied the Gospel of Luke have concluded that Dr. Luke was extremely accurate in his writings. Luke is careful to emphasize that he wrote his Gospel based upon reliable, firsthand sources (Luke 1:1-4). He wanted to make sure that the truth was known about Jesus Christ in an ordered and accurate way.

Many scholars have pointed to how relevant it is that a doctor wrote this Gospel. As a doctor, Luke would be interested in scientific and historical accuracy. As a doctor, he was certainly fully aware that a woman does not get pregnant without having relations with a man. It is therefore highly significant that he expresses unflinching belief in his Gospel that Jesus was virgin born and that Mary became pregnant as a result of the Holy Spirit overshadowing her (Luke 1:35). Further, it is highly significant that Luke as a doctor expressed unflinching belief in the many miracles of Jesus (see 4:38-40; 5:15-25; 6:17-19; 7:11-15).

Luke's Gospel has a warm tone, showing Jesus as not only a *divine* being but also as a *human* being with a big heart. This Gospel shows Jesus helping the sick, helpless, poor, downtrodden, social outcasts, women, and children. The love of Jesus shines in this Gospel. This love is not just for one group of people (such as the Jews) but for *all* people.

Joy is a common theme throughout the book. For example, Mary expressed joy after being informed that she would give birth to the divine Messiah (Luke 1:47). A pregnant Elizabeth said the child in her womb (John the Baptist) leapt for joy when she heard Mary's voice (1:44). The angels rejoice when sinners repent (15:7). Jesus was full of joy through the Holy Spirit (10:21). Jesus desires that His followers be full of joy (6:23; 10:20; 15:6,9). Truly, the Jesus story is a story of joy on many different levels, and Luke wants us to understand something of this joy.

L

M

Magic and Witchcraft

All throughout human history, people have desired success in life—healthy bodies, prosperity, and all the good things life has to offer. Many individuals, not content to seek these things by natural means or according to God's laws, have sought to use magic and occultism to bring them about. Magic was often used in ancient times for selfish purposes. It was viewed as a means of harnessing the power of a particular deity and was quite popular in pagan cultures (see Ezekiel 13:20; Revelation 21:8; 22:15).

One particular incident in the New Testament involving a magician relates to Simon Magus, who at one time amazed the Samaritans with his magic. After becoming a Christian, apparently still fascinated with such phenomena, he witnessed Peter's bestowal of the Holy Spirit and tried to buy this gift from him. For this, he was immediately condemned and rebuked by Peter (Acts 8:20).

Scripture indicates that God condemns all forms of occultism, including magic (Exodus 22:18; Leviticus 19:31; Deuteronomy 18:9-13; Ezekiel 13:18; Acts 19:19-20; Galatians 5:20; Revelation 9:21; 21:8). Magic is not only an affront to God; it is also a distraction from trust in God. Furthermore, God is greater than any form of magic. This is evident in the incident Moses had with the magicians of Egypt. The Egyptian sorcerers were not able to duplicate all the miracles Moses performed by the power of God (see Exodus 7–9).

Malachi, Book of

The book of Malachi was written by a prophet of the same name between 433 and 400 B.C. The name Malachi means "my messenger" or "the Lord's messenger," a good name for a prophet of God. His is the last book in the Old Testament.

Malachi's ministry took place following the rebuilding of the temple (515 B.C.). The people had returned to their homeland from exile, but this had not translated into a desire to walk closely with God. They practiced empty rituals without attaching any real meaning to them.

Malachi begins his book by assuring the people of God's constant and unchanging love for them (Malachi 1:1-5). This was necessary because the people were so disillusioned. They were complacent and had lost national pride. Poverty was widespread, there was drought, famine, and ruined crops, and the people had been brutalized by foreign powers. Past promises of restoration had not yet come to pass, and so the people were discouraged. They were even wondering whether the prophets of the past had gotten things right. They began to wonder if God cared for them anymore. Spiritual lethargy was at an all-time high. So God assured them through Malachi that, indeed, His love for them is unending.

M

To compound the problem, however, the people in their discouragement were not living as they should before a holy God. They were living in deep, deep sin. There was social corruption, temple worship was a sham, and priests were ignoring their duties (see Malachi 1:6–2:17). Hence, Malachi utters not only words of God's love, but words of stern warning. He spoke forceful and indicting words designed to move the people to faithfulness to the covenant God had established with them. If they continued to live like they were, more judgment was surely on the horizon. Repentance was therefore in order!

Manuscripts of Bible Books

1. Examples of Biblical Manuscripts ◆ 2. Quotations from Church Fathers ◆ 3. Manuscript Variants

1. *Examples of Biblical Manuscripts.* There are more than 5000 partial and complete manuscript copies of the New

Testament. These manuscript copies are very ancient, and they are available for inspection now. Following are some highlights:

- The Chester Beatty papyrus (P45) dates to the third century A.D. It contains the four Gospels and the book of Acts (chapters 4–17). ("P" stands for "papyrus.")

- The Chester Beatty papyrus (P46) dates to about A.D. 200 and contains ten Pauline epistles (all but the Pastorals) and the book of Hebrews.

- The Chester Beatty papyrus (P47) dates to the third century A.D. and contains Revelation 9:10–17:2.

- The Bodmer Papyrus (P66) dates to about A.D. 200 and contains the Gospel of John.

- The Bodmer Papyrus (P75) dates to the early third century and contains Luke and John.

- The Sinaiticus uncial manuscript dates to the fourth century and contains the entire New Testament.

- The Vaticanus uncial manuscript dates to the fourth century and contains most of the New Testament except the end of Hebrews, the Pastoral Epistles, Philemon, and Revelation.

- The Washingtonianus uncial manuscript dates to the early fifth century and contains the Gospels.

- The Alexandrinus uncial manuscript dates to the fifth century and contains most of the New Testament.

- The Ephraemi Rescriptus uncial manuscript dates to the fifth century and contains portions of every book except 2 Thessalonians and 2 John.

- The Bezae/Cantabrigiensis uncial manuscript dates to the fifth century and contains the Gospels and Acts.

M

- The Claromontanus uncial manuscript dates to the sixth century and contains the Pauline epistles and Hebrews.

- The Itala version (versions were prepared for missionary purposes) dates to the third century.

- The Vulgate version dates to the fourth century and later.

- The Syriac version dates to the second through sixth centuries.

- The Coptic version dates to the third and fourth centuries.

- The Armenian version dates to the fifth century.

- The Georgian version dates to the fifth century.

M

2. Quotations from Church Fathers. There are some 86,000 quotations of the New Testament from the early church fathers and several thousand lectionaries (church-service books containing Scripture quotations used in the early centuries of Christianity). In fact, there are enough quotations from the early church fathers that even if we did not have a single manuscript copy of the Bible, scholars could still reconstruct all but eleven verses of the entire New Testament from material written within 200 years of the time of Christ.

3. Manuscript Variants. In the thousands of manuscript copies we possess of the New Testament, scholars have discovered that there are some 200,000 "variants." This may seem like a staggering figure to the uninformed mind. But to those who study the issue, the numbers are not so damning as it may initially appear. Indeed, a look at the hard evidence shows that the New Testament manuscripts are amazingly accurate and trustworthy.

216

To begin, out of these 200,000 variants, 99 percent hold virtually no significance whatsoever. Many of these variants simply involve a missing letter in a word; some involve reversing the order of two words (such as "Christ Jesus" instead of "Jesus Christ"); some involve the absence of one or more insignificant words. Really, when all the facts are put on the table, only about 40 of the variants have any real significance—and even then, no doctrine of the Christian faith or any moral commandment is affected by them.

In more than 99 percent of the cases, the original text can be reconstructed to a practical certainty. By practicing the science of textual criticism—comparing all the available manuscripts with each other—we can be sure of what the original document likely said. The sheer volume of manuscripts we possess greatly narrows the margin of doubt.

Mark, Gospel of

M

The Gospel of Mark was written by Mark between A.D. 50 and 60, most likely around A.D. 55. Mark is said to be a son of Mary (Acts 12:12) and a cousin of Barnabas (Colossians 4:10). He went with the apostle Paul and Barnabas on their first missionary tour (Acts 12:25; 13:5).

Mark probably derived much of his material from the apostle Peter. In fact, Justin Martyr, a church father, referred to Mark's Gospel as "the memoirs of Peter." Because Peter referred to Mark as "my son Mark" (1 Peter 5:13), many believe it was Peter who initially led Mark to Christ. Mark's close association with the apostle Peter served to give apostolic backing to Mark's Gospel.

Mark's Gospel is the shortest of the four Gospels and was probably written first. His is certainly the fastest paced and most action packed of the four. It is bustling with life and action. Indeed, scholars have noted that this Gospel focuses more on Jesus' actions (especially His miracles) than on His teachings. By so doing, Mark demonstrates that Jesus is who He claimed to be—the divine Son of God. About one-third of Mark's Gospel focuses on the last week of Jesus' life on earth, concluding with His death and resurrection.

Unlike the Gospel of Matthew, which targeted Jewish readers, Mark's Gospel was written for Gentile readers—probably Romans. Mark went to great lengths in explaining Jewish customs, something he would not have done if he were targeting Jewish readers (see Mark 7:3-4; 14:12; 15:42). As well, there are fewer references to the Old Testament in this Gospel than there are in Matthew, and Mark left out things (such as a genealogy of Jesus) that would not be of much interest to Gentile readers. Moreover, there are fewer descriptions of hostile encounters with Pharisees and scribes, something one might expect if the Gospel were targeting Gentiles.

Marriage

1. Betrothal and Marriage ◆ 2. Divorce

1. *Betrothal and Marriage.* Marriage is an institution founded by God. In Genesis 2:18 God affirmed, "It is not good for the man to be alone. I will make a helper suitable for him." Adam and Eve were the first married couple. Since then, men and women have continued to be united in marriage: "For this reason a man will leave his father and mother and be united to his wife, and they will become one flesh" (Genesis 2:24).

Most men in Jewish society got married, and did so quite young. In fact, in biblical times Jewish authorities determined that marriages could take place when the boy was 13 and the girl was just 12 years of age. Often parents arranged these marriages. Typically, a boy's parents would select their son's bride, and the bride would become a part of the boy's clan. The bride was chosen not just in terms of compatibility with the boy, but with the family as well. This would help ensure a successful marriage and family relationship.

The Torah did not permit Israelites to marry someone from a different nation that worshiped other gods (see Exodus

34:10-16; Deuteronomy 7:3-4; see also 2 Corinthians 6:14). Incestuous relationships were also forbidden by the law (Leviticus 18:6-8; 20:19-21).

In biblical times, people first become betrothed to get married, and this betrothal was much stronger than engagements are today. In fact, to break a betrothal, one had to obtain a divorce. The betrothal contract was essentially as binding as a marriage.

Prior to the marriage, it was common for the groom or groom's family to pay the bride's father a sum of money. This money was considered a compensation for losing some of the "work force" of the family (Genesis 34:12; Exodus 22:16-17).

The wedding would generally take place after the groom had prepared a place for them to live, often in his father's house. After a place was prepared, he would go back to the bride's house and bring her back to the new dwelling, after which there would be a wedding ceremony. Following this ceremony would be a large wedding feast at the home of the bridegroom or his parents. The wedding feast could last up to a week (see Genesis 29:27).

2. Divorce. In ancient Jewish marriages, the wife did not have the legal option of divorcing her husband. Divorce was a privilege granted to the husband alone. According to the popular Rabbi Hillel (who lived in New Testament times), the husband could be granted a "bill of divorcement" for just about any infraction on the part of the wife. Even burning a meal was considered grounds for divorce. Rabbi Shammai, another influential rabbi, was more strict. He said a man could divorce his wife only if she was guilty of marital unfaithfulness. The wife had none of these rights. Only if the husband died was the wife relieved of her legal marriage commitment to her husband.

Contrary to such "easy" divorces, Scripture is clear that God Himself created the institution of marriage, and He intended it to be permanent (Genesis 2:18-25; Matthew 19:4-6). Divorce was never a part of God's original plan, and Scripture

219

says God hates divorce (Malachi 2:16). The marriage relationship was intended to be dissolved only when one of the marriage partners died (Romans 7:1-4; 1 Corinthians 7:8-9; 1 Timothy 5:14).

When sin entered the world, this affected God's ideal in marriage and many other things. Scripture tells us that even though divorce was not God's ideal, He nevertheless allowed it because of man's sinfulness (Deuteronomy 24:1-4; Matthew 19:7-8).

From a biblical perspective, divorce is allowed only under two circumstances: 1) One of the marriage partners is unfaithful (Matthew 19:9); 2) The unbelieving partner deserts the believing partner (1 Corinthians 7:15-16). Divorce for any other reason is a violation of God's ideal.

Even in cases in which a person clearly has biblical permission to divorce, God's desire is that the person, if at all possible, forgive the offending spouse and be reconciled to him or her. This follows from God's command to forgive others of their wrongs toward us (Ephesians 4:32; Colossians 3:13).

Of course, God forgives us of all our sins, including the sin of divorce (Colossians 2:13). However, simply because God forgives us does not remove the painful consequences of our actions on ourselves or on others. There is a heavy price to pay for violating God's ideal.

Mary

Mary was the mother of Jesus as well as His follower. She was a "bondslave of the Lord" (Luke 1:38 NASB), a humble servant of God. The Greek word for bondslave *(doulos)* speaks of one who serves another to the disregard of her own interests. Mary was truly a godly woman.

Scripture indicates that Mary was well versed in the Old Testament Scriptures. Her scriptural literacy is more than evident in the Magnificat (Luke 1:46-55). She was also "blessed" among women (Luke 1:48). This blessedness was due not to something intrinsically within her, but rather was related entirely on what God Himself chose to do by allowing her to give birth to the Messiah.

After the angel Gabriel informed Mary that the Holy Spirit would overshadow her so she would become pregnant with the divine child, she responded in humble obedience, "May it be to me as you have said" (Luke 1:38). Following Jesus' birth, she raised the divine child, though we are told very few details in Scripture. After a description of His infancy (see 2:1-39), Mary and Joseph do not appear again with Jesus until Jesus is 12 years old, having been left behind in the temple speaking with the rabbis (2:41-52). Mary was also with Jesus when he performed His first miracle, turning water into wine in Cana (John 2:1-12). Much later, we find Mary at the foot of the cross, witnessing her son's death (John 19:25-27). And still later, after Christ's resurrection and ascension into heaven, we find Mary in Jerusalem praying in the Upper Room, awaiting the coming of the promised Holy Spirit (Acts 1:14). Details of her death are unknown.

M

Matthew, Gospel of

The Gospel of Matthew was written by Matthew, son of Alphaeus, between A.D. 50 and 60, prior to the destruction of the Jewish temple by the Romans. By trade, Matthew had the unpopular job of being a tax collector. When Jesus called Matthew to follow Him, he left everything in obedience to the call (Mark 2:14; Luke 5:27-28). Perhaps his immediate decision to follow Jesus was motivated by previously hearing Jesus speak on several occasions. Matthew's name means "gift of the Lord." He was selected by Jesus to be one of the 12 disciples.

Matthew, himself a Jew, wrote this Gospel to convince Jewish readers that Jesus is the promised Messiah. It contains about 130 Old Testament citations and allusions, more than any other Gospel (for example, 2:17-18; 4:13-15; 13:35; 21:4-5; 27:9-10). Matthew's genealogy of Jesus is particularly relevant in this regard. Since Matthew's Gospel was written to Jews, he needed to prove to Jews that Jesus was the fulfillment of the Abrahamic Covenant (Genesis 12:1-3) and the Davidic Covenant (2 Samuel 7:12-16). By tracing Jesus' lineage to Abraham and David in the opening genealogy, Matthew accomplished this end.

Though Matthew was writing to convince the Jews that Jesus was the divine Messiah, he does not confine the good news to his own people, the Jews. Indeed, he emphasizes that the Gospel is for *all* people. Any who respond to Jesus by faith can become a part of the family of God (Matthew 28:19).

Two of Jesus' primary discourses are found in Matthew's Gospel—the Sermon on the Mount (Matthew 5–7) and the Olivet Discourse, in which Jesus speaks about the end times (24–25). Jesus also gave specific instruction to His disciples (10; 18) and taught through parables (for example, 13:3-52). This Gospel is rich in the teachings of Jesus.

M Medicine—See *Health and Healing.*

Merchants and Merchandise—See *Commerce and Trade.*

Messiah

The word "Messiah" comes from the Hebrew term *masiah,* which means "the anointed one." The Greek parallel to this term is "Christ" *(christos).* That the terms are equated is clear from John 1:41, where Andrew is portrayed as saying to Peter, " 'We have found the Messiah' (that is, the Christ)."

The New Testament is clear that Jesus is the promised divine Messiah. Recall that when the angel announced the birth of Jesus to the shepherds in the field, he identified Jesus this way: "Today in the town of David a Savior has been born to you; he is Christ the Lord" (Luke 2:11). Later, Simeon, who was filled with the Holy Spirit, recognized the babe Jesus as Christ, in fulfillment of God's promise to him that "he would not die before he had seen the Lord's Christ" (Luke 2:26).

Hundreds of messianic prophecies in the Old Testament point to a single Messiah or Christ—Jesus Christ. For example, Isaiah predicted the Messiah's virgin birth (Isaiah 7:14), His deity and kingdom (9:1-7), His reign of righteousness (11:2-5), His vicarious suffering and death on the cross (52:13–53:12), and much more. The evidence is conclusive:

- These hundreds of Old Testament messianic prophecies were written hundreds of years before they occurred.

- They could never have been foreseen.

- They depended upon factors outside human control for their fulfillment.

- They all perfectly fit the person and life of Jesus Christ.

Jesus had to be the Messiah.

Certainly others recognized that Jesus was the Christ or the prophesied Messiah. Peter recognized Jesus as being the Christ (Matthew 16:16), as did Martha (John 11:25-27). Further, on these two occasions, Jesus made His identity as the Christ the primary issue of faith. Jesus often warned that others would come falsely claiming to be the Christ (Matthew 24:4-5,23-24).

It is significant that after Jesus was arrested, He stood before Caiaphas the high priest, who demanded: "Tell us if you are the Christ, the Son of God." Jesus answered forthrightly, "Yes, it is as you say" (Matthew 26:63-64). For giving that answer, He paid with His life. But as promised, the divine Messiah resurrected from the dead (John 2:19-22).

Metallurgy

When the Israelites were delivered from Egypt by the hand of Moses, they took with them a tremendous amount of gold and silver—as well as skills in metallurgy. That they had the skill to mold these metals into particular objects seems obvious since Aaron himself participated in molding a golden calf using metallurgy skills (Exodus 32:1-5). This was clearly a *misuse* of metallurgy.

Once Israel settled in the Promised Land, the most common use of metallurgy related to producing tools (like sickles), utensils, and even weapons, all made of copper and bronze. There was certainly plenty of copper in early Israel, and metallurgists found that by mixing some tin (Numbers 31:22) with the copper (Deuteronomy 8:9; Job 28:2), the result—*bronze* (Genesis 4:22; Exodus 25:3)—ended up being a stronger metal and had a lower melting point. This proved useful, for the melted metal could easily be poured into molds to make the tools and utensils (see Exodus 38:3; Numbers 16:39; Jeremiah 52:18).

Micah, Book of

M

The book of Micah was written by a prophet of the same name in about 700 B.C. The name Micah means "who is like the Lord?" He was a contemporary of fellow prophets Amos, Hosea, and Isaiah in the eighth century B.C., and he carried on his ministry during the reigns of kings Jotham, Ahaz, and Hezekiah. He preached to Samaria and Jerusalem.

Micah was a simple farmer whose prophetic message was rooted in the injustices and exploitation he had witnessed. His primary message was that those who were rightly related to God should be interested in social justice and reach out to help the poor and disenchanted. But instead of this, those who claimed to be right with God in his day continued to ignore social injustices and, indeed, exploited the poor. Micah indicted Samaria and Jerusalem, as well as the leaders and people of Israel and Judah. He communicated that God hates injustice. God's desire for people is this: "To act justly and to love mercy and to walk humbly with your God" (Micah 6:8).

Micah thundered a stern message that things would not be allowed to continue the way they were going. Judgment would fall—a judgment so severe, Micah said, that even

Jerusalem's temple would be destroyed. Bad times were coming! Following this judgment, however, Micah said God would restore His people and bring about a kingdom of peace (see Micah 5:2).

Millennial Kingdom—See *End Times.*

Miracles

1. Mighty Works ◆ 2. Signs ◆ 3. Wonders ◆ 4. Works ◆ 5. Defining Miracles ◆ 6. The Purpose of Miracles

1. *Mighty Works.* There are four primary Greek words the New Testament uses for "miracle." The first of these is *dunamis,* which literally means "strength," "inherent power," or "power for performing miracles." Whoever the human instrument is (such as an apostle), the mighty power itself is of God alone. In the New Testament the word can be translated "miracles" or "mighty works." In Acts 19:11, for example, we read that "God did extraordinary miracles through Paul."

2. *Signs.* The Greek word *semeion* literally means "sign," "mark," "token," "that by which a person or a thing is distinguished from others and is known." A "sign" is a miracle with a meaning in the sense that it always points beyond itself to attest God and His messengers. For example, Jesus' miracle of turning water into wine was a "sign" that revealed His glory (John 2:11). In contexts dealing with the apostles, the signs attested that these individuals were genuine messengers of God (Hebrews 2:3-4).

3. *Wonders.* The Greek word *terata* literally means "wonder." It refers to something that evokes astonishment or amazement in the beholder. In its 16 New Testament usages, the word "wonder" is used side by side with the word "sign" (see,

M

225

for example, Acts 2:22). It makes sense that these words are often found side by side in Scripture. After all, the miracles are often so incredible that they 1) cause astonishment *(wonder)*, and 2) cause one to recognize that the person performing the miracle must be a spokesman for God *(sign)*.

4. Works. The Greek word *erga* literally means "works." The word is used by Jesus to describe His distinctive works that no one else has done. For example, we read that "when John had heard in the prison the works of Christ, he sent two of his disciples, and said unto him, Art thou he that should come, or do we look for another?" (Matthew 11:2-3 KJV). These are works that no mere human can do.

5. Defining Miracles. On the basis of the four Greek words above, we might concisely define a miracle as a unique and extraordinary event awakening wonder *(terata)*, wrought by divine power *(dunamis)*, accomplishing some practical and benevolent work *(erga)*, and authenticating or signifying a messenger and his message as from God *(semeion)*.

6. The Purpose of Miracles. Scripture indicates there are a number of purposes for miracles. For example, miracles accredit God's messengers (Hebrews 2:3-4), bring glory to God and Jesus (John 2:11), demonstrate the presence of God's kingdom (Matthew 12:28), promote faith among God's people (Exodus 14:31; John 20:30-31), demonstrate God's sovereignty (Exodus 7:5; Deuteronomy 29:5-6), and help people in need (for example, Matthew 14:14; 20:30-34).

Money

1. The Emergence of Coinage ◆ 2. Money Changers ◆ 3. A Typical Jewish Budget ◆ 4. Biblical View of Money.

1. The Emergence of Coinage. In Old Testament times, merchandise in many cases was bought and sold without the use of money. The bartering system was often used, and people exchanged food, clothing items, livestock, grain, oil, wine, and various kinds of building materials.

The use of metal (in raw form) came into prominence for bartering purposes before the time of Abraham (Genesis 17:12-13; 20:16; 25:15-16). Both silver and gold were used in major transactions (see, for example, 2 Samuel 24:24; 1 Kings 9:13-14). Copper, too, was used for bartering for less expensive items. The term "shekel" was used to describe pieces of silver and gold of varying sizes. For example, there were both heavy and light silver shekels, and heavy and light gold shekels.

It was not long before standardized coinage became increasingly popular. In about the seventh century B.C., Israel started to use coins. Late in Old Testament history, silver shekel coins came into wide use. By New Testament times, coins from other nations were also in use. Each of the large cities in biblical times produced their own coins, and these coins were worth varying amounts. Common coins used in New Testament times include the Roman *denarius* (a silver coin worth a day's wage) and the Greek *drachma* (a day's wage, and probably the "lost coin" of Jesus' parable in Luke 15:8-10). Other coins include the *tetradrachma* (about the size of an American half-dollar), which was a four-drachma piece, and the *didrachma*, which was a two-drachma piece. These latter coins were often used to pay temple taxes.

2. Money Changers. In view of the fact that there was no single currency in biblical times, the services of money changers became necessary. The currency of Palestine used the silver coins of Tyre. Consequently, a Jew in Jerusalem that came from another location would have to go to a money changer and, for a (sometimes exorbitant) fee, have his own coins exchanged into the silver coins of Tyre because the temple in Palestine accepted only such coins (see Matthew 21:12).

M

3. A Typical Jewish Budget. In biblical times, a significant part of one's income went to paying taxes. There were imperial Roman taxes, local administration taxes, and temple taxes. In some cases up to 20 percent of one's income went toward paying various taxes. Typically, aside from taxes, people living in New Testament times would spend about 30 percent of their income on clothing, 20 percent on food, 10 percent on charity, 10 percent on religious festivals, and perhaps 10 percent on other miscellaneous items.

4. Biblical View of Money. It is not a sin to be wealthy! (Some very godly people in the Bible—Abraham and Job, for example—were quite wealthy.) But God does condemn a *love* of possessions or riches (Luke 16:13; 1 Timothy 6:10; Hebrews 13:5). A love of material things is a sure sign that a person is living according to a temporal perspective, not an eternal perspective.

M

Scripture tells us that a love of money and riches can lead to sure destruction. The apostle Paul flatly stated that "people who want to get rich fall into temptation and a trap and into many foolish and harmful desires that plunge men into ruin and destruction" (1 Timothy 6:9). Jesus understandably warned His followers: "Watch out! Be on your guard against all kinds of greed; a man's life does not consist in the abundance of his possessions" (Luke 12:15). He then urged His followers to have an eternal perspective, exhorting: "Do not store up for yourselves treasures on earth, where moth and rust destroy, and where thieves break in and steal. But store up for yourselves treasures in heaven" (Matthew 6:19-20).

Our present attitude should be that whether we are rich or poor (or somewhere in between), we are simply stewards of what God has provided us. Our attitude should mirror that of the apostle Paul, who said: "I know what it is to be in need, and I know what it is to have plenty. I have learned the secret of being content in any and every situation, whether well fed or hungry, whether living in plenty or in want. I can do everything through him who gives me strength" (Philippians 4:12-13).

Moses

1. Rescued from the Nile ♦ 2. Sympathy for
Fellow Hebrews ♦ 3. Shepherd ♦ 4. Deliverer ♦
5. Prefigures Christ

1. *Rescued from the Nile.* Moses was a Hebrew, the son of
Amram and Jochebed, and brother of Aaron and Miriam
(Exodus 6:20; Numbers 26:59). Soon after his birth he was
hidden in a basket and put in the Nile River to prevent his pre-
mature death. (The Hebrews were reproducing so rapidly that
the pharaoh felt threatened by them and ordered the death of
Hebrew infant boys.) Moses received his name when Pharaoh's
daughter, by God's providence, drew him out of the Nile River;
"Moses" comes from a Hebrew word meaning "to draw out"
(Exodus 2:10). He was literally adopted into royalty in Egypt.
He was "educated in all the wisdom of the Egyptians and was
powerful in speech and action" (Acts 7:22).

M

2. *Sympathy for Fellow Hebrews.* Though Moses grew up
in Egypt and was trained and cultured as an Egyptian, he
witnessed the unfair treatment of his own Hebrew people and
did not like it. After killing an Egyptian taskmaster for treating
a Hebrew harshly, he fled into the wilderness where he
became a shepherd (see Exodus 2:11-15). How quickly circumstances changed! This happened when Moses was 40
years old (Acts 7:23-29).

3. *Shepherd.* Moses spent the next 40 years as a shepherd
in the land of Midian. This served to be a time of education
for him. Previously, he had studied under the Egyptians.
Now God taught him about how to survive in the desert and
how to be a good shepherd. These are skills he would need
in shepherding the Israelites out of Egypt toward the
Promised Land. Eventually, God appeared to Moses in a
burning bush and commanded him to go to Egypt to deliver
His people (Exodus 3). Moses was hesitant at first, but God

assured him that He would be with him and that he would succeed in his task.

4. *Deliverer.* Moses, a humble man (Numbers 12:3), subsequently returned to Egypt. God, through the hand of Moses, worked ten mighty miraculous judgments against prideful Pharaoh and the Egyptians, and the people were eventually released (see Exodus 5–12). After sojourning through the wilderness for three months, the people finally arrived at Mount Sinai, where God delivered to Moses the Ten Commandments to govern the lives of the people. God also provided instructions for the building of the tabernacle. It was at Mount Sinai that the Israelites finally became a nation, and the laws delivered to them through Moses constituted God's covenant stipulations, which He expected them to obey (Exodus 19–20). (See *Covenants.*)

M

5. *Prefigures Christ.* Moses prefigures Christ in many ways. For example, Moses as a child was in danger of death, just as the child Jesus was in danger of death (Exodus 1:15-16; Matthew 2:13). By God's sovereign choice, both were chosen to be deliverers of the people of God (Exodus 3:7-10; Acts 7:25). Both were rejected by many of their brethren (Exodus 2:11-15; John 1:11; Acts 7:23-28). Moreover, both were prophets (Deuteronomy 18:15; Matthew 13:57; John 12:29; 21:11; Acts 3:22-23), intercessors (Exodus 17:1-6; Hebrews 7:25), and rulers (Deuteronomy 33:4-5; John 1:49).

Music, Musicians, Musical Instruments

1. Purposes of Music ◆ 2. Wind Instruments ◆
3. Stringed Instruments ◆ 4. Percussion
Instruments ◆ 5. Temple Worship

1. *Purposes of Music.* People in Old Testament times played music and sang songs for a variety of purposes, including the celebration of military victories. For example, God's victory over Egypt was viewed by Moses as a military victory, so he and the rest of the Israelites sang a song of victory (Exodus 15). The men of Judah and Jerusalem celebrated their victory over Ammon and Moab by going into the temple of the Lord "with harps and lutes and trumpets" (2 Chronicles 20:27-28).

Music was played for the homecoming party of the prodigal son (Luke 15:25) and was also used at banquets and feasts (Isaiah 5:12; 24:8-9), as well as for laments (Matthew 9:23). Music was performed at the coronation of kings (2 Chronicles 23:11-13), as well as temple ceremonies (1 Chronicles 16:4-6; 2 Chronicles 29:25). Music was often performed during pilgrimages (2 Samuel 6:5). Sometimes music was used to enable a prophet to enter into a trance so he could receive divine oracles (see 2 Kings 3:15).

The singing of songs was a common form of worship (see Ephesians 5:19; Colossians 3:16). Songs were also sung at the construction of wells (Numbers 21:17-18) and to deflect evil powers (1 Samuel 16:16-23).

M

2. Wind Instruments. There were a variety of musical instruments used in ancient Israel, including wind instruments, stringed instruments, and percussion instruments. Examples of wind instruments include the *halil*, which was basically a hollow pipe made of cane or wood that utilized a reed to make a musical sound. The *geren* was a form of trumpet, made from the horn of an animal (see Leviticus 25:9; Joshua 6:4). A trumpet made from a ram's horn was called a *shofar* and was used for special occasions during the Jewish year, particularly on New Year's Day and on the Day of Atonement. Flutes were common as well (1 Samuel 10:5; Isaiah 5:12; Jeremiah 48:36).

3. Stringed Instruments. Stringed instruments included the *kinnor*, which is essentially a harp or lyre (see Genesis 4:21; 1 Kings 10:12; 2 Samuel 6:5). It was made from a wooden frame that had strings on it, and may have been plucked like modern harps are today. Another similar stringed instrument was the *nebel*. David, the shepherd king of Israel, was apparently able to play both of these instruments. In fact, David often used such instruments to soothe the nerves of King Saul (1 Samuel 16:16,23).

4. Percussion Instruments. Percussion instruments included the *meziltaim*, akin to modern cymbals (1 Chronicles 25:1; Nehemiah 12:27), and the *menaanim*, a wooden frame in which were suspended a series of disks that would rattle when shaken. *Castanets* were pieces of pottery containing pellets (2 Samuel 6:5 NASB). *Tambourines* were also quite common (2 Samuel 6:5; 1 Samuel 10:5). *Gongs* were sometimes used at weddings and other happy occasions (1 Corinthians 13:1). *Timbrels* were instruments beaten by the hand and were associated with processions and merrymaking (Genesis 31:27 NASB).

M

5. Temple Worship. These various instruments were often used in producing music as a part of worship in the temple. Along with the music, dancing was also a part of the people's worship. An example of this is when David and other Jews danced fervently in celebration of the Ark of the Covenant being brought to Jerusalem (2 Samuel 6:14-15).

N

Nahum, Book of

The book of Nahum was written by a prophet of the same name in about 650 B.C. Aside from the fact that he was a prophet of God and that he was a contemporary of Zephaniah, Jeremiah, and Habakkuk, we know little of his life. History is not even clear as to where he came from. But the important thing was the message he preached.

Nahum's ministry took place toward the end of Josiah's reign. His book describes the fall and destruction of Nineveh, the Assyrian capital, in graphic language. About a hundred years previously, the Ninevites had repented under the preaching of Jonah. But now Nineveh had returned in full force to idolatry, paganism, and brutality (Nahum 3:1-4). Nineveh pridefully believed in its own intrinsic power and failed to recognize that the only true ultimate power in the universe is that of the one true God.

Nahum thus prophesied that even though the Assyrians might seem invincible, their days were numbered, for judgment was rapidly approaching. Nineveh is pictured as a prostitute that had hurt others and must now be punished as a prostitute. Just as Nahum prophesied, Assyria was utterly destroyed in 612 B.C.

Names, Significance of

In the ancient world, a name was not a mere label as it is today. A name was considered as equivalent to whoever or whatever bore it. The sum total of a person's internal and external pattern of behavior was gathered up into his name. Indeed, knowing a person's name amounted to knowing his essence. This is illustrated in 1 Samuel 25:25: "Nabel...is just like his name—his name is Fool, and folly goes with him."

We also see this illustrated in the names of major Bible characters. The name "Abraham," for instance, means "father of a multitude" and was quite fitting since Abraham was the father of the Jewish nation. The name "David" means "beloved" and was fitting because David was a king specially loved by God. The name "Solomon" comes from a word meaning "peace" and is fitting because Solomon's reign was characterized by peace. In each case, we learn something about the individual from his name.

It is interesting to observe how Scripture often views the *name* and *being* of God as being inseparable. The Psalms in the Old Testament often use parallelism to emphasize this. (A parallelism is a literary form indicating a close parallel relationship.) For example: "Therefore I will praise you among the nations, O LORD; I will sing praises to your name" (Psalm 18:49); "Sing to God, sing praise to his name, extol him who rides on the clouds—his name is the LORD—and rejoice before him" (68:4); "Remember how the enemy has mocked you, O LORD, how foolish people have reviled your name" (74:18); "I will praise you, O Lord my God, with all my heart; I will glorify your name forever" (86:12). Clearly, Scripture portrays God and His name as inseparable. To know one is to know the other.

Nehemiah, Book of

Nehemiah wrote this book between 445 and 425 B.C. His name literally means "comfort of Yahweh." Under Nehemiah's leadership, the people would indeed be comforted and given a hope.

Like the book of Ezra, the book of Nehemiah focuses on the return of the exiles from Babylon. Nehemiah had been a cupbearer for the Persian king Artaxerxes but moved on to become the governor of Jerusalem in 445 B.C. Among his contributions were his leadership in repairing the shattered wall of Jerusalem. The task was completed in a mere 52 days. It would take much longer, however, to rebuild the spiritual lives of the people in Jerusalem. Nevertheless, Nehemiah's work served to raise the morale of the people, who had been utterly demoralized at seeing their beloved city in ruins. He laid the foundation for Josiah's religious reforms.

New Covenant—See *Covenants.*

New Testament

1. Significance ♦ 2. The New Covenant ♦ 3. Summary

1. Significance. The New Testament is a collection of 27 books and epistles composed over a 50-year period by a number of different authors. The primary personality of the New Testament is Jesus Christ. The primary theme is salvation in Jesus Christ, based on the new covenant.

2. The New Covenant. The word "testament" carries the idea of "covenant" or "agreement." The Old Testament focuses

N

The New Testament

Gospels	History	Paul's Epistles	General Epistles	Apocalyptic
Matthew	Acts	Romans	Hebrews	Revelation
Mark		1 and 2 Corinthians	James	
Luke		Galatians	1 and 2 Peter	
John		Ephesians	1, 2, and 3 John	
		Philippians	Jude	
		Colossians		
		1 and 2 Thessalonians		
		1 and 2 Timothy		
		Titus		
		Philemon		

on the old covenant between God and the Israelites. According to that covenant (the Sinai Covenant), the Jews were to be God's people and were to be obedient to Him, and in return God would bless them (Exodus 19:3-25). Israel failed over and over again and continually violated this covenant. So even in Old Testament times, the prophets began to speak of a new covenant that would focus not on keeping external laws but on an inner reality and change in the human heart (Jeremiah 31:31-34). Unlike the old covenant, the new covenant was to make full provision for the forgiveness of sins.

When Jesus ate the Passover meal with the disciples in the Upper Room, He spoke of the cup as "the new covenant in my blood" (Luke 22:20; see also 1 Corinthians 11:25). Hebrews 7 demonstrates that Christ's priesthood is superior to the old, and it logically follows that such a superior priesthood would have a superior ministry. Such a ministry is provided for in the new covenant. Jesus has done all that is necessary for the forgiveness of sins by His once-for-all sacrifice on the cross. This new covenant is the basis for our relationship with God in the New Testament.

N

3. Summary. The first four books of the New Testament are the Gospels: Matthew, Mark, Luke, and John. Each of these contains an account of the life of Christ. While none of these portrays all the details of His life, when they are taken together, we can reconstruct a fairly full account.

Each author included different details in his Gospel depending upon the purpose of that Gospel. For example, the Gospel of Matthew has more allusions and citations from the Old Testament than any other Gospel because Matthew sought to prove to the Jews that Jesus is the promised Messiah of the Old Testament. Mark's Gospel, by contrast, had no such Jewish motivation, but rather sought to portray Jesus in action rather than as a teacher. Luke's Gospel stresses the wonderful blessings of salvation for all people. John's Gospel focuses heavily on the identity of Jesus, and thoroughly demonstrates His divine origin and deity.

Following the Gospels is the book of Acts, which focuses on the spread of Christianity following the death and resurrection of Christ. Though the book is traditionally called The Acts of the Apostles, it is probably more appropriately called The Acts of the Holy Spirit, for truly it is the Holy Spirit who seems to be active in just about every chapter of the book.

Following the book of Acts are the Epistles or letters. The apostle Paul wrote 13 of these, and the rest were written by other followers of Jesus. Paul's epistles typically responded to particular issues that a specific church needed help on. Even so, these epistles are relevant to us today because many of the problems that existed in the early church are still issues that we struggle with today. The other (non-Pauline) epistles are more general in nature.

The final book of the New Testament is the book of Revelation, which is an apocalyptic book full of prophecy. This book was written to persecuted believers for the purpose of giving them hope, inspiration, and comfort, so that they would be able to patiently endure the persecution and struggle they were facing. The book clearly demonstrates that in the end God wins, and we will live face-to-face with Him forever in a new heaven and a new earth.

N

Noah's Ark

Noah's ark was a floating vessel constructed by Noah in which a remnant of the human race (Noah and his family), along with two each of the various animals, were preserved from the coming flood that engulfed the entire world (see Genesis 6:14–9:18). The vessel was constructed from either cypress or pine wood ("gopher wood" in some versions of the Bible) according to the specifications that God gave Noah (6:14-16).

The ark was a rather large vessel—about 450 feet long, 75 feet wide, and 45 feet high. There were three stories in the ark, which means that it had plenty of room to carry many animals (Genesis 6:16).

Noah was given a warning time of 120 years before the flood began, which means Noah had to build the ark by faith, since no catastrophe of this magnitude had every occurred in earth's history. This long time frame also demonstrated God's patience regarding the heinous sins of humankind.

The ark rested on the mountains of Ararat when the floodwaters receded (Genesis 8:4). To date, it has not been found.

Numbers, Book of

Moses wrote the book of Numbers between 1445 and 1405 B.C. (see Numbers 33:2; 36:13). The title of this book derives from the two censuses that are recorded in the book, one at Mount Sinai (the original Exodus generation) and one on the plains of Moab (the generation that grew up in the wilderness and conquered Canaan) (see Numbers 1 and 26). Obviously, censuses involve "numberings" or "countings" of people.

Aside from these censuses, the book also contains a listing of the tribes of Israel (Numbers 2), regulations for the priests and the Levites (3–8), information about the Passover (9), a chronicle of Israel moving from Mount Sinai to Moab on the border of Canaan (10–21), a record of Balaam and Balak (22–32), and the Israelites' journey coming to an end (33–36).

One thing that stands out in this book that has practical value for believers today is that God blesses obedience to His laws but brings discipline to those who are disobedient. Though the people of Israel initially had faith in God as they were delivered from Egyptian bondage, their faith soon gave way to perpetual grumbling and rebellion, which brought God's judgment. This judgment caused an 11-day journey (about 220 miles) to last a lifetime of travel—40 years' worth. Had they been obedient, the trip would have been much shorter, and the majority of the original Exodus generation would have entered the Promised Land instead of a mere handful. As it was, only the children of these grumblers would enter the land and enjoy the promises that had originally been made to them.

O

Oaths

An oath is a solemn promise. Oaths were taken quite seriously in biblical times (Exodus 20:7; Leviticus 19:12), and lying about an oath could end up in death (Ezekiel 17:16-18).

Oaths are sprinkled throughout both the Old Testament (Leviticus 5:1; Numbers 30:2-15; Deuteronomy 23:21-23) and the New Testament (Acts 2:30; 18:18; Hebrews 6:16-18; 7:20-22). The apostle Paul, for example, said, "I call God as my witness..." (2 Corinthians 1:23). Hence, there is biblical precedent for taking vows.

Some dispute this, citing Jesus' words in Matthew 5:33-37 ("...let your 'Yes' be 'Yes,' and your 'No,' 'No'..."). The problem Jesus was dealing with in these verses is rooted in Pharisaism. The Pharisees promoted the use of oaths to affirm that one was telling the truth, and the oath always involved some type of curse if one's word was not true or the promise was not fulfilled. It got to the point that one assumed someone was not telling the truth if an oath was not attached to the statement.

Jesus was against *this* use of oaths. In Matthew 5:34-37 He was telling His followers that their character, their reputation for honesty, and the words they speak should be so consistently true, undefiled, and without duplicity that no one would ever think it necessary to make them swear an oath, for no one would suspect them of deception. By constantly adding oaths to our verbal statements, we are implying to others that our usual speech is untrustworthy. It should not be that way.

Christ thus told His followers that when they were communicating with others they should let their *yes* be *yes* and their *no* be *no*. Yes cannot mean no, and no cannot mean yes. We should be as good as our word and have no duplicity!

Obadiah, Book of

The book of Obadiah was written by a prophet of the same name between 848 and 841 B.C. Obadiah ministered during King Jororam's reign in Judah. His name means "servant of the Lord." Aside from these brief facts, we know little of this obscure prophet. He may have been a contemporary of Elijah and Elisha.

In his prophecies, Obadiah spoke of the coming downfall of Edom, a mountainous area directly southeast of the Dead Sea. The Edomites had invaded Judah when Jerusalem was being overrun and destroyed by the Babylonians in 587 B.C. Obadiah indicated that the Edomites would thus be destroyed. While Edom was to be destroyed, the Israelites would one day be restored to their land.

It is interesting to observe that the Edomites were descendants of Esau. As the biblical record indicates, Esau struggled with his brother Jacob even within their mother's womb (Genesis 25:22-23). As the book of Obadiah clearly demonstrates, the descendants of these brothers continued to struggle.

O

Offerings, Sacrificial

1. Types of Offerings ◆ 2. Propitiatory Offerings ◆ 3. Dedicatory Offerings ◆ 4. Communal Offerings

1. *Types of Offerings.* Sacrificial offerings were offerings brought to God daily or periodically to atone for sins, bring ritual purity, show dedication to God, or render thanks to God. Offerings in the Old Testament include *propitiatory offerings* (sin offering, guilt offering), *dedicatory offerings* (burnt offering, cereal offering, drink offering), and *communal offerings* (peace offering, voluntary offering).

2. Propitiatory Offerings. These offerings were required when an Israelite had become ceremonially unclean or had knowingly or unknowingly sinned against God or his neighbor. There are two types:

A. *Sin Offering.* This offering was presented under three circumstances: 1) for ritual cleansing, 2) for unintentional sins against God, and 3) for the Hebrew festivals (including the Day of Atonement). In making this offering, a sacrifice was given (see Leviticus 4:5-12). The defilement caused by sin had to be cleansed, and the sacrifice accomplished this end. The blood was sprinkled upon the altar as a sign that the stain of sin had been removed through the death of the sacrificial animal. A portion of the meat of the sacrifice was then eaten as food by the priest, and when the worshiper witnessed this, it was regarded as a confirmation that God accepted the sacrifice. This offering presumes a repentant heart on the part of the offerer (Numbers 15:30).

B. *Guilt Offering.* This offering was a means of making restitution when social, religious, or ritual expectations had not been observed. In this offering, one's guilt is vicariously transferred to the animal through the symbolism of laying hands on the animal.

3. Dedicatory Offerings. Dedicatory offerings were a means of expressing homage to God. God did not accept them unless those offering them had first presented the required propitiatory offerings. There are three types:

A. *Burnt Offering.* This offering symbolized the worshiper's homage and total dedication to God. An animal (in perfect condition) would be sacrificed whole (Leviticus 8:21). The worshiper would have first placed his hands on the sacrificial animal as an indication that the animal was being sacrificed for the worshiper's own failings.

B. *Cereal Offering.* Also called the "meal offering" since the offering was presented to God as a meal, this offering expressed homage and thankfulness to God. It was a good-will offering to God.

C. *Drink Offering.* This offering of a liquid, such as wine (Exodus 29:40), was intended to bring pleasure to God and was expected as a daily offering, as well as on the Sabbath, new moon, and annual festivals.

4. Communal Offerings. These offerings did not atone for sins but were considered complementary to the propitiatory offerings and the dedicatory offerings. There are two types:

A. *Peace Offering.* The Hebrew name indicates "peace" or "well-being," and these sacrifices are sometimes seen as communion or fellowship rites. They were intended to express the desire to maintain right relations between God, man, and neighbor. For this offering, the fat of the animal (considered by Jews to be the best portion of the animal) was burnt on the altar. The meat would be eaten by the worshipers and their families (see Deuteronomy 12:18; 16:11; Judges 20:26; 21:4).

B. *Voluntary Offering.* Voluntary offerings were considered appropriate responses to the goodness of God. Since it was voluntary, an imperfectly developed ox or sheep was acceptable.

O

Old Testament

The word "testament" carries the idea of "covenant" or "agreement." The Old Testament focuses on the old covenant between God and the Israelites. According to that covenant (the Sinai Covenant), the Jews were to be God's people and were to be obedient to Him, and in return God would bless them (Exodus 19:3-25). The various books of the Old Testament provide information related to this old covenant and its outworking in history. Of course, Old Testament history reveals that Israel failed over and over again, continually violating the covenant.

The Old Testament as a body of literature is the "entire Bible" of the Jews but only "Part One" of the Christian Bible. It is interesting to note that Jews do not like the designation

The Old Testament

Law	History	Poetry	Major Prophets	Minor Prophets
Genesis	Joshua	Job	Isaiah	Hosea
Exodus	Judges	Psalms	Jeremiah	Joel
Leviticus	Ruth	Proverbs	Lamentations	Amos
Numbers	1 and 2 Samuel	Ecclesiastes	Ezekiel	Obadiah
Deuteronomy	1 and 2 Kings	Song of Solomon	Daniel	Jonah
	1 and 2 Chronicles			Micah
	Ezra			Nahum
	Nehemiah			Habakkuk
	Esther			Zephaniah
				Haggai
				Zechariah
				Malachi

"Old Testament" because of the implication that there must be a New Testament (which they reject). To them, the books that constitute the Old Testament comprise the entire Word of God. Christians, however, note that even in Old Testament times, the prophets began to speak of a new covenant that would focus not on keeping external laws but on an inner reality and change in the human heart (Jeremiah 31:31-33). Unlike the old covenant, the new covenant was to make full provision for the forgiveness of sins. This new covenant is the focus of the New Testament (see 1 Corinthians 11:25; 2 Corinthians 3:6; Hebrews 8:13).

Interestingly, in Luke 24:44, Jesus said the entire Old Testament referred to Him.

Original Sin—See *Sin and Guilt.*

Parables

1. *Definition.* Though Jesus' teachings take a variety of forms, a full third of His recorded teachings involved the use of parables. The word "parable" literally means "a placing alongside of" for the purpose of comparison. A parable is a teaching tool. Jesus would often tell a story from real life—involving, for example, a woman who lost a coin, a shepherd watching over sheep, or a worker in a vineyard—and use that story to illustrate a spiritual truth.

By taking such a story and "placing it alongside" a spiritual truth, the process of comparison helps us to understand Jesus' spiritual teaching more clearly. For example, Jesus' story of the good shepherd helps us to understand that Jesus watches over us and guides us, just as a shepherd watches over and guides sheep.

P

2. *Kinds of Parables.* There are several kinds of parables in the New Testament. Understanding a little about these different forms helps us to interpret Jesus' intended meaning more accurately.

A. *Some parables are similes.* These involve a likeness that employs the words "like" or "as." An example is Matthew 10:16, where Jesus said, "I am sending you out like sheep among wolves. Therefore be as shrewd as snakes and as innocent as doves."

B. *Some parables are metaphors.* In this type of parable, there is an implied likeness of some sort. An example is John 10:7, where Jesus said, "I am the gate for the sheep." This metaphor teaches that Jesus is the way of salvation.

C. *Some parables are similitudes.* In this type of parable, Jesus takes what we already know in the natural world and uses it as a word picture to teach us some new spiritual truth. We see this in Matthew 13:33, where Jesus said, "The kingdom of heaven is like yeast that a woman took and mixed into a large amount of flour until it worked all through the dough." Here Jesus refers to yeast to illustrate the growth of the kingdom of heaven and the penetrating power of the Gospel.

D. *Some parables are stories.* This was Jesus' most common type of parable in teaching His followers. In such a parable, Jesus would tell a story about a person in order to teach an important spiritual concept. For example, in Luke 15:11-32 Jesus told a story of a man who had two sons, one of which was the "prodigal son." Through this story Jesus taught that God always has His arms wide open to receive into fellowship those who repent and come to Him in contriteness.

Passover—See *Festivals, Annual.*

Patriarchs

---

1. Abraham ◆ 2. Isaac ◆ 3. Jacob ◆ 4. Joseph

P

1. *Abraham.* The word "patriarchs" is a term that refers to the leaders of Israel preceding the time of Moses, including Abraham, Isaac, Jacob, and the sons of Jacob. Abraham was the most important patriarch. His name means "father of a multitude," and he lived around 2000 B.C., originating from the city of Ur, in Mesopotamia, on the Euphrates River. He was apparently a very wealthy and powerful man.

God called Abraham to leave Ur and go to a new land—the land of Canaan, which God was giving Abraham and his descendants (Genesis 11:31). Abraham left with his wife, Sarah, and his nephew Lot. Upon arriving in Canaan, his first act was to construct an altar and worship God. This was typical of Abraham; God was of first importance.

God made a pivotal covenant with Abraham in which He promised that he would have a son and that his descendants would be as numerous as the stars in the sky (Genesis 12:1-3; 13:14-17). Abraham was also promised that he would be personally blessed, that his name would become great, that those who bless him would be blessed and those who curse him would be cursed, and that all the families of the earth would be blessed through his posterity.

Abraham lived 175 years, and then "breathed his last and died at a good old age" (Genesis 25:7-8).

2. *Isaac.* God fulfilled His promise to give Abraham and Sarah a son when they were very old (Abraham was 100 years old, Sarah was 90), far beyond normal childbearing age (Genesis 17:17; 21:5). Their son was named Isaac. As promised, an entire nation eventually developed from his line. "Isaac" means "laughter," and the name is fitting because it points to the joy derived from this child of promise. Recall that when Abraham and Sarah heard they would have a son in their old age, they laughed (see Genesis 17:17-19; 18:9-15).

Isaac carried on the covenant first given to his father, Abraham. The New Testament calls him a child of promise (Galatians 4:22-23), and he was a man of good character. He was a man who trusted in God (Genesis 22:6-9), practiced regular prayer (Genesis 24:63; 26:25), and sought peace (Genesis 26:20-22).

In a famous episode in the Bible, Abraham's faith was stretched when he was commanded by God to sacrifice his beloved son of promise, Isaac, which command he obeyed without hesitation. In his heart, Abraham believed God would provide a substitute lamb for the burnt offering (Genesis 22:8). God, of course, intervened before his son was actually sacrificed, but the episode served to demonstrate the tremendous faith Abraham had in God.

Isaac grew up, and at age 40 married Rebekah, who gave birth to twin sons: Esau and Jacob.

3. Jacob. Jacob, a son of Isaac, was appropriately named. His name means "he supplants," and indeed, Jacob was a supplanter, for he took hold of his brother Esau's birthright (Genesis 25:29-34), his father's blessing and inheritance (27:1-29), and his father-in-law's flocks (30:25-43). More specifically, Jacob talked a hungry and exhausted brother—Esau, Isaac's firstborn son—into giving him his birthright, along with the greater inheritance that accompanies the birthright, in exchange for a mere bowl of food. Jacob then tricked Isaac into giving him Esau's inheritance when Isaac was a very old man and could not see well. Once a blessing is given, it cannot be taken back, so Isaac's blessing of Jacob was a final transaction. In this way, then, Jacob became part of the hereditary line through which God would establish a great nation. Jacob had many sons.

4. Joseph. A famous (eleventh) son of Jacob was Joseph, whose name means "May God give increase." Joseph, Jacob's favorite son (Genesis 37:3), was well known as a dreamer whose dreams often focused on his own future elevation to power (37:5-11). Understandably, this did not go over well with his brothers, who eventually sold him into slavery to get rid of him. Jacob became convinced by his other sons that Joseph had been killed and eaten by a wild animal, and he grieved deeply for his loss (37:34-35).

P

Meanwhile, Joseph came into the service of Potiphar, an Egyptian official who had a large house (Genesis 39:1-6). Joseph rose to a position of prominence in running the entire household for Potiphar until Potiphar's wife falsely accused him of seduction. Joseph was subsequently imprisoned. Even in prison, however, "God was with Joseph" and gave him favor in the eyes of others (39:21). It seems that no matter where Joseph found himself, God was with him, and he succeeded in whatever he did.

As a result of his dream-interpreting abilities, Joseph was eventually called out of prison by Pharaoh to interpret a disturbing dream he had, a dream which no one else under

Pharaoh's command could interpret. After providing the proper interpretation, which related to a famine that would one day come upon the land, Joseph was elevated to a position of power in Egypt, thus fulfilling the dreams Joseph earlier had regarding his rise to power (Genesis 41:37-57).

Joseph was eventually reconciled with his family when his brothers showed up in Egypt in hopes of getting much-needed food for the family of Jacob. At the time they did not recognize Joseph, but Joseph recognized them. Joseph finally revealed himself to them and brought the entire family to Egypt where he cared for them (Genesis 45).

Paul, Apostle

1. Hebrew of Hebrews ◆ 2. Well Educated ◆
3. Conversion ◆ 4. Missionary

1. *Hebrew of Hebrews.* Paul called himself a "Hebrew," an "Israelite," and one of "Abraham's descendants" (2 Corinthians 11:22). He was "circumcised on the eighth day, of the people of Israel, of the tribe of Benjamin, a Hebrew of Hebrews; in regard to the law, a Pharisee" (Philippians 3:5). Paul excelled at keeping the law.

2. *Well Educated.* Paul was well educated as a Jew. Though born and raised in Tarsus in Cilicia (a Gentile city, Acts 22:3), he had studied in Jerusalem at the feet of Gamaliel, one of the outstanding Jewish rabbis of the day (Acts 5:34). He was known as a brilliant student (Galatians 1:14) and a zealous Pharisee (Philippians 3:5-6). Following his conversion to Christianity, Paul's background as a Jew put him in a unique position to be able to explain how Jesus and Christianity fulfilled the Old Testament Scriptures.

3. *Conversion.* Paul is first introduced at Stephen's stoning (Acts 7:58). After becoming a Christian, he acknowledged to

P

God in prayer that "when the blood of your martyr Stephen was shed, I stood there giving my approval and guarding the clothes of those who were killing him" (Acts 22:20). In addition to Paul's involvement in Stephen's death, he appears to have been involved in others. He later acknowledged: "On the authority of the chief priests I put many of the saints in prison, and when they were put to death, I cast my vote against them" (26:10).

Paul had not been content to persecute Christians in the Jerusalem area alone. He went to the high priest for a letter authorizing him to arrest Christians in Damascus and bring them back to Jerusalem where they could be tried by the Sanhedrin for acquittal or death (Acts 9:2).

When Paul was on his way to Damascus, a "light from heaven flashed around him," and the risen Jesus confronted him: "Saul, Saul, why do you persecute me?" (Acts 9:3-4). ("Saul" was Paul's former name.) Paul later revealed that the light he saw was none other than Jesus Himself (Acts 9:27; 22:14-15; 26:16; 1 Corinthians 9:1; 15:7-8). This is important because to be an apostle, one must have seen the resurrected Lord (1 Corinthians 9:1).

Paul reverently responded to Jesus' question with another question: "Who are you, Lord?" (Acts 9:5). After finding out it was Jesus, a dumbfounded and blinded Paul was led by hand into Damascus.

Paul's discovery that he had been persecuting the risen Jesus all along must have been traumatic for him, for he could not eat or drink for three days after this. This is understandable since all that he previously believed as a zealous Pharisee came tumbling down into a pile of rubbish.

Meanwhile, God appeared in a vision to another man in Damascus named Ananias. God commissioned him to go to "Straight Street" and ask for Paul of Tarsus (Acts 9:11). This probably refers to the same Straight Street that runs east to west through Damascus today. God told Ananias that Paul, too, was having a vision regarding his coming. God instructed him that Paul's sight was to be restored through their meeting.

P

Ananias was understandably hesitant because Paul was well known for his persecution of the church. Ananias was also apparently aware of the letter from the high priest giving Paul authority to arrest Christians and haul them off to Jerusalem. The Lord Jesus responded to Ananias' hesitancy by informing him that Paul would be His chosen vessel for bringing the Gospel to the Gentiles and their kings, as well as the people of Israel. Paul was a chosen instrument in the Lord's hand (Acts 9:15-16).

Paul had formerly set out to do all he could to extinguish those who believed in Jesus Christ. Yet, following his encounter with the risen Jesus, he became a mighty instrument through whom God communicated His truth to both Gentiles and Jews.

4. Missionary. Paul went on three missionary tours, spreading God's Word in strategic cites like Antioch, Perga, Iconium, Lystra, Derbe, Troas, Philippi, Thessalonica, Berea, Athens, Corinth, Ephesus, Galatia, and Miletus. One of Paul's strategies was to visit major Roman capitals that were easily reached by existing trade routes, a strategy that resulted in the Gospel spreading out to other areas through these routes. By God's providence, Paul ended up being thrown into jail a lot, during which time he wrote many of his letters to different churches (Ephesians, Colossians, Philippians, and so forth). God accomplished great things through Paul!

Pentateuch

The first five books of the Bible—Genesis, Exodus, Leviticus, Numbers, and Deuteronomy—were written by Moses and are sometimes called "The Pentateuch." This word derives from two Greek words literally meaning "five scrolls" or "five volumes." The Jews refer to these five books as "Torah," a word meaning "instruction" or "guidance" (see *Torah*).

The Pentateuch is foundational to the rest of the Bible. It includes such important teachings as the creation account, human beings' creation in the image of God, the reality of the Fall and the sin problem, Noah and the Flood, God's calling of Abraham, the development of the nation of Israel, God's deliverance of the Jews from Egyptian bondage, the wilderness wanderings, the Ten Commandments, God's covenant with Israel, and the sacrificial system, which ultimately points forward to the work of Christ on the cross. Quite obviously, one cannot properly understand major portions of the rest of the Bible without a foundational understanding of the Pentateuch.

Though some liberal scholars have tried to challenge the Mosaic authorship of these books, conservative scholars believe there is very strong evidence for Mosaic authorship. For example, the writing of these books was attributed to Moses in postexilic writings (Nehemiah 8:1; 2 Chronicles 25:4; 35:12). Jesus Himself strongly affirmed that Moses authored these books (Mark 10:4-5; Luke 24:44; John 5:46-47). Since Jesus is God and is therefore all-knowing, Jesus cannot be wrong on this issue. Further, ancient Jewish tradition affirms that Moses was the author, and archaeological evidence is consistent with this. Moreover, many parts of the Pentateuch claim to have been written by Moses (for example, Exodus 17:14; 24:4; 34:27-28). In keeping with this, the apostle Paul affirmed that Moses was the author of Exodus (Romans 10:5). Finally, Moses was certainly qualified to write the Pentateuch in terms of educational training, for he was "educated in all the wisdom of the Egyptians" (Acts 7:22).

(See *Genesis, Exodus, Leviticus, Numbers, Deuteronomy.*)

Pentecost

One feast the Israelites celebrated annually was the Feast of Harvest (Exodus 23:16a), which was held in the spring at the beginning of the wheat harvest (see Exodus 34:22). In this feast, two loaves made of new grain were to be presented to the Lord (Leviticus 23:15-21). In this way, the people gave thanks to God for the grain He provided them. Elsewhere in

Scripture this feast is called the Feast of Weeks (Exodus 34:22) because it was held seven weeks (or 50 days) after the Feast of Unleavened Bread. In later Judaism, the Feast of Harvest came to commemorate the giving of the law at Mount Sinai (though no Old Testament passage substantiates this). In New Testament times, the feast was called "Pentecost" (Acts 2:1), which means "50."

In Acts 2, we read that on the day of Pentecost, 50 days after Passover, a group of about 120 people—including the 12 disciples, Mary (the mother of Jesus), and Jesus' brothers—were gathered in a house in Jerusalem. Suddenly, they heard something that sounded like a strong wind, and they saw tongues of fire resting upon each of them (Acts 2:2-3). The disciples then began to speak in other tongues (languages). The commotion quickly attracted the attention of Jews who had come into Jerusalem from various other nations, and each heard the disciples speaking in his own native language (verses 4-12). Some of the people were astonished, noting that these were Galileans who were speaking other languages. Others derided the disciples, saying they were drunk (verse 13).

Peter then took the opportunity to address the crowd before him and said that no one was drunk. Indeed, he said that what was being witnessed was related to the prophecy of Joel 2:28-32 (see Acts 2:16-21). What we see in Acts 2 is an example of what is called prophetic foreshadowing. Joel 2:28-32 will be ultimately and finally fulfilled in the end times, but in Acts 2 we witness a prophetic foreshadowing, which, scholars believe, is a common prophetic occurrence in Scripture. Just as the Holy Spirit will act in a big way in the end times, so the Holy Spirit acted in a big way on the day of Pentecost.

Peter's Pentecost sermon persuaded some 3000 people to be baptized that day, and on this day we witness the birth of the church (see Acts 2; see also 1:5; 11:15; 1 Corinthians 12:13). It is likely that some of the converts were those who heard the message of the disciples *in their own languages* when the disciples started to speak in other tongues.

Peter, 1 and 2

Peter was a fisherman who became one of the 12 men who were with Jesus right through to the end of His ministry. He was one of the "inner three" who saw some of Jesus' greatest miracles and who were allowed to see Him in His true glory (Mark 9:1-8; 2 Peter 1:16-18). Jesus appeared to Peter before any of the other apostles after the resurrection, most likely because He knew of Peter's great remorse in denying Him three times (Matthew 26:69-75). At the end of his life, Peter was crucified upside down in Rome during Emperor Nero's persecution, which began in A.D. 64.

First Peter, written in A.D. 63 or 64, was sent to scattered groups of Christians in the five Roman provinces that covered the greater part of modern Turkey. Peter probably wrote from Rome at the outbreak of Nero's persecution. Having already endured beating at Herod's hands, Peter wrote his brethren in Asia to encourage and strengthen them in facing the Neronian persecution. It may well be that Peter recalled his Lord's injunctions: "Strengthen your brothers" (Luke 22:32), and "Feed my sheep" (John 21:15-17).

Peter's letter was apparently intended for Gentile readers. He reminded them that although formerly "not a people," they were now the people of God (1 Peter 2:10). He described their past life as having been lived in the sinful lusts of the Gentiles (4:3-4). But now they were believers, and his letter would help them maintain patient endurance in the midst of their suffering. Peter reminded them that suffering can have the beneficial effect of purifying their faith (1:7).

In 2 Peter, written in A.D. 66 to the same group as his first letter, the apostle addressed some errors that had penetrated certain churches. These errors involved the ideas that morality is unimportant and that Jesus Christ would not return. Apparently there were some mystics who were placing more weight on their own spiritual experiences than on revelations received from prophets and apostles that Jesus would one day return. Peter rebuked these ideas and emphasized that since

P

Jesus *will* in fact return one day, we should live "holy and godly lives" (2 Peter 3:11).

Pharisees—See *Jewish Sects.*

Philemon, Book of

Paul addressed this letter, written about A.D. 63, to a friend and leader of the church at Colossae named Philemon, a prominent man who had owned a slave named Onesimus. Apparently, Onesimus had stolen some money (verse 18) and escaped, probably to Rome. Perhaps Onesimus reasoned that in the booming population of Rome, no one would notice him. Onesimus ended up meeting the apostle Paul in prison (we are not told how this meeting actually came about). Under Paul's leading, Onesimus became a Christian.

Paul ended up developing a sincere love for young Onesimus (verses 12,16). Paul was fully aware that, under Roman law, Onesimus could be executed as a runaway slave. But amends had to be made. Paul sent Onesimus back to Philemon with a letter urging him to set Onesimus free as a brother in Christ so that he could return to help Paul in his work of ministry.

P

Philippians

The apostle Paul wrote the epistle to the Philippians in A.D. 63. Philippi, in northern Greece, was named after Philip II of Macedon, the father of Alexander the Great. The city, which lay about ten miles inland from the Gangites River, was originally established by Philip as a center of operations for the nearby mining of gold and silver. Because of its strategic location, Philippi experienced tremendous growth—so much so that it was later described as "the leading city of that district of Macedonia" (Acts 16:12).

Many of the inhabitants of Philippi were retired Roman soldiers who were given free land in return for the Roman "military presence" they represented. And because of Philippi's close ties to Rome, the citizens enjoyed special privileges such as self-government, freedom from imperial taxation, and the same rights as citizens of Rome. It is interesting to note that Philippi was respected for its medical advances, and this may have been the hometown of Dr. Luke.

Because Philippi was a Roman colony, there were apparently too few Jews to warrant the establishment of a synagogue, which required a minimum of ten adult Jewish men (women were not allowed to act as substitutes). The Jews therefore met for prayer by the river Gangites on the Sabbath (at "the place of prayer," Acts 16:13,16), and it was at this location that Paul addressed the first converts of the city during his second missionary tour.

After a time, the Philippian church developed some problems. It came to suffer under intense rivalries (Philippians 2:3-4), disturbances caused by Judaizers (3:1-3), and libertinism (3:18-19). These internal problems severely hindered spiritual growth, and the Philippian church as a whole needed to deal with and overcome them. That is one of the reasons Paul wrote this letter.

Paul also wrote to thank the Philippians for their support to his ministry (Philippians 1:3). Paul urged them to be full of joy and rejoice in their relationship with Jesus Christ (2:18; 3:1). Paul was full of joy, even in the prospect of death. He acknowledged that to depart this earthly life and be with Christ is better by far. But he noted it was more necessary for him to stay on earth a time further for the Philippians' benefit (1:21-26).

Philistines

Philistia was located directly to the southwest of Canaan. No Philistine literature has survived to the present, and little is known about their origins except for what is found in the Bible. What is known is that they were a pagan nation that stood against the people of God in biblical times.

Like the Canaanites, the Philistines believed in false pagan gods, including Dagon, Ashtoreth, and Beelzebub (see Judges 16:23; 1 Samuel 5:1-7; 2 Kings 1:2). Images of these gods were often carried into battle by Philistine soldiers, thinking it would give them victory over opponents with weaker gods.

Apparently, the Philistines were governed by a representative for each city who exercised complete control during wartime and peacetime. This type of government served to unify the Philistines and keep the nation strong. The Israelites, in contrast, were often loosely organized.

The Philistines were apparently gifted in the art of goldsmithing. They were involved in the manufacture and distribution of iron implements and weapons, such as the metal armory and equipment used by the Philistine Goliath in his short battle with David.

There are a number of interesting references to the Philistines in the Old Testament. For example, David became instantly famous for killing Goliath, the giant Philistine warrior (1 Samuel 17). Also, during the time of Samuel, the Philistines were able to capture the Ark of the Covenant in battle. When the Ark caused the head of their god Dagon to fall off and afflicted their people with tumors, they got rid of it as quickly as possible (1 Samuel 5).

Samson is said to have killed a thousand Philistines with the jawbone of a donkey (Judges 15:15). Samson's downfall was that he fell in love with a Philistine woman, Delilah, who eventually betrayed the secret he told her about his hair (Judges 16). The Philistines had bribed her to find out the secret of Samson's strength, and she was all too happy to oblige. Samson's hair was cut while he slept, and he was captured and imprisoned by the Philistines. He lost all of his strength (see *Samson*).

Plagues and Pestilences

In the Bible, a plague is generally a disease, epidemic, or some other form of infliction caused by God to judge a nation or simply to bring about His sovereign purposes. The Hebrew word for "plague" literally means "to strike" or "to smite."

There are many plagues mentioned throughout the Bible, but perhaps the most well known are those that were inflicted by God through the hand of Moses on Pharaoh and the Egyptians. After Moses initially approached Pharaoh about releasing the Israelites from bondage, Pharaoh asked, "Who is the LORD, that I should obey him and let Israel go?" (Exodus 5:2). To convince Pharaoh of God's identity and might, Moses (with God's power) smote the Egyptians with ten plagues, each of which grew progressively worse. It is interesting to observe that over the course of the ten plagues, many of Egypt's false gods were judged.

An example is the first plague, which turned the Nile's water into blood (Exodus 7:14-25). This constituted a judgment against one of Egypt's most prominent gods. The Nile itself was worshiped as a god, and as its water was virtually the lifeblood of Egypt, this blow was devastating. More specifically, this plague was a judgment against the Egyptian sacred river god, *Nilus*. As the Exodus account reveals, this alleged god was impotent in the face of the true God of Scripture.

Another example is the second plague, in which God produced a swarm of frogs (Exodus 8:1-15). Frogs in Egypt were associated with the gods *Hapi* and *Heqt*. As frogs were sacred to the Egyptians, it must have been abominable for them in that everywhere they stepped, they crushed a frog. Again, God demonstrated that there is no one like Him in all the universe.

Yet another example is the fifth plague, which resulted in many animals becoming diseased (Exodus 9:1-7). This was probably a murrain plague on the Egyptian cattle, representing a judgment against *Apis* and *Hathor*, the Egyptian sacred bull and cow. Again, Egypt's gods and sacred idols were no match for the God of Moses.

One final example is the ninth plague, in which darkness enveloped the whole land (Exodus 10:21-29). This was a judgment against the Egyptian sun god, *Re*. The sun god was not only regarded as the creator, father, and king of the gods,

257

but his singular and exceptional character as creator and sustainer of all living things caused him to be looked upon as the most excellent, most distinguished god in the pantheon, and to be praised as the god who was stronger, mightier, and more divine than the other gods. But Re was nowhere to be found when the true God of Scripture darkened the land.

In these and all the other plagues inflicted by God throughout Scripture, God brought about His purposes and judged sinful humanity.

Poetry and Wisdom Literature

1. Poetry ◆ 2. Wisdom Literature

1. *Poetry.* Poetry is found in a number of Old Testament books, including Job, Psalms, Proverbs, the Song of Solomon, Lamentations, as well as the messages of many of Israel's prophets, such as Isaiah and Jeremiah. About 40 percent of the Old Testament is poetic in nature. Much Old Testament poetry is about God. Sometimes this poetry is used in celebratory praise of God, while at other times it is used to communicate God's will as spoken through the prophets. In the case of the book of Proverbs, poetic statements communicate wisdom for living.

Biblical poetry did not contain the elements often appreciated in modern poetry—such as alliteration, meter, and rhyme. Rather, the most common feature of Hebrew poetry was parallelism. The two poetic lines in each verse usually have a parallel relationship of some kind. There are a number of kinds of parallelism in Hebrew poetry:

> A. In *synonymous parallelism,* the words or concepts in one line are paralleled by similar words or concepts in the second line. Proverbs 2:11 is an example: "Dis-

258

cretion will protect you, and understanding will guard you" (see also Genesis 4:23; Psalm 2:4; 51:2-3).

B. In *antithetical parallelism,* one line is the opposite of (or contrasts with) the other line. Proverbs 10:1 is an example: "A wise son brings joy to his father, but a foolish son grief to his mother" (see also Psalm 1:6; 34:10).

C. In *emblematic parallelism,* one line illumines or makes clear the other line by using a simile or a metaphor. Proverbs 10:26 is an example: "As vinegar to the teeth and smoke to the eyes, so is a sluggard to those who send him."

D. In *synthetic parallelism,* the second line simply continues (or "synthesizes" with) the same thought of the first line. There are two varieties of this type of parallelism:

   1. Sometimes the second line indicates the result of what is mentioned in the first line. Proverbs 3:6 is an example of this variety: "In all your ways acknowledge him, and he will make your paths straight."

   2. At other times the second line merely describes something mentioned in the first line. Proverbs 15:3 is an example of this variety: "The eyes of the LORD are everywhere, keeping watch on the wicked and the good."

New Testament poetry includes the Beatitudes (Matthew 5:3-10), Mary's Magnificat (Luke 1:46-55), and the prophecy of Zacharias (Luke 1:68-79). As was true with Old Testament poetry, there are a variety of forms of parallelism in New Testament poetry (see, for example, Matthew 7:6; John 6:32-33).

2. Wisdom Literature. The "wisdom books" of the Bible include the book of Proverbs, Job, Ecclesiastes, the Song of

Solomon, and some of the Psalms (1, 19, 37, 49, 104, 107, 112, 119, 127, 128, 133, 147, and 148). Proverbs provides wisdom on daily living, Job and Ecclesiastes provide wisdom on understanding the inequalities of life and making sense of suffering, the Song of Solomon provides wisdom on human love, and the Psalms provide wisdom on praise and prayer to God.

Israel did not produce the only wisdom literature in the ancient world; it was also quite common to both Egypt and Babylon. Examples of Egyptian wisdom literature include *The Instruction of the Vizier Ptah-Hotep* (ca. 2450 B.C.), which contains advice on how to be a successful state official; *The Instruction of Amen-em-Het* (ca. 2000 B.C.), which contains a father's words to his son regarding how certain people he had favored disappointed him; and *The Instruction of Amen-em-Ope* (ca. 1300–900 B.C.), which contains a king's teachings to his son about various issues in life. It utilizes some words and phrases quite similar to those in Proverbs (for example, "Listen, my son," "path of life," and so forth).

The Babylonian collections of wisdom literature include *Counsels of Wisdom* (ca. 1500–1000 B.C.), *Akkadian Proverbs* (ca. 1800–1600 B.C.), and *The Words of Ahiqar* (ca. 700–400 B.C.). Many of the proverbs contained in these works are secular in nature, and some are even quite crass in their moral tone.

The most significant difference between Proverbs and the wisdom literature of Egypt and Babylon is that the Hebrew concept of wisdom, as set forth in Proverbs, is rooted in the *fear of the Lord.* The Hebrews considered this the "beginning of knowledge." Without such fear of the Lord, no one—according to Solomon—can truly be called "wise" (Proverbs 1:7; 9:10; 15:33).

Poverty and Wealth—See *Money.*

Prayer

1. Components of Prayer ♦ 2. Biblical Principles
of Prayer ♦ 3. Effectiveness of Prayer

1. *Components of Prayer.* Prayer is not just asking for things from God. Prayer also involves thanksgiving, praise, worship, and confession.

A. *Thanksgiving.* In prayer we ought always to give thanks to God for everything we have (Ephesians 5:20; Colossians 3:15). We should "enter his gates with thanksgiving" (Psalm 100:4; see also Psalm 95:2).

B. *Praise.* Like David, we should always have praise for God on our lips (Psalm 34:1). We should praise God in the depths of our heart (Psalm 103:1-5,20-22), and continually "offer to God a sacrifice of praise" (Hebrews 13:15). One means of praising God is through spiritual songs (Psalm 69:30).

C. *Worship.* Like the psalmist of old, we should bow down in worship before the Lord our Maker (Psalm 95:6). We are to worship Him "who made the heavens, the earth, the sea and the springs of water" (Revelation 14:7). We should worship Him with "reverence and awe" (Hebrews 12:28) and worship Him alone (Exodus 20:3-5; Deuteronomy 5:7).

D. *Confession.* Confession in prayer is wise, for "he who conceals his sins does not prosper, but whoever confesses and renounces them finds mercy" (Proverbs 28:13). We are promised that "if we confess our sins, he is faithful and just and will forgive us our sins and purify us from all unrighteousness" (1 John 1:9).

E. *Requests.* Certainly we can also go to God for specific requests. In the Lord's Prayer, we are exhorted to pray for our daily bread (Matthew 6:11). The apostle Paul wrote: "Do not be anxious about anything, but in everything, by prayer and petition, with thanksgiving, present your requests to God. And the peace of God, which transcends all understanding, will guard your hearts and your minds in Christ Jesus" (Philippians 4:6-7).

P

2. Biblical Principles of Prayer. Scripture provides a number of principles for effective praying.

- We must remember that all our prayers are subject to the sovereign will of God. If we ask for something God does not want us to have, He will sovereignly deny that request. First John 5:14 instructs us, "This is the confidence we have in approaching God: that if we ask anything according to his will, he hears us."

- Prayer should not be an occasional practice but rather a continual habit. We are instructed in 1 Thessalonians 5:17 to "pray continually."

- Recognize that sin is a hindrance to prayer being answered. Psalm 66:18 says, "If I had cherished sin in my heart, the LORD would not have listened."

- Living righteously, on the other hand, is a great benefit to prayer being answered. Proverbs 15:29 says, "The LORD is far from the wicked but he hears the prayer of the righteous."

- A good model prayer is the Lord's Prayer found in Matthew 6:9-13. In this one prayer we find praise (verse 9), personal requests (verses 11-13), and an affirmation of God's will (verse 10).

- Be persistent. In Matthew 7:7-8, Jesus said, "Ask and it will be given to you; seek and you will find; knock and the door will be opened to you. For everyone who asks receives; he who seeks finds; and to him who knocks, the door will be opened." The tenses in the Greek for this verse actually carry the idea, *Keep on asking* and it will be given, *keep on seeking* and you will find, *keep on knocking* and the door will be opened.

- Pray in faith. As Mark 11:22-24 puts it, we need to place our faith in God and believe that we have

P

received what we have asked for. If what we have asked for is within God's will, we will receive it.

• Pray in Jesus' name (John 14:13-14). Jesus is the "bridge" between humanity and God the Father. We have the wonderful privilege of going to the Father and praying in the name of His dear Son.

• If your prayer seems unanswered, keep trusting God no matter what. He has a reason for the delay. You can count on it.

3. *Effectiveness of Prayer.* God promises that He answers the prayers of His people. Below are just a few of the benefits of prayer:

• Prayer can bring enlightenment regarding God's purposes for us (Ephesians 1:18-19).

• Prayer can help us understand God's will (Colossians 1:9-12).

• Prayer can increase our love for other people (1 Thessalonians 3:10-13).

• Prayer can bring about encouragement and strength (2 Thessalonians 2:16-17).

• Prayer can keep us from harm and pain (1 Chronicles 4:10).

• Prayer can bring about deliverance of people from their troubles (Psalm 34:15-22).

• Prayer can keep us from succumbing to lies and falsehood (Proverbs 30:7-9).

• Prayer can bring about our daily food (Matthew 6:11).

• Prayer can help us to live righteously (1 Thessalonians 5:23).

• Prayer can bring about healing (James 5:14-15).

P

Priests

1. Qualifications ◆ 2. Aaronic Descent ◆
3. Responsibilities ◆ 4. Dress

1. Qualifications. The priests were the official worship leaders and ministers for the nation of Israel. They served to represent the people before God and were in charge of the various rituals and offerings prescribed by God. (See *Offerings, Sacrificial.*)

The Old Testament stipulates certain qualifications regarding Israel's priests. For example, they were not to be immodest (Exodus 20:26). They were to keep free from all sin and defilement (Leviticus 21:1-15; 22:1-9), and refrain from strong drink (Leviticus 10:8-11). They were also to wear special garments (Exodus 28:3; 31:10; Leviticus 16:4,23-24).

2. Aaronic Descent. Aaron and his four sons can be regarded as the forerunners of the priests in Israelite history (Exodus 28:1). Aaron was a Levite, and the Levites were set apart for priestly and religious duties. Obviously, considering the sheer number of Levites, not all of them could participate as priests, so many of them performed supportive, less important duties.

3. Responsibilities. Responsibilities of the priest were important. For example, in addition to overseeing various rituals, the priests were to teach the people God's law and serve as judges (Deuteronomy 17:8-12). They were also to oversee the care of the sanctuaries where incense and sacrifices were offered on behalf of the people (Leviticus 2:16; 5:12-18; 6:19–7:21; Numbers 3:21-38). In many ways, the priesthood constituted the religious heart of the nation.

4. Dress. The high priest was splendidly dressed, almost royal in appearance. For example, he wore an ephod, which was a beautiful, multicolored garment made of twisted linen

(Exodus 28:6-14). It was joined at the shoulders by two straps and had a skillfully woven waistband to girdle it around the waist. On each shoulder strap was an onyx stone engraved with the names of six of the 12 tribes of Israel. Hence, the high priest carried the 12 tribes before God whenever he entered the tabernacle.

The high priest also wore a multicolored breastplate that had four rows and three columns of precious stones (totaling 12 stones), each one representing one of Israel's 12 tribes (Exodus 28:15-21). It was attached to the ephod's shoulder straps by rings and gold chains. The square cloth on which the stones were placed was folded upward, much like a pouch, and in this pouch were kept the Urim and Thummin. These were precious stones that were used like lots to determine God's will on a particular matter.

Under the ephod, the high priest wore a violet-colored robe that reached below the knees and had bells on its hem (Exodus 28:31-35). When the high priest went into the holy place to make an offering, the bells let them know he was still alive. (This was a real concern, since the high priest could die if there was some uncleanness in his life while making an offering.)

Normal priests wore much simpler clothing— tunics, girdles or sashes, caps, and linen breeches. Though most of these clothes were commonplace, the priests were distinguished by the particular sash they wore, which was decorated according to the priest's rank. The clothing of both the high priest and normal priests had to be anointed before serving God in the tabernacle.

Promised Land

In the covenant God made with Abraham, God promised to give him and his descendants the land of Canaan, a land flowing with milk and honey, "as an everlasting possession" (Genesis 17:8). After the wilderness sojourn, the entrance into the Promised Land became a reality—but only for a handful of the original Exodus crowd (most of the disobedient Israelites perished during the sojourn).

There are many passages in the Old Testament that speak of inheriting the Promised Land. Psalm 37 is typical. Who will "inherit the land" (verses 9,11,22,29), that is, live on to enjoy the blessings of the Lord in the Promised Land? Will the wicked, who plot (verse 12), scheme (verses 7,32), default on debts (verse 21), use raw power to gain advantage (verse 14), and seem thereby to flourish (verses 7,16,35) inherit it? Or will the righteous, who trust in the Lord (verses 3,5,7,34) and are humble (verse 11), blameless (verses 18,37), generous (verses 21,26), upright (verse 37), peaceable (verse 37), and from whose mouth is heard the moral wisdom that reflects meditation on God's law (verses 30,31) inherit it?

The obvious answer is that the righteous will "inherit" the Promised Land and experience God's blessing there. This is ultimately a fulfillment of the covenant stipulations God made with the Israelites at Sinai, for God promised blessing for obedience and punishment for disobedience (Deuteronomy 28:15-68). (See *Captivity and Exile*.)

Property—See *Land and Property*.

Prophecy—See *End Times*.

Prophets

1. Spokesmen for God ◆ 2. Messages of Judgment and Comfort ◆ 3. Different Styles ◆ 4. Major and Minor Prophets

1. *Spokesmen for God.* The Hebrew word for "prophet," *nabi*, refers to a person taken over by the power of God and who spoke forth God's words to the people. Often their words were directed at specific situations or problems that needed to be dealt with. They would typically preface their words with, "Thus saith the LORD," thereby indicating that their words were not their own but came from God.

These prophets were called into service directly by God, some even before birth (Jeremiah 1:5; Luke 1:13-17). They came from all walks of life, from farmers (Amos 7:14) to princes (Genesis 23:6). Whatever their background, the prophets were messengers of the Lord (Isaiah 44:26) who served God and shepherded God's people (Jeremiah 17:16; Amos 3:7; Zechariah 11:4,7).

2. Messages of Judgment or Comfort. Some prophets carried out their work prior to Israel going into captivity. Because of Israel's sin and complacency, these prophets warned that a time of judgment was coming. God would not permit the sins of His people to continue (see, for example, Amos 9:1-10). Though the prophets called the people to repentance, however, the people became hardened in their sin, and therefore judgment inevitably came.

During the time the Israelites were in captivity and the people started to perceive the clear message that God had them there on purpose (because of their sins), some of the people became despondent because they realized they had brought this on themselves. At this time, the prophets spoke soothing words of comfort and promised them that God still had a plan for their future and would one day deliver them from their suffering (see Isaiah 6:13; 28:5; 29:5; 31:5).

3. Different Styles. Prophets received messages from God in various ways, including visions, dreams, and even hearing God's voice. Likewise, the means that the prophets used to deliver their messages varied. Sometimes it involved a simple proclamation of the message in a sanctuary, at other times speaking face-to-face with an individual, and at other times acting out a message (see Jeremiah 19). Isaiah even went barefoot and naked for three years in pointing to the shame of his people (Isaiah 20:2-3). Regardless of the means in which the message was delivered, the people were expected to hear and obey.

P

4. *Major and Minor Prophets.* The prophetic books are divided into two categories—the Major Prophets and the Minor Prophets. The Major Prophets were Isaiah, Jeremiah, Ezekiel, and Daniel. The Minor Prophets were Hosea, Joel, Amos, Obadiah, Jonah, Micah, Nahum, Habakkuk, Zephaniah, Haggai, Zechariah, and Malachi. Interestingly, the book of Isaiah is longer than all the Minor Prophets combined.

Proverbs

1. Purpose ◆ 2. Method ◆ 3. Author

1. *Purpose.* The book of Proverbs is a "wisdom book" and contains maxims of moral wisdom. The maxims found in this book were engineered to help the young in ancient Israel acquire mental skills that promote wise living. Both the content of the proverbs and their structure contributed to the students' development.

In Solomon's thinking, wise living was essentially synonymous with godly living, for one who is godly or righteous in his daily behavior is wise in God's eyes. By contrast, a wicked or unrighteous person is foolish. Indeed, Solomon often equates the "path of wisdom" with the "path of righteousness" and the "path of folly" with the "path of wickedness" (see Proverbs 2–4; 6:1-19).

Linguists tell us that the main Hebrew word for wisdom in the Old Testament is *hokmah*. It was used commonly for the skill of craftsmen, sailors, singers, administrators, and counselors. *Hokmah* pointed to the experience and efficiency of these various workers in using their skills. Similarly, a person who possesses *hokmah* in his spiritual life and relationship to God is one who is both knowledgeable and experienced in following God's way. Biblical wisdom involves skill in the art of godly living. This wisdom, which makes for skilled living, is broad in its scope, teaching students how to be successful at home, at work, in human relationships, regarding money, regarding death and the afterlife, and much more. In the book of Proverbs, the reader learns how to think and act wisely in all of these areas.

2. Method. The word "proverb" literally means "to be like" or "to be compared with." A proverb, then, is a form of communicating truth by using comparisons or figures of speech. The proverbs, in a memorable way, crystallize and condense the writers' experiences and observations about life. The reward of meditating on these maxims is wisdom.

The book of Proverbs is rich in poetic parallelism. This means that the lines in each proverb usually have some kind of parallel relationship with each other. Some forms of parallelism in Proverbs include synonymous parallelism, antithetical parallelism, emblematic parallelism, and synthetic parallelism. (See *Poetry and Wisdom Literature* for descriptions of these forms of parallelism.)

3. Author. The majority of the proverbs were written by Solomon, the wisest man who ever lived (1 Kings 3; 4:29-34). Solomon is known to have spoken some 3000 proverbs during his life. His wisdom was unparalleled. He was a master of *hokmah*, and he passed on this *hokmah* to students in the Proverbs.

Solomon composed his proverbs between 971 and 931 B.C. (the time of his reign as king). King Hezekiah's scribes compiled additional proverbs written by Solomon and added them to the book sometime between 729 and 686 B.C. (the time of Hezekiah's reign). It is reasonable to conclude that the book of Proverbs was completed by 700 B.C. or shortly thereafter.

Psalms

The book of Psalms seems to be a compilation of five smaller collections or books: 1–41, 42–72, 73–89, 90–106, and 107–150. Each of the five collections closes with an ascription of praise. Book 1 (Psalms 1–41) contains primarily personal psalms relating to David. Books 2 and 3 (Psalms 42–72 and 73–89) are primarily national psalms, some of them relating to when the nation was divided into the northern kingdom and the southern kingdom. Books 4 and 5 (Psalms 90–106 and 107–150) are primarily worship psalms. The psalms were written from about 1410 to 450 B.C.

It seems clear that David was the author of many of the psalms (at least half of them), for many bear his name. Elsewhere we are told that David was a talented musician and poet, and so it would have been natural for him to compose such psalms (see, for example, 1 Samuel 16:23). The sons of Korah, Asaph, Solomon, Moses, Heman, and Ethan wrote other psalms (for example, Psalm 82 was written by Asaph).

The Psalms were collected for use in temple worship and were typically set to the accompaniment of stringed instruments. Within the Psalms one will find prayers, poetic expressions, liturgies, hymns, and just about every emotion known to man—including happiness, serenity, peace, hatred, vengeance, bitterness, and much more. In the Psalms, we find human beings struggling honestly with life and communicating honestly with God without holding anything back. Because we today struggle with the same kinds of problems and emotions that the ancients did, the book of Psalms is one of the most relevant and loved books in the entire Bible to modern Christians. The Psalms are indeed timeless.

Punishment—See *Crime and Punishment.*

R

Races

God created all races of man. All human beings are completely equal—equal in terms of their creation (Genesis 1:28), the sin problem (Romans 3:23), God's love for them (John 3:16), and God's provision of salvation for them (Matthew 28:19). The apostle Paul affirmed, "From one man he made every nation of men, that they should inhabit the whole earth; and he determined the times set for them and the exact places where they should live" (Acts 17:26). Moreover, Revelation 5:9 tells us that God's redeemed will be from "every tribe and tongue and people and nation." There is thus no place for racial discrimination, for all men are equal in God's sight.

As for differences in skin color, scientists tell us this is all related to genetics as the human races grew from generation to generation. Further, it is important to note that the Bible nowhere says that skin color is a sign of superiority or inferiority.

Reading and Writing—See *Education.*

Religion in the Ancient World

Religion in the ancient world was predominantly polytheistic. Typically, it was believed that there were a variety of gods and goddesses that were behind the world of nature, controlling rainfall, sunshine, and various events (such as military battles). Therefore, the people went to great efforts to give offerings—sometimes human sacrifices—to these gods in hopes of placating them.

The chief deities among the Canaanites included El, Asherah, Hadad, Baal, Mot, and Yomm. Baal was the most significant of these deities and was believed to be in control of vegetation and fertility. His blessing was coveted in order to obtain good crops.

The Assyrians believed that their many gods had the power to give them military victories over other nations. The national god of Assyria was Ashur, the king of the gods. Ashur and various other gods were believed to control all natural phenomena, including the sun, the moon, and the weather. Assyrians also practiced divination, consulting astrologers to predict the future.

Philistine gods included Dagon, Ashtoreth, and Beelzebub (see Judges 16:23; 1 Samuel 5:1-7; 2 Kings 1:2). Images of these gods were often carried into battle by Philistine soldiers who trusted the idols to give them victory over opponents with weaker gods.

Egypt, too, was polytheistic. In Egyptian religion, the god at the top of the totem pole was the sun god, Re. He was considered the creator, father, and king of the gods. Next in line was the pharaoh of Egypt, who was considered to be the son of Re. In addition to these were a variety of gods, believed to control various aspects of the world of nature, including Sekhmet (a god who could control epidemics), Osiris (a god of agriculture), Shu (the god of the atmosphere), Seth (the god of the crops), and Serapis (who supposedly protected the land from locust invasions).

In view of such polytheism, it becomes clear why God continually emphasized that He was the only true God throughout Old Testament history: "I am the LORD, and there is no other; apart from me there is no God" (Isaiah 45:5).

Repentance

The Greek word for repentance, *metanoe*, means "to change one's mind." The ancients used the word to refer to a religious or ethical change in the way a person thinks and acts. It carries the idea of changing one's way of life as a result of a change in the way one thinks, particularly in regard to the issues of sin and righteousness (see Matthew 4:17; Luke 1:16; 24:47; Acts 3:19; 9:35; 11:21; 14:15; 15:19; 26:18-20; 1 Thessalonians 1:9; 1 Peter 2:25). In some cases, the "changing of mind" had to do not with sin but with the identity of Jesus, as is apparently the case in Acts 2:38 with reference to the Jews who had rejected Jesus as the divine Messiah.

Well-known personalities in the Bible spoke often of repentance. John the Baptist's primary preaching message was, "Repent, for the kingdom of heaven is near" (Matthew 3:2). Jesus, too, placed a heavy emphasis on repentance (see, for example, Matthew 18:3; Luke 13:3,5). A famous example of repentance in the Old Testament is that of David, who committed adultery with Bathsheba and had her husband Uriah killed. David's prayer of repentance is found in Psalm 51.

Resurrection

1. Significance ◆ 2. Biblical Evidence

1. Significance. The resurrection of Christ is the foundation stone of the Christian faith. The apostle Paul wrote to the Corinthians: "If Christ has not been raised, our preaching is useless" (1 Corinthians 15:14). He wrote: "If Christ has not been raised, your faith is futile; you are still in your sins" (verse 17). If the resurrection did not really happen, the apostles were false witnesses, our faith is futile, we are still lost in our sins, the dead in Christ have perished, and we are the most pitiful people on the face of the earth—to say nothing of the fact that there's no hope for any of us beyond the grave.

2. Biblical Evidence. The biblical testimony tells us that Jesus first attested to His resurrection by appearing to Mary Magdalene (John 20:14)—a fact that is a highly significant indicator of the authenticity and reliability of the resurrection account. If the resurrection story were a fabrication, made up by the male disciples, no one in a first-century Jewish culture would have invented it this way. A woman's testimony was unacceptable in any Jewish court of law except in a very few circumstances. A fabricator would have been much more likely to portray Peter or the other male disciples at the tomb. But our biblical text tells us that the Lord appeared first to Mary because that was the way it actually happened.

Following this, Mary promptly told the disciples the glorious news. That evening, the disciples had gathered in a room with the doors shut for fear of the Jews (John 20:19). This fear was well founded, for after Jesus had been arrested, Annas the high priest specifically asked Jesus about the disciples (John 18:19). Jesus had also previously warned the disciples in the Upper Room: "If they persecuted me, they will persecute you also" (John 15:20). These facts no doubt lingered in their minds after Jesus was brutally crucified.

But then their gloom turned to joy. The risen Christ appeared in their midst and said to them, "Peace be with you" (John 20:19b). This phrase was a common Hebrew greeting (1 Samuel 25:6). But on this occasion there was added significance to Jesus' words. After their conduct on Good Friday (they all fled after Jesus' arrest), the disciples may well have expected a rebuke from Jesus. Instead, He displayed compassion by pronouncing peace upon them.

Jesus immediately showed the disciples His hands and His side (John 20:20). The risen Lord wanted them to see that it was truly He. The wounds showed that He did not have another body but the same body. He was dead, but now He was alive forevermore.

All this is highly significant. By all accounts, the disciples came away from the crucifixion frightened and full of doubt. And yet, following Jesus' resurrection appearance to the disciples, their lives were transformed. The cowards became bulwarks of courage, fearless defenders of the faith. The only thing that could account for this incredible transformation was the resurrection.

As the days passed, Jesus continued to make many appearances and prove that He had indeed resurrected from the dead. Acts 1:3 says, "He showed himself to these men and gave many convincing proofs that he was alive. He appeared to them over a period of forty days and spoke about the kingdom of God." Moreover, "He appeared to more than five hundred of the brothers at the same time, most of whom are still living" (1 Corinthians 15:6). It seems clear that the resurrection of Christ is one of the best-attested historical events of ancient times.

Revelation

1. General Revelation ◆ 2. Special Revelation

There are two primary ways God has revealed Himself: *general* revelation and *special* revelation.

1. *General Revelation.* "General revelation" refers to revelation that is available to *all persons* of *all times.* An example of this would be God's revelation of Himself in the world of nature (Psalm 19). By observing the world of nature around us, we can detect something of God's existence and discern something of His divine power and glory. We might say that the whole world is God's "kindergarten" to teach us the ABCs of the reality of God. Human beings cannot open their eyes without being compelled to see God. Indeed, God has engraved unmistakable marks of His glory on His creation.

There are, of course, limitations to how much we can learn from general revelation, for it tells us nothing about God's cure for man's sin problem. It tells us nothing of the "gospel message." These kinds of things require *special* revelation. But general revelation does give us enough information about God's existence that if we reject it, and refuse to turn to God,

R

God is justified in bringing condemnation against us (Romans 1:20).

2. *Special Revelation*. Special revelation refers to God's *very specific* and *clear* revelation in such things as His mighty acts in history, the person of Jesus Christ, and His message spoken through Old Testament prophets (like Isaiah and Daniel) and New Testament apostles (like Paul and Peter).

A. *God's Revelation in History.* God is the *living* God, and He has communicated knowledge of Himself through the ebb and flow of historical experience. The Bible is first and foremost a record of the history of God's interactions among Abraham, Isaac, Jacob, the 12 tribes of Israel, the apostle Paul, Peter, John, and all the other people of God in biblical times.

The greatest revelatory act of God in Old Testament history was the deliverance of Israel from bondage in Egypt. God, through Moses, inflicted ten plagues on the Egyptians that thoroughly demonstrated His awesome power (Exodus 7–12). God's demonstration of power was all the more impressive since the Egyptians believed their many false gods had the power to protect them from such plagues.

Note that the historical miracles and events wrought by God were always accompanied by spoken words. The miracle or event was never left to speak for itself. Nor were human beings left to infer whatever conclusions they wanted to draw from the event. God made sure that when a significant event occurred there was a prophet at hand to interpret it. For example, Moses was there to record everything related to the Exodus. The apostles were there to record everything related to the life, death, and resurrection of Jesus. God has revealed Himself in history, and He always made sure that His historical actions were adequately recorded!

B. *God's Ultimate Revelation in Jesus Christ.* The only way for God to be able to *fully* do and say all that He wanted was to actually leave His eternal residence and enter the arena of humanity. This He did in the person of Jesus Christ. Jesus was God's ultimate "special" revelation.

R

276

Scripture indicates that God is a Spirit (John 4:24). And because He is a Spirit, He is invisible (Colossians 1:15). With our normal senses, we cannot perceive Him apart from what we can detect in general revelation. Further, man is spiritually blind and deaf (1 Corinthians 2:14). Since the Fall of man in the Garden of Eden, man has lacked true spiritual perception. So humankind was in need of special revelation from God in the worst sort of way.

Jesus—as eternal God—took on human flesh so He could be God's fullest revelation to man (Hebrews 1:2-3). Jesus was a revelation of God not just in His person (as God) but in His life and teachings as well. By observing the things Jesus *did* and the things Jesus *said,* we learn a great deal about God. For example, God's awesome power was revealed in Jesus (John 3:2). God's incredible wisdom was revealed in Jesus (1 Corinthians 1:24). God's boundless love was revealed and demonstrated by Jesus (1 John 3:16). And God's unfathomable grace was revealed in Jesus (2 Thessalonians 1:12).

These verses serve as the backdrop as to why Jesus told a group of Pharisees, "When a man believes in me, he does not believe in me only, but in the one who sent me" (John 12:44). Jesus likewise told Philip that "anyone who has seen me has seen the Father" (John 14:9). Jesus was the ultimate revelation of God!

C. *God's Revelation in the Bible.* Another key example of "special" revelation is the Bible. In this one book, God has provided everything He wants us to know about Him and how we can have a relationship with Him.

God is the one who caused the Bible to be written (2 Timothy 3:16; 2 Peter 1:21). And through it He speaks to us today just as He spoke to people in ancient times when those words were first given. The Bible is to be received as God's words to us and revered and obeyed as such. As we submit to the Bible's authority, we place ourselves under the authority of the living God.

277

Revelation, Book of

The book of Revelation is the only apocalyptic book in the New Testament. The author is the apostle John, who was imprisoned on the isle of Patmos (in the Aegean Sea) for the crime of sharing Jesus Christ with everyone he came into contact with (Revelation 1:9). It was on this island that John received the "revelation." The book was apparently written around A.D. 95.

The recipients of the book of Revelation were undergoing severe persecution, with some of them even being killed (see Revelation 2:13). Things were about to get even worse. John wrote this book to give his readers a strong hope that would help them patiently endure suffering. At the time, it seemed as if evil was prevailing at every level. However, Revelation indicates that evil will one day come to an end. At the Second Coming, Christ will overthrow wicked governments, cast the wicked into a place of horrible suffering, and bring about an eternal state where Satan will be forever banished. There will be no further sin, sorrow, or death, and fellowship with God will be perpetual and uninterrupted.

This book promises that God's people will enjoy His presence forever in a "new heaven and a new earth" (Revelation 21:1). Jesus promises, "I am coming soon" (22:20). Such a wonderful promise helps suffering believers see "the big picture" regarding the future so they can patiently endure in the present.

R

Righteousness—See *Justice and Righteousness.*

Romans

1. Significance ◆ 2. Author ◆ 3. Date and Place of Writing ◆ 4. Recipients ◆ 5. Occasion ◆ 6. Content

1. *Significance.* Rome, in terms of trade and commerce, was a hub city connected by road to numerous other cities in the ancient world. There was a constant coming and going. Obviously, Rome was a strategic city in the spread of the Gospel.

2. Author. Romans was written by the apostle Paul (Romans 1:1). Paul's authorship was never disputed by any of the early church fathers. Scholars have pointed out that the doctrines Paul discusses in this letter are similar to those he discusses in his other letters (1 and 2 Corinthians and Galatians). Common doctrines include salvation, justification by faith in Christ, spiritual gifts, and the church as the body of Christ.

Moreover, the historical references in the letter are in full agreement with what we know of Paul and his activities as a missionary. For example, Romans 15:25-27 makes reference to Paul's collection of money for the Jerusalem church. This is in agreement with other historical references found in Acts 19:21; 20:1-5; 21:15-19; 1 Corinthians 16:1-5; 2 Corinthians 8:1-12; and 9:1-5.

3. Date and Place of Writing. Paul wrote his letter to the Romans in about A.D. 57. Paul was presently busy in Corinth collecting money for the poverty-stricken Christians in Jerusalem (Romans 15:25-27), and it is from this city that he wrote to the Romans. We know he was in Corinth because he makes reference to Gaius, his host, who was a Corinthian (Romans 16:23).

R

4. Recipients. Scholars are unsure of who founded the church at Rome. Some have suggested it may have been founded by people who were converted on the Day of Pentecost. (Acts 2:10 makes reference to "visitors from Rome." These visitors may have been among the 3000 converts that day.) Others say it may have been founded by converts of the apostle Paul or one of the other apostles. Regardless of who founded the church, it quickly became well known for its faith warriors (Romans 1:8).

The church at Rome was predominantly made up of Gentile believers (Romans 1:5,13; 11:13; 15:15-16). However, there was also a strong minority of Jewish believers (2:17; 9–11; 14).

5. Occasion. The church at Rome was well known (Romans 1:8), and the apostle Paul had a strong desire to visit it (1:10-15). Apparently Paul wrote this letter to the Roman Christians primarily to prepare the way for his eventual visit to the city (15:14-17,23-24).

It may be that the doctrines Paul covers in this letter serve as a theological introduction to the teaching and ministry he hoped to accomplish among them when he visited. It may also be that Paul intended that the Roman church would become a base of missionary operations in that strategic part of the world. Hence, his letter would give them a chance to digest his missionary Gospel-message before his arrival.

6. Content. Romans is the most theological of all of Paul's letters. Among other things, Paul speaks of humankind's sin problem and the universal need for righteousness (Romans 1:18–3:20); salvation and how one is declared not guilty before God by placing faith in Christ (3:21–5:21); how a believer experientially grows in righteousness in daily life, how he is freed from the power of sin, and how he is freed from the domination of the law (6:1–8:39); how the Jews have a special place in God's plan (9:1–11:12); instructions on spiritual gifts (12:3-8); the need for respecting the government (13:1-7); and unity between Jews and Gentiles (15:5-13). With such broad theological themes, it is easy to see how immensely practical this letter is for the Christian life.

Rome

1. Significance ◆ 2. High Slave Population ◆
3. Moral Degradation ◆ 4. Dominance in Palestine
◆ 5. Religion

1. Significance. Rome, the capital city of the Roman Empire, was home to over a million people. It was an imperial capital city of an empire that stretched from Britain to Arabia. The city was wealthy and was considered the trade center of the ancient world. Large buildings and impressive architecture were common throughout the city. To facilitate easy trade, there were excellent roads connecting Rome to other major cities. There was also water transportation via the Mediterranean Sea. The city was apparently named after its founder and first king, Romulus, in 753 B.C.

2. High Slave Population. Relatively few people in Rome were citizens with full rights. Slaves made up a large part of the population. In fact, less than half of Rome's inhabitants were free men.

3. Moral Degradation. Rome was characterized by moral degradation. Bloody contests between men and beasts—or between men and men—were featured regularly. It seems that increasingly perverted forms of entertainment became necessary to satisfy the hedonistic crowds.

4. Dominance in Palestine. Though the Jews in Palestine disliked the presence of the Romans, the reality is that the presence of Roman soldiers brought stability and order to the area. History reveals that four legions of Roman soldiers were stationed in Palestine. However, the Jews had to pay heavy taxes to the Romans for such "services."

R

5. Religion. Similar to other pagan nations of the day, the Romans believed that there were a variety of gods behind the world of nature and everyday events. Every conceivable aspect of life was considered to have a god involved behind the scenes.

Despite the fact that the Romans believed in many different gods, this belief in itself had little impact on the way the Romans lived their lives. Whereas Christianity always made a profound ethical impact on the lives of its followers, Roman religion did not require such ethical changes. In fact, the gods were generally considered to be distant deities who were to be respected and honored, but were not too interested in morality.

One of the unique aspects of Roman religion is that the emperors were worshiped as gods. This served to instill loyalty among the people to the government. Obviously, to disobey the leader of Rome was to disobey a god of Rome. Eventually, the worship of the emperor as a god became a test of loyalty, a test Christians could not pass since they would not worship him. Christians in Rome thus had to be willing and ready to suffer and die for their faith.

Ruth, Book of

The book of Ruth was likely written during the time of the judges in about 1000 B.C. Some scholars believe the book was written by the prophet Samuel, but there is no hard proof of this. The name "Ruth" is probably a derivative of the Hebrew term *reuit*, which means "friendship." The name is appropriate, for it describes Ruth's character.

According to this book, Elimelech and his wife, Naomi, migrated from Bethlehem to Moab during a time of famine. (Moab is northeast of the Dead Sea.) They were accompanied by his two sons, who both married Moabite women. Eventually the father and sons died in Moab. This left Naomi in a predicament as to what to do. In biblical times, women were dependent upon fathers and husbands for provisions in life. A woman without a father or husband was in a dire situation. Naomi decided to return to Bethlehem, and her Moabite daughter-in-law, Ruth, decided to go with her (see Ruth 1:6-18).

Upon their arrival, they found themselves in poverty (Ruth 1:19-22). But God led Ruth to a distant relative of her first husband's family named Boaz (2:1-7). Boaz ended up fulfilling his family duty and married Ruth, despite the fact that Ruth was not an Israelite (4:1-12).

It is noteworthy that Ruth, the Moabite, was the great-grandmother of David, the king of Israel, and hence an ancestress of Jesus (Matthew 1:1,5). Hence, even though Ruth did not know it at the time, her lineage was very important to the unfolding plan of God. It is also noteworthy that this is one of two books in the Bible named after a woman (the other is Esther).

R

Sabbath

1. Significance ◆ 2. Formalization ◆ 3. Jewish Legalism ◆ 4. Replaced by the Lord's Day

1. *Significance.* The Hebrew word for "Sabbath" means "cessation." The Sabbath was a holy day and a day of rest for both man and animals (Exodus 20:8-11). This day was to commemorate God's rest after His work of creation (Genesis 2:2). God set the pattern for living—working six days and resting on the seventh. The Sabbath thus finds its ultimate origins in the Creation account.

2. *Formalization.* At Mount Sinai, the Sabbath—already in existence—formally became a part of the law and a sign of God's covenant relationship with Israel (Exodus 20:8-11). Keeping the Sabbath was a sign that showed submission to God, and honoring it brought great blessing (Isaiah 58:13-14). By contrast, to break the Sabbath law was to rebel against Him, and this was a sin that warranted the death penalty (see Exodus 31:14). God provided detailed instructions for Sabbath observance in Leviticus 25, Numbers 15:32-36, and Deuteronomy 5:13-15.

Some may find it odd that Sabbath observance is commanded in the Ten Commandments, while the Sabbath was already known among God's people (Exodus 20:8-11). However, an examination of the fourth commandment (which says, "*Remember* the Sabbath...") suggests that though the concept of the Sabbath was already known to the Israelites, it now needed formal statement and clarification. Such clarification would have been necessary because the Israelites were probably not allowed to observe the Sabbath during their time in Egypt.

3. *Jewish Legalism.* By the time of Jesus, Jewish legalists had added all kinds of new rules and regulations for properly keeping the Sabbath. The Sabbath thus became a burden instead of a blessing. These legalistic Jews put their own laws in place of divine law (see Matthew 15:9). Jesus stood against such legalism.

4. *Replaced by the Lord's Day.* Keeping the Sabbath is the only one of the Ten Commandments not repeated after the Day of Pentecost (Acts 2). The early church made Sunday the day of worship for a number of reasons:

- New Testament believers are not under the Old Testament Law (Romans 6:14; Galatians 3:24-25; Hebrews 7:12).

- Jesus resurrected and appeared to some of His followers on the first day of the week (Sunday) (Matthew 28:1).

- Jesus continued His appearances on succeeding Sundays (John 20:26).

- The descent of the Holy Spirit took place on a Sunday (Acts 2:1).

- The early church was thus given the pattern of Sunday worship, and this they continued to do regularly (Acts 20:7; 1 Corinthians 16:2).

- Sunday worship was further hallowed by our Lord who appeared to John in that last great vision on "the Lord's day" (Revelation 1:10).

- In Colossians 2:16 we read, "Therefore do not let anyone judge you by what you eat or drink, or with regard to a religious festival, a New Moon celebration or a Sabbath day." This verse indicates that the distinctive holy days of the Old Testament are no longer binding on New Testament believers.

S

Sacraments

1. Two Sacraments ◆ 2. The Lord's Supper ◆
3. Baptism

1. *Two Sacraments.* There are two sacraments spoken of in the New Testament—the Lord's Supper and baptism. Some theologians prefer not to call them "sacraments" because this word seems to imply the conveyance of grace in participating in the rituals. These theologians prefer the word "ordinances."

2. *The Lord's Supper.* Jesus instituted the Lord's Supper at the Last Supper where He shared bread and wine with the disciples prior to His crucifixion (Mark 14:12-26). The timing is highly significant. After all, at Passover, the Jews celebrated their ancestors' escape from Egyptian bondage (salvation). Jesus, with the bread and wine, instructed the disciples that these elements would serve to remind them of the significance of His death (which would bring salvation) (1 Corinthians 11:25).

There are four primary views of the significance of the Lord's Supper:

A. *The Roman Catholic view* is known as Transubstantiation. This view says that the elements actually change into the body and blood of Jesus Christ at the prayer of consecration of the priest. It is said to impart grace to the recipient. Jesus is viewed as literally present. There is no change in the appearance of the elements, but the elements nevertheless change.

There are a number of problems with this view. First, note that Jesus was present with the disciples when He said the elements (bread and wine) were His body and blood (Luke 22:17-20). Obviously He intended that His words be taken figuratively. Further, one must keep in mind the scriptural teaching that drinking blood is forbidden to anyone (Genesis

9:4; Leviticus 3:17; Acts 15:29). Still further, the idea that Jesus' body and blood are physically present in Roman Catholic churches all over the world each Sunday would imply the omnipresence of the physical body of Christ. Scripturally, omnipresence is an attribute of Christ's divine nature only.

B. *The Lutheran view* is known as Consubstantiation. This view says that Christ is present *in, with,* and *under* the bread and wine. There is a real presence of Christ but no change in the elements. The mere partaking of the elements after the prayer of consecration communicates Christ to the participant along with the elements.

C. *The Reformed view* is that Christ is spiritually present at the Lord's Supper, and it is a means of grace. There is said to be a dynamic presence of Jesus in the elements made effective in the believer as he partakes. The partaking of His presence is not a physical eating and drinking, but an inner communion with His person.

D. *The memorial view* (my view) is that there is no change in the elements, and that the ordinance is not intended as a means of communicating grace to the participant. The bread and wine are symbols and reminders of Jesus in His death and resurrection (1 Corinthians 11:24-25). It also reminds us of the basic facts of the Gospel (11:26), our anticipation of the Second Coming (11:26), and our oneness as the body of Christ (10:17).

3. Baptism. Baptism was not a new concept in New Testament times. In fact, whenever a person converted to Judaism in biblical times, he had to be baptized in water, by immersion, as a sign of his cleansing. Christianity gave baptism a deeper significance.

A. *Significance of Baptism.* There are at least three views that Christians have regarding the significance of baptism. The first of these is the sacramental view espoused by Roman Catholics and Lutherans. In this view, God conveys grace to the believer through the sacrament of baptism. As a result of

S

this ritual, the believer's sins are allegedly remitted and he is given a new nature.

A second view is the covenantal view, which holds that New Testament baptism is essentially a counterpart to Old Testament circumcision as a sign of the covenant. Contrary to the sacramental view, this view does not see baptism as a means of salvation. Rather, baptism is a *sign* of God's covenant to save humankind, and is a *means* of entering into that covenant (and enjoying its benefits).

A third view (my view) is the symbolic view. This view says that baptism does not produce salvation, does not convey grace, but rather is a symbol pointing to the believer's complete identification with Jesus Christ. It is a public testimony that shouts to the world that a change in status has occurred in the person's life: formerly, the person was identified with the world and was lost, but now the person is identified with Jesus Christ. The immersion into the water and the coming up out of it symbolizes death to the old life and resurrection to the new life in Christ (Romans 6:1-4).

B. *Baptism by Immersion or Sprinkling?* Christians are divided on this issue. Those who argue for sprinkling point out that a secondary meaning of the Greek word *baptizo* is "to bring under the influence of." This fits sprinkling better than immersion. Moreover, it is argued, baptism by sprinkling better pictures the coming of the Holy Spirit upon a person.

It is also suggested that immersion would have been impossible in some of the baptisms portrayed in Scripture. In Acts 2:41, for example, it would have been impossible to immerse all 3000 people who were baptized. The same is said to be true in regard to Acts 8:38, 10:47, and 16:33.

Those who hold to the immersion view (like I do) respond by pointing out that the primary meaning of the Greek word *baptizo* is "to immerse." And the prepositions normally used in conjunction with *baptizo* (such as "into" and "out of" the water) clearly picture immersion and not sprinkling. The Greek language has perfectly acceptable words for "sprinkling" and "pouring," but these words are never used in the context of baptism in the New Testament.

As noted above, the ancient Jews practiced baptism by immersion. Hence, it is likely that the Jewish converts to Christianity (including the disciples, who came out of Judaism) would have followed this precedent.

Certainly baptism by immersion best pictures the significance of death to the old life and resurrection to the new life in Christ (Romans 6:1-4). And, despite what sprinkling advocates say, in every instance of water baptism recorded in the New Testament, immersion was practiced. Arguments that there was not enough water to accomplish immersion are weak and unconvincing. Archaeologists have uncovered ancient pools all over the Jerusalem area.

Though immersion is the biblical norm of baptism, it is not necessarily an inflexible norm. God accepts the believer on the basis of his or her faith in Christ and the desire to obey Him, not on the basis of how much water covers the body at the moment of baptism.

C. *Infant Baptism.* Some Christians have argued in favor of infant baptism by saying it is analogous to circumcision in the Old Testament, which was done to infant boys (see Genesis 17:12). Moreover, it is argued that household baptisms in the New Testament must have included infants (Acts 16:33). As well, Jesus Himself clearly blessed the children in Mark 10:13-16 and said that to such belong the kingdom of God.

Other Christians (including myself) disagree with this view and point out that the biblical pattern is that a person always get baptized *following* his or her conversion experience (see, for example, Acts 2:37-41; 8:12; 10:47; 16:29-34; 18:8; 19:4-5). Moreover, household baptisms such as described in Acts 16:33 do not specify the presence of any infants. Having said that, it is certainly permissible and right for young children who have trusted in Christ to get baptized.

S

Sacrifice

1. Animal Sacrifices Costly ◆ 2. Substitutionary
Sacrifices ◆ 3. Typological of Christ

1. *Animal Sacrifices Costly.* Among the ancient Jews, sacrificing an animal to the Lord was no small sacrifice. Indeed, animals were very expensive, and for that reason the average Jewish family's diet was often vegetarian. On special occasions, such as having a guest over or perhaps having someone in the family get married, meat would be served. Otherwise, primarily vegetables would be served on the table each night.

According to the law, the animals offered in sacrifice could not be "second best"—that is, they could not have blemishes. Indeed, only unblemished animals could be used (see Leviticus 1:3). Anything less than this would show great disrespect.

2. *Substitutionary Sacrifices.* In the sacrificial system, the animal being sacrificed substitutionally represented the one making the offering. When the offerer placed his hand upon the animal's head, he was symbolically transferring the guilt of sin onto the animal, and hence the animal was dying in the place of the offerer.

Scripture indicates that the blood itself makes atonement. Leviticus 17:11 states: "For the life of a creature is in the blood, and I have given it to you to make atonement for yourselves on the altar; it is the blood that makes atonement for one's life." The Jews accordingly believed:

A. The blood used for sacrifice is a *divine provision.*

B. The shedding of the blood of sacrifice is a *price-paying act.*

C. The shedding of the blood of sacrifice is a *substitutionary act.*

3. *Typological of Christ.* A type is a figure or representation of something to come. More specifically, a type is an Old Testament institution, event, person, object, or ceremony that has reality and purpose in biblical history, but which also, by divine design, foreshadows something yet to be revealed.

That the animal sacrifices were typological of Christ is evident in the apostle Paul's affirmation that Christ, our Passover lamb (John 1:29), has been sacrificed (1 Corinthians 5:7). He gave His life as a ransom for our sins (Mark 10:45). By His blood we are purified from our sins (1 John 1:7). Indeed, it is by His blood that humanity has been delivered from slavery to sin (Hebrews 9:12). (See *Offerings, Sacrificial.*)

Sadducees—See *Jewish Sects.*

Salvation

1. Threefold Salvation ◆ 2. Salvation Words ◆
3. The Necessity of Faith in Christ ◆ 4. Secure in
Our Salvation

1. *Threefold Salvation.* The salvation we have in Christ is threefold, involving the past, present, and future. In terms of the past, God has delivered us from the *penalty* of sin and has wiped our slate clean. This happens the moment we trust in Christ for salvation (Acts 16:31). The present aspect of salvation involves deliverance from the *power* of sin in our daily lives (Romans 8:13; Philippians 2:12). In the future, when we enter into glory, we will be finally delivered from the very *presence* of sin (Romans 13:11; Titus 2:12-13).

2. *Salvation Words.* Scripture uses a number of salvation words to describe the wonder and all-encompassing nature

S

of our new status in Christ, including "born again," "justified," "reconciled," "forgiven," and "adopted."

A. *Born Again.* Being "born again" literally means to be "born from above." It refers to the act of God by which He gives eternal life to the one who believes in Christ (Titus 3:5). Just as a *physical* birth places a new baby into a family, so a *spiritual* birth places one into the family of God (see John 3:1-5; 1 Peter 1:23).

B. *Justified.* God "declares righteous" all those who believe in Jesus. Because of Christ's work on the cross—taking our place and bearing our sins—God acquits believers and pronounces a verdict of "not guilty." Romans 3:24 tells us that God's "declaration of righteousness" is given to believers "freely by his grace." The word "grace" literally means "unmerited favor." It is because of God's unmerited favor that believers can freely be "declared righteous" before God.

This does not mean God's declaration of righteousness has no objective basis. God did not just subjectively decide to overlook man's sin or wink at his unrighteousness. Jesus died on the cross for us. He died in our stead. He *paid* for our sins (Mark 10:45).

C. *Reconciled.* By believing in Jesus, who paid for our sins at the cross, we are reconciled to God. The alienation and estrangement that formerly existed is done away with (2 Corinthians 5:19).

D. *Forgiven.* One of the greatest blessings of salvation is that we are truly forgiven of all our sins. God said, "Their sins and lawless acts I will remember no more" (Hebrews 10:17). We are told, "For as high as the heavens are above the earth, so great is his love for those who fear him; as far as the east is from the west, so far has he removed our transgressions from us" (Psalm 103:11-12).

There is a definite point that is "north" and another that is "south"—the North and South Poles. But there are no such points for "east" and "west." It does not matter how far you go to the east; you will never arrive where east begins because by definition east is the opposite of west. The two never meet.

To remove our sins "as far as the east is from the west" is by definition to put them where no one can ever find them. That is the forgiveness God has granted us.

E. *Adopted.* Believers are adopted into God's forever family. We become a "son of God" (Romans 8:14). Being a "son of God" makes one a member of God's family. God adopts into His family *any* who believe in His Son, Jesus Christ. This is noticeably different from human adoptions, for human adults generally seek to adopt only the healthiest and best-behaved children. But *all* are welcome in God's family.

Because of this new relationship with God, believers are called "heirs of God" and "co-heirs with Christ" (Romans 8:17). In a typical family, each child in the family receives a share in their parents' estate. This makes each child an "heir," and the children as a group are "co-heirs." As God's children we are "heirs," and collectively we are "co-heirs" with Christ (Galatians 4:7).

3. *The Necessity of Faith in Christ.* Scripture indicates that the means of receiving the wonderful package of salvation described above is by faith in Christ. Recall that in Acts 16:31 the jailer asked Paul and Silas how to be saved. They responded, "Believe in the Lord Jesus, and you will be saved." The jailer believed and immediately became saved. Close to 200 times in the New Testament, salvation is said to be by faith alone (see, for example, John 3:15; 5:24; 11:25; 12:46; 20:31).

4. *Secure in Our Salvation.* Though some Christians have debated back and forth on this issue, it seems to be the teaching of Scripture that once a person trusts in Christ and becomes a part of God's forever family, he or she is saved forever (Romans 8:28-30). No matter what that child of God does henceforth, he or she is saved.

That does not mean the Christian can get away with perpetual sinning. If children of God sin and refuse to repent, God brings discipline—sometimes very severe discipline—

S

into their lives to bring them to repentance (Hebrews 12:4-11). Christians will either respond to God's light or they will respond to His heat.

There are many scriptural evidences for security in salvation. For example, Ephesians 4:30 indicates that we are sealed unto the day of redemption by the Holy Spirit (see also Ephesians 1:13). This seal—which indicates ownership, authority, and security—cannot be broken. The seal guarantees our entry into heaven.

Besides this, we are told that the Father keeps us in His sovereign hands, and no one can take us out of His hands (John 10:28-30; 13:1 NASB). God has us in His firm grip. And that grip will never let us go.

Further, the Lord Jesus Himself regularly intercedes and prays for us (Hebrews 7:25). His work of intercession, as our divine High Priest, is necessary because of our weaknesses, our helplessness, and our immaturity as children of God. And His prayers are always answered!

Samaritans—See *Jewish Sects.*

Samson

At birth, Samson, the son of Manoah, was set apart for God's service by a Nazirite vow, a vow signified by the fact that his hair was never to be cut (see Judges 13:2-5; 16:17). He is famous for his incredible strength, which, amazingly, was related to the length of his hair. His strength powerfully showed itself when he defeated the Philistines all alone.

When he was attacked by a young lion, Samson, in his mighty strength, killed it with his bare hands (Judges 14:5-6). He killed a thousand Philistines with the jawbone of a donkey (15:15). He tied 300 foxes together, attached torches to their tails, and had them run through Philistine fields, burning up their crops (15:4-5). His strength was unparalleled.

Samson lived during a time of moral and spiritual decline. As Judges 17:6 (NASB) puts it, "Every man did what was right in his own eyes." The people of Israel had fallen into lawlessness and were completely unfaithful to God. During much of this time (20 years), Samson served as a judge.

Samson's downfall was that he fell in love with a Philistine woman, Delilah, who eventually betrayed the secret he told her about his hair (Judges 16). The Philistines had bribed her to find out the secret of Samson's strength, and she was all too happy to oblige. Samson's hair was cut while he slept, and he was captured and imprisoned by the Philistines. He lost all of his strength.

Samson was blinded and then enslaved by the Philistines, forced to perpetually work by grinding grain. During this time, he came to realize that God had given him this special strength in order to serve Him. He prayed to God for renewed strength, and this strength showed itself when he brought down a Philistine temple with his bare hands. He was chained between two pillars that supported the temple, and he pulled these chains till the pillars collapsed, bringing the whole temple down. He thus exacted his revenge against the Philistines (Judges 16:28-31).

Samuel, 1 and 2

The books of 1 and 2 Samuel were written by a prophet of the same name sometime after 931 B.C. Samuel was a wonderful prophet—the last and greatest of the judges of Israel. He ruled Israel his entire life and is noted for bringing the Israelites back to God's laws.

The two books of Samuel chronicle Israel's history from the time of the judges through the reign of King David (who reigned from 1011 to 971 B.C.)—about 135 years of history. It was during this time that Israel demanded a king like the nations around them, and it was Samuel who anointed the first king, Saul, who reigned from 1052 to 1011 B.C. These books, then, chronicle the transition in leadership from judges to kings in the life of Israel.

Originally, 1 and 2 Samuel were a single book, known as the "Book of Samuel." But the translators of the Septuagint—the Greek translation of the Hebrew Old Testament that predates Christ—divided it into two parts.

One thing that is obvious in these books is that God is the true King. So long as the human king (whether Saul or David) obeys the divine King's orders, the nation prospers and succeeds. However, if he departs from the will of God, as did Saul, the nation is judged and the king is dethroned. We learn from this that the power of earthly kings is not to be compared with the power of the divine King.

Satan

1. A Powerful Creature ◆ 2. Scriptural Descriptions ◆ 3. Lucifer's Fall

1. *A Powerful Creature.* Satan, formerly known as Lucifer, is a fallen angel who is aligned against God and His purposes, and he leads a vast company of fallen angels, called demons. Though he possesses creaturely limitations (he is not omnipresent, omnipotent, or omniscient like God is), Satan is nevertheless pictured in Scripture as being extremely powerful and influential in the world. He is called the "ruler of this world" (John 12:31 NASB) and "the god of this age" (2 Corinthians 4:4). He is called the "ruler of the kingdom of the air" (Ephesians 2:2). He is also said to deceive the whole world (Revelation 12:9; 20:3). He is portrayed as having power in the governmental realm (Matthew 4:8-9), the physical realm (Luke 13:11,16; Acts 10:38), the angelic realm (Ephesians 6:11-12; Jude 9), and the ecclesiastical (church) realm (Revelation 2:9; 3:9). Clearly Satan is a being that Christians should be very concerned about.

296

2. Scriptural Descriptions. We learn much about Satan and his work by the various names and titles used of him:

- Satan is called the *accuser of our brothers* (Revelation 12:10). The Greek of this verse indicates that accusing God's people is a continuous, ongoing work of Satan. He never lets up. He brings charges against believers before God (Zechariah 3:1), and he accuses believers to their own conscience.

- Satan is called our *adversary* (1 Peter 5:8 NASB). This word indicates that Satan opposes us and stands against us in every way he can.

- Satan is called *Beelzebub* (Matthew 12:24). This word literally means "lord of the flies," carrying the idea, "lord of filth." The devil corrupts everything he touches.

- Satan is called the *devil* (Matthew 4:1). This word carries the idea of "adversary" as well as "slanderer." The devil was and is the adversary of Christ; he is the adversary of all who follow Christ. Satan slanders God to man (Genesis 3:1-7) and man to God (Job 1:9; 2:4).

- Satan is called our *enemy* (Matthew 13:39). This word comes from a root meaning "hatred." It characterizes Satan's attitude in an absolute sense. He hates both God and His children.

- Satan is called the *evil one* (1 John 5:19). He opposes all that is good and is the promoter of all that is evil. Indeed, he is the very embodiment of evil.

- Satan is called the *father of lies* (John 8:44). The word "father" is used here metaphorically of the originator of a family or company of persons animated by a deceitful character. Satan was the first and greatest liar.

- Satan is called a *murderer* (John 8:44). This word literally means "man killer" (see 1 John 3:12,15). Hatred is the motive that leads one to commit murder. Satan

S

297

hates both God and His children, so he has a genuine motive for murder.

• Satan is called the *god of this age* (2 Corinthians 4:4). This does not mean that Satan is deity. It simply means that this is an evil age, and Satan is its "god" in the sense that he is the head of it.

• Satan is called the *prince of the power of the air* (Ephesians 2:2 NASB). It would seem that the "air" in this context is that sphere in which the inhabitants of this world live. This sphere represents the very seat of Satan's authority.

• Satan is called the *prince of this world* (John 12:31; 14:30; 16:11). The key word here is "world." This word refers not to the physical earth but to an anti-God system that Satan has promoted and that conforms to his ideals, aims, and methods.

• Satan is called a *roaring lion* (1 Peter 5:8-9). This graphic simile depicts Satan's strength and destructiveness.

• Satan is called the *tempter* (Matthew 4:3). His constant purpose is to incite man to sin. He whispers the most plausible excuses for sinning against God.

• Satan is called a *serpent* (Genesis 3:1; Revelation 12:9). This word symbolizes the origin of sin in the Garden of Eden, as well as the hatefulness and deadly effect of sin. The serpent is characterized by treachery, deceitfulness, venom, and murderous proclivities.

3. Lucifer's Fall. Many scholars believe Ezekiel 28 and Isaiah 14 provide insights regarding how Lucifer fell and became Satan. The being described in Ezekiel 28 is portrayed as having the nature of a cherub (verse 14), as being initially blameless and sinless (verse 15), as being on the Holy

Mount of God (verses 13-14), as being cast out of the mountain of God and thrown to the earth (verse 16), and is said to have been full of wisdom, perfect in beauty, and a model of perfection (verse 12). Since such things cannot be said of a mere human being, many believe this is a reference to Lucifer.

Our text tells us that he was created in a state of perfection (Ezekiel 28:12,15), and he remained perfect in his ways until wickedness was found in him (verse 15b). What was this iniquity? We read in verse 17, "Your heart became proud on account of your beauty, and you corrupted your wisdom because of your splendor." Lucifer apparently became so impressed with his own beauty, intelligence, power, and position that he began to desire for himself the honor and glory that belonged to God alone. The sin that corrupted Lucifer was self-generated pride. This seems to be confirmed in Isaiah 14:12-17, which describes the five boastful "I wills" of Lucifer.

God rightfully judged this mighty angelic being: "I threw you to the earth" (Ezekiel 28:17). As a result of this heinous sin, Lucifer was banished from living in heaven (Isaiah 14:12). He became corrupt, and his name changed from Lucifer ("morning star") to Satan ("adversary"). His power became completely perverted (14:12,16-17). And his destiny, following the Second Coming of Christ, is to be bound in a pit during the thousand-year millennial kingdom over which Christ will rule (Revelation 20:3), and he will eventually be thrown into the Lake of Fire (Matthew 25:41; Revelation 20:10).

S

Scribes—See *Jewish Sects.*

Second Coming of Christ

1. The Promise ◆ 2. A Visible Event ◆ 3. Timing

1. *The Promise.* The Second Coming is that event when Jesus Christ—the King of kings and Lord of lords—returns to earth in glory at the end of the present age and sets up His kingdom. The very same Jesus who ascended into heaven will come again at the Second Coming. In Acts 1:11 some angels appeared to Christ's disciples (after the ascension) and said to them: "Men of Galilee, why do you stand here looking into the sky? This same Jesus, who has been taken from you into heaven, will come back in the same way you have seen him go into heaven."

Jesus also told the disciples the night prior to His crucifixion: "Do not let your hearts be troubled. Trust in God; trust also in me. In my Father's house are many rooms; if it were not so, I would have told you. I am going there to prepare a place for you. And if I go and prepare a place for you, I will come back and take you to be with me that you also may be where I am" (John 14:1-3). There are some 300 additional references to the Second Coming in the New Testament.

2. A Visible Event. The Second Coming will involve a visible, physical, bodily coming of the glorified Jesus. A key Greek word used to describe the Second Coming of Christ in the New Testament is *apokalupsis.* This word carries the basic meaning of "revelation," "visible disclosure," "unveiling," and "removing the cover from something that is hidden." The word is used of Christ's Second Coming in 1 Peter 4:13 (NASB): "But to the degree that you share the sufferings of Christ, keep on rejoicing; so that also at the *revelation* of his glory, you may rejoice with exultation."

Another Greek word used of Christ's Second Coming in the New Testament is *epiphaneia,* which carries the basic meaning of "to appear," "to shine forth." In Titus 2:13 (NASB) Paul speaks of "looking for the blessed hope and the *appearing* of the glory of our great God and Savior, Christ Jesus." In 1 Timothy 6:14, Paul urges Timothy to "keep this command without spot or blame until the *appearing* of our Lord Jesus Christ." Significantly, Christ's first coming—which was both bodily and visible ("the Word become flesh")—was

S

called an *epiphaneia* (2 Timothy 1:10). In the same way, Christ's Second Coming will be both bodily and visible.

The Second Coming will be a universal experience in the sense that "every eye" will witness the event. Revelation 1:7 says, "Look, he is coming with the clouds, and every eye will see him, even those who pierced him; and all the peoples of the earth will mourn because of him." Moreover, at the time of the Second Coming, there will be magnificent signs in the heavens (Matthew 24:29-30).

3. Timing. The timing of the Second Coming is entirely in God's sovereign hands. Before His ascension into heaven, Jesus said to the disciples: "It is not for you to know the times or dates the Father has set by his own authority" (Acts 1:7). In Matthew 24:36 Jesus said: "No one knows about that day or hour, not even the angels in heaven, nor the Son, but only the Father." In view of this, it should be a matter of constant expectancy for all Christians.

Sermon on the Mount

The Sermon on the Mount (Matthew 5–7) is one of five major discourses of Jesus Christ recorded in the Gospel of Matthew; the others are recorded in chapters 10, 13, 18, and 23–25. This sermon is called the "Sermon on the Mount" because He

S

The Sermon on the Mount

Subject	Verses	Subject	Verses
The Beatitudes	5:3-12	Avoiding Judging	7:1-6
Salt and Light	5:13-16	Praying Rightly	7:7-12
True Righteousness	5:17-48	Choosing the Narrow Way	7:13-14
Avoiding Hypocrisy	6:1-18	Bearing Fruit	7:15-20
Kingdom Priority	6:19-34	Good Deeds	7:21-29

delivered it on a mountainside (Matthew 5:1). It presents the highest standard of Christian living.

Perhaps the most famous verse in the Sermon on the Mount is Matthew 7:12, which is widely known as the Golden Rule: "So in everything, do to others what you would have them do to you, for this sums up the Law and the Prophets." Since this verse summarizes God's requirements in the Law and the Prophets, its relevance to righteous living is obvious.

Sex and Sexuality

1. God Created Sex for Marriage ◆ 2. Fornication and Adultery Condemned ◆ 3. Homosexuality Condemned

1. *God Created Sex for Marriage.* God created human beings as sexual beings. Sex was a part of God's "good" creation. Indeed, God created sex and "everything created by God is good" (1 Timothy 4:4). But it is good *only* within the confines of the (male-female) marriage relationship, which He Himself ordained (see Hebrews 13:4; see also Genesis 2:24; Matthew 19:4-5; 1 Corinthians 6:16; Ephesians 5:31). Sexual intercourse is actually one of God's first commands to Adam and Eve: "Be fruitful and multiply; fill the earth" (Genesis 1:28). So important is sex in the marriage relationship, the apostle Paul said, that husbands and wives should always be available to each other (1 Corinthians 7:1-5).

2. *Fornication and Adultery Condemned.* Christians are commanded to abstain from fornication (Acts 15:20). The apostle Paul strongly affirmed that sexual immorality is not what the body is created for, but it is a sin against the body, and believers should flee from it (1 Corinthians 6:13-18). We must not forget that the body is the temple of the Holy Spirit (1 Corinthians 6:19). The Ephesians were instructed that fornication should not be even once named or spoken of among them (5:3 NASB).

Adultery is also strongly condemned in Scripture: "You shall not commit adultery" (Exodus 20:14). In the Old Testament, adulterers were to be put to death (Leviticus 20:10). Jesus pronounced adultery wrong even in its basic motives (Matthew 5:27-28). Paul called it an evil work of the flesh (Galatians 5:19), and John envisioned in the Lake of Fire those who practiced it (Revelation 21:8).

One particularly heinous form of fornication in Old Testament times involved the pagan worship of Baal. Because Baal was considered the god of fertility, there were male and female prostitutes in Baal temples. It was believed that worshipers, by having sex with temple prostitutes, could obtain from Baal the things they wanted in life. Such Baal worship is condemned in the strongest possible terms in the Bible (see 1 Kings 15:12).

3. Homosexuality Condemned. The Bible states that "neither fornicators...nor homosexuals...will inherit the kingdom of God" (1 Corinthians 6:9 NASB). The Scriptures repeatedly and consistently condemn homosexual practices (see Leviticus 18:22 and Romans 1:26-27). The Bible condemns *all* types of fornication—which would therefore include homosexuality (Matthew 15:19; Mark 7:21; Galatians 5:19-21; 1 Thessalonians 4:3). Again, God intends sex only for the (male-female) marriage relationship (Hebrews 13:4).

Shema

The Shema (literally "Hear thou") was an early Hebrew confession of faith whose beginning is found in Deuteronomy 6:4: "Hear, O Israel: The LORD our God, the LORD is one." This verse is probably better translated from the Hebrew, "Hear, O Israel! The LORD is our God, the LORD alone." The entire Shema can be found in Deuteronomy 6:4-9, 11:13-21, and Numbers 15:37-41.

For a nation surrounded by pagan nations who believed in many false gods and idols—including the Egyptians, who held the Israelites in bondage for over 400 years—the Shema would have been particularly meaningful, for it emphasized that the Lord alone is God. The importance of the Shema is reflected in the Hebrew practice of requiring children to memorize it at a very early age. Jesus once quoted from the Shema during a dispute He had with the scribes (Mark 12:28-30).

Sheol—See *Hell.*

Signs and Wonders—See *Miracles.*

Sin and Guilt

1. Original Sin ◆ 2. Guilt and Alienation ◆ 3. Sin Yields Death ◆ 4. The Nature of Sin ◆ 5. Jesus on Sin ◆ 6. The Wonder of Salvation

1. *Original Sin.* When Adam and Eve sinned, it did not just affect them in an isolated way. It affected the entire human race. In fact, ever since then, every human being born into the world has been born in a state of sin. The apostle Paul said that "sin entered the world through one man, and death through sin, and in this way death came to all men, because all sinned" (Romans 5:12). Indeed, "through the disobedience of the one man the many were made sinners..." (Romans 5:19; see also 1 Corinthians 15:21-22).

2. *Guilt and Alienation.* When Adam and Eve sinned, they immediately sensed an alienation from God and even went so far as to try to hide themselves from Him (Genesis 3:8). They sinned and, in their panic, frantically tried to do the impossible: They tried to withdraw and avoid having to face God altogether. This sense of separation from God and the accompanying shame is one of the worst results of man's sin problem. Tragically, in consequence of the Fall, it is now human nature to do over and over again what Adam and Eve did in Genesis 3. That is, people sin and then try to hide from God so as to avoid having to face the guilt.

3. Sin Yields Death. When Adam and Eve sinned, they passed immediately into a state of spiritual death—spiritual separation from God. They were evicted from the Garden of Eden, and a sword-bearing angel was posted to guard the entrance.

The full penalty for sin, though, includes both spiritual and physical death (Romans 6:23; 7:13). Death, in the biblical sense, literally means "separation." Spiritual death, then, is spiritual separation from God. Physical death is separation of the soul from the body. Physical death is the inevitable result of spiritual death. The fall into sin introduced the process of age and decay, leading ultimately to death.

Adam and Eve's expulsion from the Garden of Eden gave geographical expression to humankind's spiritual separation from God—our unfitness to stand before Him and enjoy the intimacy of His presence (Genesis 3:23). Because of our sin, God's presence becomes a place of dread. The fiery sword of the guarding angel—which barred the way back to Eden—represents the terrible truth that in his sin man is separated from God (Romans 1:18).

4. The Nature of Sin. Though there are many ways Scripture speaks of sin, two of the more important are "missing the target" and "falling short of God."

A. *Missing the Target.* Sin is failure to live up to God's standards. All of us miss the target. There is not one person who is capable of fulfilling all of God's laws at all times (Romans 3:23). There may be some people whose behavior is more righteous than others'. But all of us fall short of God's infinitely perfect standards. None of us can measure up to His perfection.

S

Human sin shows up in the presence of God's holiness. The "light" of His holiness reveals the darkness of human imperfection. This is illustrated in the life of Isaiah. He was a relatively righteous man, but when he beheld God in His infinite holiness, his own personal sin came into clear focus and he could only say, "Woe to me! I am ruined! For I am a man of unclean lips, and I live among a people of unclean lips" (Isaiah 6:5).

When we measure ourselves against other human beings, we may come out looking okay. In fact, to measure ourselves against other human beings might lead us to believe that we are fairly righteous. But other human beings are not our moral measuring stick. God is. And as we measure ourselves against God in His infinite holiness and righteousness, our sin shows up in all of its ugliness. We "miss the target."

B. *Falling Short of God.* The apostle Paul stressed that all human beings fall short of God's glory (Romans 3:23). The words "fall short" are a single word in the Greek and are present tense. This indicates continuing action. Human beings perpetually fall short of God's glory. The word "glory" here refers not just to God's splendor but to the outward manifestation of His attributes, including His righteousness, justice, and holiness. Human beings perpetually fall short of God in these and other areas.

5. *Jesus on Sin.* The seriousness of man's sin problem comes into clearest focus in the teachings of Jesus. He taught that as a result of the Fall human beings are evil (Matthew 12:34) and that man is capable of great wickedness (Mark 7:20-23). Moreover, He said that man is utterly lost (Luke 19:10), that he is a sinner (Luke 15:10), and that he is in need of repentance before a holy God (Mark 1:15).

Jesus often spoke of sin in metaphors that illustrate the havoc sin can wreak in one's life. He described sin as blindness (Matthew 23:16-26), sickness (Matthew 9:12), being enslaved in bondage (John 8:34), and living in darkness (John 8:12; 12:35-46). Moreover, Jesus taught that this is a universal condition and that all people are guilty before God (Luke 7:37-48).

Jesus also taught that both inner thoughts and external acts render a person guilty (Matthew 5:28). He taught that from within the human heart come evil thoughts, sexual immorality, theft, murder, adultery, greed, malice, deceit, envy, slander, arrogance, and folly (Mark 7:21-23). Moreover, He affirmed that God is fully aware of every person's sins, both external acts and inner thoughts; nothing escapes His notice (Matthew 22:18; John 4:17-19).

6. *The Wonder of Salvation.* It is in view of the horrific nature of sin that the wonder of the salvation provided in Jesus Christ comes into clear focus. For Scripture indicates that those sinners who come to Christ and place their faith in Him are recipients of the most wonderful gift in the world—the free gift of eternal salvation (Ephesians 2:8-9). (See *Salvation.*)

Sinai Covenant—See *Covenants.*

Slavery

1. Slavery in Ancient Times ◆ 2. The Biblical View

S

1. *Slavery in Ancient Times.* The practice of human slavery was a way of life among the ancients. In fact, every ancient people of which there are historical records practiced slavery: Egyptians, Sumerians, Babylonians, Assyrians, Phoenicians, Syrians, Moabites, Ammonites, Edomites, Greeks, and Romans.

People could become slaves in any number of ways. For example, enemies captured in war could become enslaved (Genesis 14:21). A person in severe debt could place himself in slavery to pay the debt (Exodus 21:2-6). A thief who could not repay what he stole could be enslaved. A child born into a family of slaves would himself become a slave (Genesis 15:3).

Among most ancient peoples, slaves were considered property without any personal rights. This was not the case among the Israelites. Though slaves were still considered property, they had definite rights as defined under the Mosaic Law. In many cases, the slave was treated as a member of the family. Indeed, in many cases the slave was better off as a slave (in terms of having food and other provisions) than not as a slave. The law provided that no Israelite (including slaves) could be treated harshly (Leviticus 25:39), and if a slave was beaten, the law said he could go free (Exodus 21:26-27).

2. The Biblical View. Contrary to what some have claimed, the Bible does not condone slavery. From the very beginning, God declared that all humans are created in the image of God (Genesis 1:27). The apostle Paul also declared that "we are God's offspring" (Acts 17:29), and "From one man he made every nation of men, that they should inhabit the whole earth" (verse 26). Hence, all of us are equal before God.

Moreover, despite the fact that slavery was countenanced in the Semitic cultures of the day, the law in the Bible demanded that slaves eventually be set free (Exodus 21:2; Leviticus 25:40). Likewise, servants had to be treated with respect (Exodus 21:20,26). Israel, itself in slavery in Egypt for a prolonged time, was constantly reminded by God of this (Deuteronomy 5:15), and their emancipation became the model for the liberation of all slaves (see Leviticus 25:42).

Further, in the New Testament, Paul declared that in Christianity "there is neither Jew nor Greek, there is neither slave nor free, there is neither male nor female; for you are all one in Christ Jesus" (Galatians 3:28). All social classes are broken down in Christ; we are all equal before God.

Though the apostle Paul urged, "Slaves, obey your earthly masters" (Ephesians 6:5; Colossians 3:22), he was not approving of the institution of slavery, but was simply

S

alluding to the *de facto* situation in his day. He was simply instructing servants to be good workers, just as believers should be today, but he was not commending slavery. Paul also instructed all believers to be obedient to government (even if unjust) for the Lord's sake (Romans 13:1; see also Titus 3:1; 1 Peter 2:13). But this in no way condones oppression and tyranny, which the Bible repeatedly condemns (Exodus 2:23–25; Isaiah 10:1).

Sodom and Gomorrah—See *Archaeology.*

Solomon

1. Wisdom ♦ 2. Kingdom ♦ 3. Temple ♦
4. Heavy Taxes ♦ 5. Foreign Policy ♦
6. Disobedience

1. Wisdom. Solomon is best known for his incredible wisdom (1 Kings 3; 4:29-34). He wrote the majority of proverbs in the book of Proverbs and is known to have spoken some 3000 proverbs during his lifetime. His wisdom was unparalleled.

2. Kingdom. Solomon, the son and successor of David, became king in 970 B.C. at about 20 years of age (1 Kings 11:42). He inherited a peaceful kingdom from his father, and he worked hard to maintain that peace via military strength. It is significant that Solomon's name literally means "peaceful." Eventually, his peaceful kingdom would expand to some 50,000 square miles.

3. Temple. Among Solomon's major accomplishments was the building of a magnificent temple of God in Jerusalem. Hiram, the King of Tyre, aided Solomon in the building of the Jerusalem temple. He supplied trees, carpenters, and expert craftsmen for this project (2 Chronicles 2:3). Solomon raised

S

up an Israelite labor force of 30,000 men to assist Hiram in Lebanon's forests (1 Kings 5:13). Solomon also had 70,000 men to carry burdens, and 80,000 gathering stone in the mountains (1 Kings 5:15). It was a gargantuan building project.

4. Heavy Taxes. Israel enjoyed a golden age under Solomon's reign. He built Israel into a powerful industrial and trading nation (see 1 Kings 1–8). However, not all was perfect. Heavy taxes were inflicted upon the people as a means of paying for Israel's impressive building projects (1 Kings 12:4). Those who could not afford to pay such taxes found themselves doing hard labor.

5. Foreign Policy. History reveals that Solomon was very aggressive in his foreign policy. In sealing treaties in ancient days, it was customary for a lesser king to give his daughter in marriage to the greater king (in this case, Solomon). Every time a new treaty was sealed, Solomon ended up with yet another wife. These wives were considered tokens of friendship and sealed the relationship between the two kings (see 1 Kings 11:1-13). It may be that Solomon was not even personally acquainted with some of his many wives, even though he was married to them.

S

6. Disobedience. In the process of marrying many wives, Solomon was disobedient to the Lord. He was apparently so obsessed with power and wealth that it overshadowed his spiritual life and he ended up falling into apostasy in his old age (1 Kings 11:1-13). He worshiped some of the false gods of the women who became married to him. What a sad end to a great life!

Son of God—See *Jesus Christ.*

Song of Solomon

The Song of Solomon, also known as the Song of Songs in ancient Hebrew versions, was written by Solomon shortly after 971 B.C. Solomon is said to have written 1005 songs (1 Kings 4:32), and hence the ancient Hebrew rendering of the title of this book as "Song of Songs" is an indication that this is his best of the bunch.

The Song of Solomon is an extended poem, full of metaphors and imagery, which shows the richness of sexual love between husband (lover) and wife (his beloved) (see Song of Solomon 1:8–2:7). The backdrop, of course, is that God Himself created male and female (Genesis 1–2), and He created them as sexual beings (see Genesis 1:28). Therefore, sex within the boundaries of marriage is God-ordained and is to be enjoyed (see Genesis 2:24; Matthew 19:5; 1 Corinthians 6:16; Ephesians 5:31). Of course, in any deep relationship, there is both joy and pain, and the Song of Solomon reflects this, pointing to both the joys and heartaches of wedded love (Song of Solomon 5:2–7:9).

Some Bible expositors throughout the centuries have interpreted the Song of Solomon allegorically, saying it points to the love relationship between God and Israel. Others have said it is an allegory pointing to the love relationship between Christ and the church (his bride). However, there is no indication in the text of the book that it is to be taken in any other way than describing an amorous relationship between husband and wife.

Songs—See *Hymns and Songs.*

Sorcery—See *Divination and Sorcery.*

S

Soul

1. Living Being ♦ 2. Seat of Emotions and
Experience ♦ 3. Immaterial Nature

1. *Living Being.* The word "soul" is used in several different ways in Scripture. For example, the Hebrew word for "soul" *(nephesh)* can be used in reference to a living being. Genesis 2:7 is clearly an example of this: "And the LORD God formed man of the dust of the ground, and breathed into his nostrils the breath of life; and man became a living soul" (Genesis 2:7 KJV).

2. *Seat of Emotions and Experience.* Besides referring to living beings, the word *nephesh* ("soul") is also used in the Old Testament as the seat of the emotions and experiences. Man's *nephesh* can be sad (Deuteronomy 28:65 NASB), grieved (Job 30:25), pained (Psalm 13:2), distressed (Genesis 42:21 NASB), embittered (Job 3:20), troubled (Psalm 6:3), and cheered (Psalm 86:4). Clearly, man's "soul" can experience a wide range of emotional ups and downs.

In this sense, the word "soul" seems to refer to the "inner man" within the human being. This is in keeping with verses like 2 Kings 4:27b (NASB): "The man of God said, 'Let her alone, for her soul is troubled within her.'" Likewise, Psalm 42:6a says, "My soul is downcast within me," and Psalm 43:5 says, "Why are you downcast, O my soul? Why so disturbed within me?"

3. *Immaterial Nature.* The word "soul" can also refer to man's immaterial nature. An example of this may be Genesis 35:18, which says: "And it came about as her soul was departing, (for she died) that she called his name Benoni: but his father called him Benjamin." This seems to be equivalent to the Greek word for "soul" in the New Testament, *psuche.* In fact, *psuche* is often used to translate the Hebrew term *nephesh* into Greek.

An example of *psuche* in the New Testament is Matthew 10:28, in which Jesus says: "Do not fear those who kill the body but are unable to kill the soul; but rather fear him who is able to destroy both soul and body in hell." In this verse, *psuche* (or "soul") clearly refers to that part of man that continues on after physical death.

Another example of *psuche* in the New Testament is Revelation 6:9-10, where we read: "When he opened the fifth seal, I saw under the altar the souls of those who had been slain because of the word of God and the testimony they had maintained. They called out in a loud voice, 'How long, Sovereign Lord, holy and true, until you judge the inhabitants of the earth?'" Notice that the souls exist and are conscious despite the fact that they had been physically slain. The word "soul" here clearly refers to that immaterial part of man that survives physical death.

In this sense, the word "soul" is interchangeable with the word "spirit." For example, in Luke 23:46 we read the words Jesus uttered as He died on the cross: "Father, into your hands I commit my spirit." In context, it is clear that "spirit" here refers to Jesus' human immaterial nature that departed from His body at the moment of death (see also Acts 7:59; 2 Corinthians 5:6-8; Philippians 1:21-23).

Sports and Games

1. Athletics ◆ 2. Games

1. *Athletics*. Familiarity with Greek athletics helps us to properly understand some of the apostle Paul's teaching in the New Testament. For example, Paul made reference to running a race with a view to winning, keeping one's eye on the finish line (1 Corinthians 9:24). Paul also referred to boxing, using it as a metaphor to buffeting his body (9:26).

Winners of these contests in Greece would receive a crown of laurel, pine, or olive boughs. Likewise, the Christian who "runs to get the prize" can look forward to receiving a crown as a reward from God (1 Corinthians 9:25). In Greek athletics,

S

a government official or even an emperor bestowed the crown to the winning athlete. But for the Christian, Christ Himself will hand out these crowns at the judgment seat of Christ (2 Corinthians 5:10).

Another popular sport in biblical times was that of wrestling. The sport was popular not only in Israel but even in pagan nations like Babylon. We find a reference in the Old Testament to Jacob wrestling with God (Genesis 32:24).

2. Games. Certainly there were games for both children and adults in biblical times. For example, slinging stones at a target was a popular pastime. In this game, a person would put a stone in a slingshot pouch and swirl it round and round until he released it toward the target, much as David did in bringing down the giant Goliath. Whoever came closest to hitting the target would win.

Another popular pastime was shooting a bow and arrow. Sometimes a target would be set up and people would compete to see who could most accurately hit the target. At other times, people would compete to see who could shoot the arrow the furthest. Jonathan once used his archery skills in sending his friend David a message (1 Samuel 20:18-23).

Children would often invent games using stones. One popular pastime involved children digging a hole in the ground, and then standing a distance away from it, trying to throw stones into the hole. The child who succeeded was the winner.

Archaeologists have uncovered toys used by children in ancient times. Many of these toys apparently made a noise, such as rattling and whistling. Archaeologists have also discovered little dolls that girls played with. Further, miniature furniture and cooking pots have been discovered that date to between 900 and 600 B.C., indicating that girls apparently also played with miniature dollhouses in ancient Israel.

Archaeological discoveries further reveal that there were variations of hopscotch, chess, dice games, and other board games that were played among the people of ancient Israel.

314

(Recall that the soldiers threw dice or cast lots at Jesus' crucifixion.) Sometimes people have a stereotype in their mind that the ancients never had much fun. Apparently, they were interested in having fun just as modern people are.

Substitutionary Atonement—See *Atonement.*

Suffering

Job was an authority on suffering. Job 5:7 tells us, "Man is born to trouble as surely as sparks fly upward." Job 14:1 likewise states, "Man born of woman is of few days and full of trouble."

Suffering can be caused by a variety of things. Christians can suffer for the sake of the Gospel (2 Timothy 1:8). They can also suffer as a result of persecution (Matthew 5:10), as a result of Satanic affliction (Job 1–2), or as a result of God's discipline (Hebrews 12:5-11).

Yet Scripture affirms that no trouble can separate Christians from Christ (Romans 8:35). Further, Christians can rejoice in suffering because it produces patience and endurance in them (see Romans 5:3 5; 1 Peter 4:12-14). Even in the midst of suffering, Christ's consolation is abundant (2 Corinthians 1:5) and God restores His people (1 Peter 5:10). Christians must ever bear in mind that no amount of human suffering is comparable to the future glory they will inherit in heaven (Romans 8:18; 2 Corinthians 4:17-18).

S

Synagogue

1. *Synagogue Defined.* A synagogue is a place of worship for Jewish congregations. The word "synagogue" comes from the Greek *synagogue,* which means "a bringing together." At first, the word was used to refer to any gathering of people (religious or secular), but eventually the term came to be used almost wholly for Jewish religious assemblies.

2. History. Synagogues emerged during the time when Israel was in captivity in Babylon. They made great sense because the Jews had to worship somewhere (see Psalm 137), and since the temple had been destroyed in Jerusalem, there was really no other option. Besides, in their captivity, they were too far away from Jerusalem (which was the only place the temple could be built).

During New Testament times, most Jews met in local synagogues on the Sabbath day. Each community among the Jews had its own synagogue, and in each was a chest that contained scrolls of God's law. Jewish leaders would read from these scrolls each Sabbath.

3. Synagogue Services. The synagogue service would generally consist of a recitation of the Shema (Deuteronomy 6:4), a Scripture reading (one from the Law and one from the Prophets), prayer while facing Jerusalem, and a closing benediction. Synagogue leaders would sit in the front and face the congregation. Men and women would be separated so they could respectively listen to the reading and exposition of the Law and the Prophets without distraction.

4. Center of Jewish Life. The synagogue served as the heart of Jewish life in each community. During the week, Jewish children would attend school at the synagogue. Social events would also take place there. Moreover, local Jewish courts would meet at the synagogue to sentence offenders and hand out punishment (Matthew 10:17).

Tabernacle

1. Significance ◆ 2. Specifications ◆ 3. Two
Rooms ◆ 4. Tabernacle Furnishings

1. Significance. The word "tabernacle" means "dwelling place." The word almost always signifies the place where God dwells among His people (Leviticus 26:11). The tabernacle was truly the heart and center of Israelite religious life following the time of the Exodus. The entire tabernacle plan was designed to show that even though God loved and cared for His people, He was separated from them by virtue of His great holiness. The only way He could be approached was in the way stipulated by Him via the tabernacle.

The tabernacle was where the God of glory came to dwell among His people. When the tabernacle was completed, the Israelites watched as the cloud of glory covered the tabernacle, and the glory of the Lord filled it (Exodus 40:34). The Lord was now actually among His people.

2. Specifications. The tabernacle building was 45 feet by 15 feet. The specifications for the tabernacle called for wooden frames at the sides, top, and back of the structure. These frames were to be made with acacia wood. This type of wood is darker than oak wood and, fortunately for the Israelites, did not attract wood-eating insects. On the top and back of this wooden structure were placed a series of curtains (Exodus 26:1,2,7,13-14).

This tabernacle was to be constructed at the center of the Israelite community, with the tents of the 12 tribes of Israel erected around it. This represented the centrality of worship for the Israelites. It was at this tabernacle that sacrifices were offered to God by all the people of the community.

THE TABERNACLE

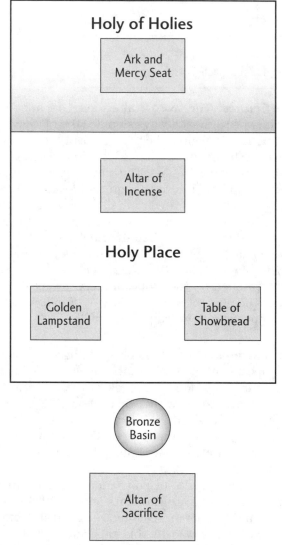

T

3. Two Rooms. The tabernacle had two rooms in it—the Holy Place (the larger room one entered upon walking through the outer door) and the inner Holy of Holies, where the presence of God dwelt (Exodus 26:33; Leviticus 16:2). The high priest was allowed to enter into the Holy of Holies only on the Day of Atonement (once a year), and there he offered a sacrifice for the sins of the people.

4. Tabernacle Furnishings. Perhaps the most important "furnishing" in the tabernacle was the Ark of the Covenant, which symbolized God's presence (1 Samuel 4:3-22). It served as the container of the covenant stones, which were a continual reminder of the covenant between God and Israel (Exodus 25:16,21). It also contained the pot of manna which symbolized the bread of God from heaven (Exodus 16:33). Aaron's rod was later placed in it as a witness to Israel of God's choice of the priesthood (Numbers 17:10). It was made of Acacia wood and was overlaid with gold. It had rings at the four corners, through which poles were inserted to make it easier to carry. The Ark stood in the Holy of Holies. It was believed that God was invisibly enthroned there.

Another furnishing, located in the Holy Place, was the altar of burnt offering, which was where sacrifices were offered to God by fire. It was made of wood and was covered by bronze. It measured about seven feet square and was about four feet high.

Another altar—the incense altar—was where incense was burned morning and evening when the priest tended to the lamp. Incense in the Bible is often representative of the prayers of God's people. The altar was made from acacia wood and overlaid with gold, just like the Ark of the Covenant.

Another furnishing in the Holy Place was the table of showbread, which, on each Sabbath, would have upon it 12 loaves of bread as a meal offering presented by the 12 tribes of Israel. The bread was not for God to eat but was a symbol of spiritual food (Leviticus 24:5-9). At the end of the week, when the

T

bread was changed, the priests were allowed to use the bread as food for themselves and their families.

One final furnishing was the golden lampstand, which was to be set on the south wall of the Holy Place (Exodus 26:35), opposite the table of showbread on the north so that the light would be reflected toward the table. The light was to burn perpetually, being serviced each evening and morning (Exodus 27:21; see also Leviticus 24:1-4). The lampstand provided light for the ministerial priests going about their duties.

Taxation

There were various kinds of taxes levied in biblical times. For example, the Mosaic law stipulated that every male adult 20 years of age was to be assessed a tax of one-half shekel to pay for expenses related to the tabernacle (Exodus 30:11-16). After Israel became a monarchy, with a king ruling, taxes included annual tributes to the king (1 Kings 4:21; 10:25) and import duties (1 Kings 10:14-15).

Israel enjoyed a golden age under Solomon's reign. He built Israel into a powerful industrial and trading nation with many beautiful buildings. However, he also inflicted heavy taxes upon the people to pay for these impressive building projects (1 Kings 12:4). Those who could not afford to pay such taxes found themselves doing hard labor (1 Kings 5:13-18).

During New Testament times, the Jews in Palestine were forced to pay heavy taxes to the Romans (see Matthew 22:21). These taxes were levied in order to pay for the presence of the four legions of Roman soldiers that were stationed there, bringing stability to the area.

The Zealots in New Testament times were a group of fanatical Jewish patriots who did not believe the Romans had the authority or right to impose such taxes on the Jewish people. Indeed, they considered it to be treason against God to pay taxes to the Roman emperor, for God was their true King. They were willing to fight to the death for their cause. They seized control of Jerusalem in A.D. 66, and this ultimately led to Rome's siege (and destruction) of the city in A.D. 70.

All in all, a significant part of one's income in biblical times went to paying taxes. In New Testament times, there were imperial Roman taxes, local administration taxes, and temple taxes. In some cases up to 20 percent of one's income went toward paying various taxes.

Teachers and Teaching—See *Education.*

Temple

1. The First Temple ◆ 2. The Second Temple ◆
3. The Third Temple

1. *The First Temple.* There were three different temples in Israel's history. David had sought to build the first temple for God, though it was not to happen because David was a warrior. It was his son Solomon who eventually built the temple (see 1 Kings 6–7; 2 Chronicles 3–4).

Built in Jerusalem, this temple was rectangular, running east and west, and measured about 87 by 30 feet. It was 43 feet high. The walls of the temple were made of cedar wood, and cherubim angels, flowers, and palm trees were carved into them. The walls were overlaid with gold. The floor was made of cypress.

Hiram, the king of Tyre, aided Solomon in the building of the Jerusalem temple. He supplied trees, carpenters, and expert craftsmen for this project (2 Chronicles 2:3-15). Solomon raised up an Israelite labor force of 30,000 men to assist Hiram in Lebanon's forests (1 Kings 5:13). Solomon also had 70,000 men to carry burdens, and 80,000 gathering stone in the mountains (1 Kings 5:15).

Like the tabernacle, Solomon's temple had a Holy Place and a Holy of Holies. In the Holy Place (the main outer room)

T

321

SOLOMON'S TEMPLE

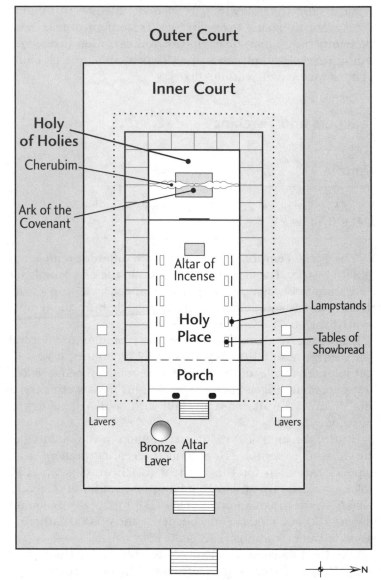

Outer Court

Inner Court

Holy of Holies

Cherubim

Ark of the Covenant

Altar of Incense

Lampstands

Holy Place

Tables of Showbread

Porch

Lavers

Lavers

Bronze Laver

Altar

N

T

was the golden incense altar, the table of showbread, and five pairs of lampstands, as well as utensils used for sacrifice. Double doors led into the Holy of Holies, in which was found the Ark of the Covenant. The Ark was between two wooden cherubim angels, each standing ten feet tall. God manifested Himself in the Holy of Holies in a cloud of glory (1 Kings 8:10-11).

This temple—the heart and center of Jewish worship for the kingdom of Judah—was eventually destroyed by Nebuchadnezzar and the Babylonians in 587 B.C.

2. The Second Temple. Following the Babylonian exile, many Jews returned to Jerusalem and constructed a smaller version of Solomon's temple. King Cyrus of Persia gave them permission to go, to return the temple vessels Nebuchadnezzar had looted, and to rebuild this temple.

The returned exiles started out well in 538 B.C., but they soon ran out of steam. The prophets Haggai and Zechariah had to work hard to encourage them, and finally, the second temple was completed in 515 B.C. However, it was not nearly as magnificent as Solomon's temple (see Ezra 3:12). It had little of its former glory and was a dim reflection of the original. This temple was without the Ark of the Covenant, which had never been recovered, and had only one seven-branched lampstand (Solomon's ten lampstands were never recovered). This temple lasted about 500 years.

3. The Third Temple. Israel's third temple in Jerusalem was built by King Herod the Great. Herod believed this ambitious building program, which he began in 19 B.C., would be a great way to earn favor with the Jews of his time (that is, his subjects), as well as impress the Roman authorities.

Completed in A.D. 64, it was much larger and more resplendent (with more gold) than Solomon's temple. It was an enormous, cream-colored temple that shone exceedingly bright during the day. It measured 490 yards (north to south) by 325 yards (east to west).

T

This magnificent temple ended up being destroyed in A.D. 70 along with the rest of Jerusalem by Titus and his Roman warriors, a mere six years after the project was completed. How ironic that those Herod sought to impress in Rome were the instigators of the temple's destruction.

Temptation

A temptation is an enticement to sin and be disobedient to God. Scripture warns that we are to be aware of the reality of temptations (Galatians 6:1) and make every effort not to let evil get the best of us (Romans 12:21). We are not to let sin control us (Romans 6:12), but rather must be cautious not to lose our secure footing (2 Peter 3:17). We are to bear in mind that if we get too close to the fire, metaphorically speaking, we may get burned (Proverbs 6:27-28).

Scripture thus exhorts us to keep alert and pray (Matthew 26:41). Indeed, we are to pray daily that we not succumb to temptation (Matthew 6:9-13) and are not overcome (Luke 22:40). Such temptations are said to emerge from our sinful nature (James 1:13-15).

One great temptation that has snared many is a love of money (1 Timothy 6:9-10; see also Deuteronomy 7:25). Sex is another temptation that has snared many (1 Corinthians 7:5). We are exhorted to not let Satan outsmart us (2 Corinthians 2:11), for he is a master tempter (Matthew 4:3; 1 Thessalonians 3:5). We are to resist his every effort (James 4:7).

Thankfully, God can prevent us from falling (Jude 24). Scripture reveals that when we are tempted, God will make a way of escape for us (1 Corinthians 10:13). Scripture also indicates that Jesus, our faithful High Priest, helps us in the midst of our temptations (Hebrews 2:14,18).

Ten Commandments

The Ten Commandments follow God's assertion that "I am the LORD your God..." (Exodus 20:1-17). These commandments would mean nothing if there were no God to whom human beings must answer. But because these laws came from a moral Lawgiver (God) who had just delivered His people from Egyptian bondage, it is good and right for His people to follow His instructions in how to live a good life.

The Ten Commandments can be broken down into two categories. The first four commandments pertain to the Israelites' relationship with God: 1) have no other gods, 2) have no graven images of God, 3) do not take the Lord's name in vain, 4) keep the Sabbath. The next six commandments deal with the Israelites' relationships with each other: 5) honor parents, 6) do not kill, 7) do not commit adultery, 8) do not steal, 9) do not bear false witness, and 10) do not covet.

In view of this, the total content of the Ten Commandments can be summarized in two briefer commandments: Love God and love your neighbor (Deuteronomy 6:5; Leviticus 19:18). For this reason, Jesus said that the greatest commandment is "Love the Lord your God," while the second is "Love your neighbor as yourself" (Matthew 22:37-39).

Theocracy

The word "theocracy" comes from the Greek *theokratia*, which is a compound word. *Theos* means "God," and *kratein* means "to rule" or "to govern." Hence, *theokratia* means "ruled by God" or "governed by God." In the Old Testament, Israel was viewed as a nation ruled by God (see Exodus 19:4-8; Deuteronomy 33:1-6).

God, as the divine King, made a covenant with His people, and the covenant contained stipulations that He expected the people to obey (see Deuteronomy 4:1-2). Of course, the people continually failed to obey the covenant stipulations, and God punished them by sending them into captivity.

There are other examples of "theocracy" in the Bible. For example, the Roman Empire was a kind of theocracy, loosely speaking, since the emperor was viewed as a god himself, a deified human king. Likewise, Egypt was a kind of theocracy,

T

loosely speaking, because the pharaoh was viewed as a god, the son of Re (the sun god).

Thessalonians, 1 and 2

The church of Thessalonica was founded around A.D. 50. Thessalonica was a capital of the Roman province of Macedonia in northern Greece. It was a very prosperous port.

Paul had visited Thessalonica for just a short time. He would have stayed longer, but Jewish resistance shortened his stay. The Jews were jealous when Paul won converts to Christianity from among their own. For Paul's own safety, the Christians in Thessalonica sent him to Berea (Acts 17:1-10).

Understandably, Paul, with a pastor's heart, very much wanted to know the situation of the young church in Thessalonica. Within a year he sent his young associate Timothy to Thessalonica to ascertain the status of the church. Timothy then delivered his report. Soon after, in early A.D. 51, Paul wrote these babes in Christ a letter in order to answer some of the questions they had about spiritual matters.

Paul had already taught them that Jesus would one day come again. But what about Christians who died before Christ came? What became of them? Apparently some of the Thessalonian Christians were very concerned about this, and Paul wrote 1 Thessalonians to comfort them in this regard. Paul assured them that the dead in Christ will indeed rise from the dead (1 Thessalonians 4:13-17), and hence there is no need to worry. Paul urged his readers to be constantly ready for the return of Christ.

Paul probably wrote 2 Thessalonians from Corinth during the summer of A.D. 51. Several months had passed since he had written 1 Thessalonians, and now he wrote 2 Thessalonians to further explain and clarify God's program of events relating to the Day of the Lord (including Christ's Second Coming) and to encourage the brethren to correct the disorders remaining among them.

More specifically, some of the Thessalonian brethren were apparently concerned that Christ had already returned, for some phony epistles had surfaced teaching this idea. Paul responded by teaching that there were certain noticeable events that would surround Christ's Second Coming, including the emergence of the Antichrist and various social upheavals (2 Thessalonians 2:1-12).

Paul also explained the proper attitude about working as one awaits the Second Coming. On the one hand, Paul clearly taught that believers should be constantly ready for Christ's coming. On the other hand, those people who were so caught up in prophetic excitement that they stopped working and lived off of others were to be rebuked (2 Thessalonians 3:6-13). Balance is necessary.

Time and Eternity

1. The Creation of Time ◆ 2. The Passing of Time ◆
3. Proper Perspective on Time ◆ 4. Eternal Life

1. *The Creation of Time.* Scripture is not clear about the relationship between time and eternity. Some prefer to think of eternity as time—a succession of moments—without beginning or ending. However, there are indications in Scripture that time itself may be a created reality—a reality that began when God created the universe.

The book of Hebrews contains some hints regarding the relationship between time and eternity. Hebrews 1:2 tells us that the Father "has spoken to us by his Son, whom he appointed heir of all things, and through whom he made the universe." This last phrase is rendered more literally from the Greek, "through whom indeed he made *the ages.*" Likewise, Hebrews 11:3 tells us that "by faith we understand that the universe was formed at God's command." This is more literally, "By faith we understand that *the ages* were formed by a word of God."

T

327

Scholars have grappled with what may be meant here by "the ages." Some conclude that this is a clear indication that time came into being when the creation came into being. Some believe it refers to not just vast periods of time, but all that transpires in them as well. Many modern theologians have thus concluded that church father and philosopher Augustine was right in saying that the universe was not created in time, but that time itself was created along with the universe. If this is correct, as Scripture seems to suggest, then it would not be correct to say that time already existed when God created the universe. Rather, the universe was created *with* time rather than *in* time.

2. *The Passing of Time.* When God created the earth and put man upon it, He Himself set boundaries for day and night (Job 26:10) and divided the year into seasons (Genesis 1:14). These are "handles" by which mere humans can orient themselves as time passes. As the days continually pass, so seasons eventually pass; and as seasons pass, so years eventually pass; and as years pass, we eventually die and enter into eternity—either an eternity with God in heaven (believers) or an eternity in hell (nonbelievers) (see Matthew 25:31-46). The decision we make about Christ during our short stay on earth thus becomes all-important.

3. *Proper Perspective on Time.* Scripture indicates that no matter what comes our way in life, our times are in God's hands (Psalm 31:15). Hence, we are to "trust in Him at all times" (Psalm 62:8). We are urged to make "the most of every opportunity, because the days are evil" (Ephesians 5:16). And because God is in sovereign control of the universe, we must ever be mindful that our plans for tomorrow are subject to God's will (James 4:13-17). Our goal should be to constantly be about the business of doing what is right, day in and day out (Psalm 106:3).

As for the prophetic future, God Himself is in control of that, and we can do nothing to change it. God has said,

"Have you not heard? Long ago I ordained it. In days of old I planned it; now I have brought it to pass..." (Isaiah 37:26). We cannot know the precise times when all God's prophetic promises will come to pass. "It is not for you to know the times or dates the Father has set by his own authority" (Acts 1:7).

4. Eternal Life. God is the only being in the universe that is eternal, never having been created. He has always existed. He never came into being at a point in time. He is beyond time altogether. He is the King eternal (1 Timothy 1:17) who alone is immortal (6:16). But those who trust in Christ are the recipients of "eternal life," and they will live with Him forever in heaven (John 3:16-17). Revelation 21:4 assures us that God "will wipe every tear from their eyes. There will be no more death or mourning or crying or pain, for the old order of things has passed away." What a day to look forward to!

Timothy, 1 and 2

Timothy was a young and trusted colleague of the apostle Paul. Already a believer, young Timothy joined Paul in Lystra and grew quickly in his spiritual life. So much did Paul trust Timothy that he appointed Timothy to be a leader in the church and even to represent Paul to others in various churches (Acts 17:14-15; 1 Corinthians 4:17).

In 1 Timothy, written in A.D. 62–64, Paul provided advice to Timothy regarding situations that might be encountered in the process of leading a church, including how to deal with false doctrine (1 Timothy 1:3-7; 4:1-3) and disorder in worship (2:1-15). Paul also discussed the qualifications for church leaders (3:1-13), and encouraged Timothy to stay focused on the work of ministry and to not get sidetracked. Paul is here speaking as a more mature, experienced pastor to a younger, inexperienced pastor.

When Paul wrote 2 Timothy (A.D. 66–67), he was in prison and expected to be executed shortly (2 Timothy 1:16; 2:9). Thus, this epistle contains the apostle's last words to Timothy

T

(see 4:6-8). The occasion for writing was no less than the need to maintain the faith, to hold on to sound doctrine, to be faithful in the work of ministry, and to preach the Gospel relentlessly (1:6,13-14; 3:14–4:5). As Moses gave the charge to Joshua, and the Lord to His apostles, so Paul gave the charge to Timothy. Paul was "passing the mantle of ministry" to his young friend. Paul also expressed his desire for his young friend to come visit him one last time (4:9,21), but there is no record of Timothy making it in time.

Tithing

The word "tithe" literally means "a tenth" in the Hebrew language. In Old Testament times, tithing was commanded by God on the basis that "the earth is the LORD's and everything in it, the world, and all who live in it" (Psalm 24:1). The tithe was a means whereby the people of God acknowledged that God owned all things and was sovereign over them. It was an acknowledgement that all the good things we have in life ultimately come from Him. Among the items God's people were commanded to tithe were the land and its produce (Leviticus 27:30; Deuteronomy 14:2), the animals (Leviticus 27:32), and new wine, oil, and honey (2 Chronicles 31:5). It is interesting to observe that withholding tithes and offerings from God is said to be robbing God (Malachi 3:8-10).

Despite the heavy emphasis on tithing in the Old Testament, many Bible expositors today do not believe that tithing is intended for the New Testament church—at least as a commandment from the law. In fact, there is not a single verse in the New Testament where God specifies that believers should give 10 percent of their income to the church. Yet this should not be taken to mean that church members should not support the church financially. The New Testament emphasis seems to be on what might be called "grace giving." We are to freely give as we have been freely given to. And we are to give as we are able (2 Corinthians 8:12). For some, this will mean less than 10 percent. But for others whom God has

330

materially blessed, this will mean much more than 10 percent.

The starting point for having a right attitude toward giving to the church is that we must first give ourselves to the Lord. The early church is our example: "They gave themselves first to the Lord and then to us in keeping with God's will" (2 Corinthians 8:5). Only when we have given ourselves to the Lord will we have a proper perspective on money.

We also read in Romans 12:1, "Offer your bodies as living sacrifices, holy and pleasing to God—this is your spiritual act of worship." The first sacrifice we make to God is not financial. First, we sacrifice our own lives. As we give ourselves unconditionally to the Lord for His service, our attitude toward money will be what it should be. God is not interested in our money until He first has our hearts.

Titus

Paul wrote this "pastoral epistle" to Titus, a young pastor and leader of the church in Crete, between A.D. 62 and 64. Titus was one of the apostle Paul's trusted inner circle of friends and ministry associates. He was a "partner and fellow worker" with Paul (2 Corinthians 8:23) and traveled with him on some of his missionary journeys. Titus was also an uncircumcised Gentile who illustrated one of Paul's teachings: Gentiles need not be circumcised to be saved.

In this short letter, Paul focused heavy attention on warning against false teachers (Titus 1:10-16) and urged Titus to pursue—along with his congregation—sound doctrine and good works (1:9; 2:1–3:11). The nature of the false teaching is not entirely clear, though it seems to relate to "Jewish fables," circumcision, genealogies, and Jewish legalism (see Titus 1:10,14; 3:9-10). At all costs, the flock (church) must be protected against such false teachers. As Paul put it, "They must be silenced" (1:11).

T

Tools

A variety of tools were used in biblical times. Metal saws with teeth were used to cut wood or stone (1 Kings 7:9); mallets and hammers were used to hammer objects (Judges 4:21; 1 Kings 6:7); chisels were used for cutting wood or stone (Isaiah 44:13); awls and drills were used for making holes (Exodus 21:6; Deuteronomy 15:17); furnaces were used for pottery and metallurgy (Isaiah 41:7); bellows were used to blow air into furnaces to make them hotter (Jeremiah 6:29); and tongs were used to handle hot objects (Isaiah 44:12).

Moreover, anvils were used as a surface against which metal could be hammered (Isaiah 41:7); axes were used for chopping purposes (Deuteronomy 19:5); knives were used for cutting objects (Genesis 22:6); files were used to sharpen metal blades (1 Samuel 13:21); nails were used to fasten objects (1 Chronicles 22:3); and planes were used to shape wood (Isaiah 44:13).

Further, a plumb line—a weight hanging on a cord—was used to ensure that a building was erected straight vertically (Amos 7:7); a compass was used for sketching circles (Isaiah 44:13); mills and millstones were used for the grinding of grain (Judges 16:21); harrows were used to plow ground (2 Samuel 12:31 KJV); yokes were used for harnessing animals for plowing purposes (1 Samuel 11:7); mattocks were used to weed gardens (1 Samuel 13:20-21); shovels were used for winnowing (Isaiah 30:24); pruning hooks were used to prune grapevines (Isaiah 18:5); sickles were used for cutting stalks of grain (Joel 3:13); and needles were used for weaving (Exodus 26:1-13). These and other such tools made life much easier for the Israelites.

Torah

The Torah refers to the first five books of the Bible: Genesis, Exodus, Leviticus, Numbers, and Deuteronomy. The word "Torah" literally means "instruction," "guidance," or "teaching."

This gives a clue as to the purpose of the Torah. This "law" from God instructs, guides, and teaches people in how they are to live. The five books in the Torah guide people in their relationships with other people, with God, the natural world around them; it also instructs people on the nature of both God and man. It is considered to teach a total way of life.

Eventually the Old Testament Torah was translated into Greek and was referred to as the Pentateuch (which literally means "five scrolls" or "five volumes"). (See *Pentateuch, Genesis, Exodus, Leviticus, Numbers, Deuteronomy.*)

Towns—See *Houses and Tents.*

Trade—See *Commerce and Trade.*

Tradition, Oral

1. Oral Tradition Among the Ancients ◆
2. Supremacy of Scripture

1. Oral Tradition Among the Ancients. Among the ancients, much attention was paid to accuracy and reliability in carrying on the oral traditions. This is less an emphasis today, for we have computers, electronic organizers, and day planners to track various details we need to remember. But among the ancients, great value was placed on accuracy in passing on the oral traditions because it was by this means that customs, practices, and teachings were handed down generation to generation by the Jews. Unfortunately, many of the Pharisees ended up making their traditions more authoritative than Scripture. Jesus stood against this mentality (Matthew 15:2-3).

2. Supremacy of Scripture. Jesus told the Pharisees and teachers of the law: "You nullify the word of God for the sake

333

of your tradition" (Matthew 15:6). There is no doubt that Jesus here prioritized the Word of God over tradition and pointed to the Word of God as the final authority. Jesus said, "Scripture cannot be broken" (John 10:35). He also said, "I tell you the truth, until heaven and earth disappear, not the smallest letter, not the least stroke of a pen, will by any means disappear from the Law until everything is accomplished" (Matthew 5:18). He said, "It is easier for heaven and earth to disappear than for the least stroke of a pen to drop out of the Law" (Luke 16:17).

Jesus used Scripture, not tradition, as the final court of appeal in every matter under dispute. To the Sadducees He said, "You are in error because you do not know the Scriptures or the power of God" (Matthew 22:29). Jesus informed some Pharisees, "You have let go of the commands of God and are holding on to the traditions of men" (Mark 7:8). To the devil, Jesus consistently responded, "It is written..." (Matthew 4:4-10). In Colossians 2:8 the apostle Paul warns: "See to it that no one takes you captive through hollow and deceptive philosophy, which depends on human tradition and the elementary principles of this world, rather than on Christ." In view of such verses, it is clear that Scripture alone is our supreme and final authority.

Travel and Transport

1. Walking ◆ 2. Chariots ◆ 3. Roman Roads ◆
4. Portable Chairs ◆ 5. Sailing ◆ 6. Caravan

1. Walking. Most traveling in biblical days was done by simple walking. Sometimes a traveling family would also bring a pack animal such as a mule to carry their belongings, but family members themselves would still walk. Generally, assuming decent traveling conditions, people could cover about 16 miles per day on foot. This would mean that Joseph and Mary's foot trip from Nazareth to Bethlehem probably took them about five days (Luke 2:1-7).

2. Chariots. Wheeled transport was quite limited, especially in Old Testament times. While the rich could afford horse-drawn chariots, they did not have modern (smooth) roads, and since much of the ground was rough and bumpy, travel by chariots was not comfortable.

3. Roman Roads. By the first century A.D., the Romans had built a road system that connected all the provinces of the Roman Empire. The roads were made as straight as possible and were paved. The practical benefit of this for the empire is that troops could be moved quickly, couriers could deliver messages quickly, wheeled chariots became more common as a means of travel, and travel for common people on foot was made easier. During this time, the Romans policed the major roads, so travel was safer. Some Roman roads survive even to the present day, indicating how well they were constructed.

4. Portable Chairs. A popular mode of transportation in biblical days was the "litter." This was basically a couch or chair with a curtain around it that rested on two poles—what one might call a "portable chair." These poles enabled the litter to be carried by one man in the front and one in the back. Of course, because most people could not afford to hire two men to be at their disposal for traveling purposes, this mode of transportation was more common among the wealthier class.

5. Sailing. In both the Old and New Testaments, sailing was a common means of transportation. The Egyptians and Phoenicians were famous for their ships, used for both warfare and trading. During the reign of Solomon, Israel developed a fleet of ships (1 Kings 9:26; see also Jonah 1; Acts

T

13:4; 27:1-44). Sailing was typically done between the months of May and September (Acts 27:9).

6. Caravan. When travelers had a long way to go, it was safest to travel with a caravan—a convoy of other travelers with pack animals. There were plenty of caravan routes connected to Palestine.

Treaties

In biblical times there were treaties or alliances between nations (1 Samuel 11:1; 27:1-12; 1 Kings 5:1-12), between individual people (Genesis 21:22-34; 31:43-55), between individual tribes of Israel (Judges 4:10; 6:35), between friends (1 Samuel 18:3-4), and between God and His people (for example, the Sinai Covenant, Exodus 19–20). At Sinai, the Israelites were forbidden by God to make any treaties with the pagan Canaanites (Exodus 23:32).

One common type of ancient treaty was the Hittite suzerainty treaty that was made between a king and his subjects. Such a treaty would always include a preamble naming the author of the treaty, a historical introduction depicting the relationship between the respective parties, a list of required stipulations explaining the responsibilities of each of the parties, a promise of either blessing or judgment depending on faithfulness or unfaithfulness to the treaty, a solemn oath, and a religious ratification of the treaty. In such treaties, the motivation for obedience to the stipulations was the undeserved favor of the king making the treaty. Out of gratitude, the people were to obey the stipulations. It is interesting to observe that the Sinai Covenant God made with the Israelites was styled after the ancient Hittite suzerainty treaties, showing that God communicated to His people in forms they were familiar with.

Trees and Shrubs

The Bible mentions a variety of trees and shrubs, which served a variety of purposes among the people. Fig trees, for example, produced figs, a popular snack in Bible times (Luke 19:4). Olive trees produced olives, which could either be eaten or pressed to extract olive oil, which was used for cooking. Olive oil was also used as a fuel for lamps and to anoint kings and priests (see Exodus 25:6; 35:8). Oak trees, which grew on the hills of Israel, produced wood used for making various objects, such as oars for boats. The cedar tree was used in Solomon's day to obtain wood for the paneling of the temple and palace he built (1 Kings 6:15-18). Fir and pine trees, which grew on the hills of Israel, also provided wood for use in the building of Solomon's temple, as well as for building the decks of ships (1 Kings 5:8). The acacia tree grows in the Sinai desert and provided the wood used in the building of the Ark of the Covenant (Exodus 25:10), as well as parts of the tabernacle. Palm trees provided clusters of dates, a tasty food. Vines produced grapes, an important fruit in biblical times. Grapes were used to make wine, which would then be stored in wineskins. Interestingly, Jesus spoke of Himself as the "true vine," providing nourishment to His followers, the branches (see John 15).

Tribulation Period—See *End Times.*

T

Trinity

1. Definition ◆ 2. Clarifying the Trinity ◆
3. Biblical Basis for the Doctrine

1. *Definition.* There is one God, but in the unity of the Godhead are three co-equal and co-eternal persons—the Father, the Son, and the Holy Spirit, who are equal in terms of the divine nature but distinct in personhood.

2. *Clarifying the Trinity.* It is important that we clarify what we *do not* mean by the word "Trinity." We must avoid two errors: 1) that the Godhead is composed of three utterly distinct persons such as Peter, James, and John, a concept that would lead to what is known as tritheism (belief in three different gods); and 2) that the Godhead is one person only and the triune aspect of His being is no more than three fields of interest, activities, and manifestations, which is referred to in theology as modalism. The fallacy of these errors will become clearer as we examine the biblical evidence for the Trinity below.

3. *Biblical Basis for the Doctrine.* The doctrine of the Trinity is based on three lines of evidence: evidence that there is only one true God, evidence that there are three persons who are God, and evidence that indicates three-in-oneness within the Godhead.

A. *Evidence for One God.* That there is only one true God is the consistent testimony of Scripture from Genesis to Revelation. It is like a thread that runs through every page of the Bible. God positively affirmed through Isaiah the prophet: "This is what the LORD says—Israel's King and Redeemer, the LORD Almighty: I am the first and I am the last; apart from me there is no God" (Isaiah 44:6; see also 46:9). The oneness of God is also often emphasized in the New Testament (John 5:44; 17:3; Romans 3:29-30; 16:27; 1 Corinthians 8:4; Galatians 3:20; Ephesians 4:6; 1 Timothy 2:5; and James 2:19).

B. *Evidence for Three Persons Who Are Called God.* While Scripture is clear there is only one God, in the unfolding of God's revelation to humankind it also becomes clear that there are three distinct persons who are called God in Scripture:

- *The Father Is God:* Peter refers to the saints "who have been chosen according to the foreknowledge of God the Father" (1 Peter 1:2).

- *Jesus Is God:* The Father said of Jesus, "Your throne, O God, will last for ever and ever, and righteousness will be the scepter of your kingdom" (Hebrews 1:8).

- *The Holy Spirit Is God:* In Acts 5:3-4, lying to the Holy Spirit is equated to lying to God.

Moreover, each of the three persons on different occasions are seen to possess the attributes of deity. For example, all three are said to be omnipresent: the Father (Matthew 6:4,6,18), the Son (Matthew 28:18-20), and the Holy Spirit (Psalm 139:7). All three are omniscient: the Father (Romans 11:33), the Son (Matthew 9:4), and the Holy Spirit (1 Corinthians 2:10). All three are omnipotent: the Father (1 Peter 1:5), the Son (Matthew 28:18), and the Holy Spirit (Romans 15:19). Furthermore, holiness is ascribed to each person: the Father (Revelation 15:4), the Son (Acts 3:14), and the Holy Spirit (John 16:7-11). Eternity is ascribed to each person: the Father (Psalm 90:2), the Son (Revelation 1:8,17-18), and the Holy Spirit (Hebrews 9:14).

C. *Three-In-Oneness in the Godhead.* In the New American Standard Bible, Matthew 28:19 reads: "Go therefore and make disciples of all the nations, baptizing them in the name of *the Father* and *the Son* and *the Holy Spirit*" (emphasis added). The word "name" is singular in the Greek, indicating that there is one God, but these are three distinct persons within the Godhead—the Father, the Son, and the Holy Spirit. Notice there is a definite article ("the") before the Father, the Son, and the Holy Spirit. These definite articles clearly show a distinction between the three. Hence, though there is one God (as indicated by the singular name), there are three persons within the Godhead (see also 2 Corinthians 13:14).

T

Twelve Tribes of Israel

The Israelites were divided into 12 tribes, descended from the 12 sons of Jacob. Different portions of the land of Canaan—the Promised Land, flowing with milk and honey—were given to each tribe. Reuben, Gad, and half of the tribe of Manasseh, settled in the east, while Asher, Naphtali, Zebulon, Issachar, Ephraim, and the other half-tribe of Manasseh settled in the northwest. Benjamin, Judah, Simeon, and Dan settled in the southwest.

T

U

Universe

1. *The Glory of the Universe.* As a young shepherd, David must have spent many nights under the open sky as he led his sheep across vast fields of green. Looking up to the starry heavens at night, waves of emotion must have swept through him as he contemplated how the Lord—his divine Shepherd—had created all of it. On one such night, David penned Psalm 19, and said: "The heavens declare the glory of God; the skies proclaim the work of his hands. Day after day they pour forth speech; night after night they display knowledge. There is no speech or language where their voice is not heard. Their voice goes out into all the earth, their words to the ends of the world" (Psalm 19:1-4). It was the Lord who created the universe. And David considered the magnificence of interstellar space a testimony to the glory of the Creator.

2. *The Majesty of the Universe.* Only about 4000 stars are visible to the human eye without a telescope. However, the Creation's true vastness becomes evident when we realize that with the giant telescopes now available, astronomers have estimated that there are about 10^{25} stars (that is, 10 million billion billion) in the known universe. It has also been estimated that there are about the same number of grains of sand in the world—essentially impossible to count. And who but God knows how many stars exist beyond the reach of our telescopes?

What is truly fascinating is that even though the stars are innumerable from man's perspective, God knows precisely

U

341

how many exist and has even assigned a name to each one of them (Psalm 147:4; Isaiah 40:26). In the same way that Adam named animals based upon the characteristics of those animals (Genesis 2:19-20), so God in His infinite wisdom named each star according to its particular characteristics.

The grandeur of the created universe is evident not only in the number of stars but also in their incredible distances from each other. The sun, for example, is about 93 million miles from earth. The moon is only about 211,453 miles way. Scientists tell us that light travels at 186,000 miles per second, so a beam of light would travel from the earth to the moon in just one and a half seconds. It would take that same beam of light 35 minutes to reach Jupiter (367 million miles away), and an hour and eleven seconds to reach Saturn (790 million miles away). It would take the light beam almost 25 days to reach the North Star, about 400 billion miles away. Even then, one has only just begun to journey into our vast universe. God created all of it.

3. *Earth: A Center of Divine Activity.* In view of the sheer vastness of the stellar universe, it is truly amazing that God sovereignly chose our tiny planet as a center of divine activity. Relatively speaking, the earth is but an astronomical atom among the whirling constellations, only a tiny speck of dust among the ocean of stars and planets in the universe. To the naturalistic astronomer, the earth is but one of many planets in our small solar system, all of which are in orbit around the sun. But the earth is nevertheless the center of God's work of salvation in the universe. For, indeed, it was on the earth that God created man and has appeared to people throughout biblical times. It was on the earth that Jesus became incarnate and died for the sins of man. It will be to the earth that the Lord Jesus comes again at the Second Coming. And He will then create the new heavens and new earth (Revelation 21:1).

The centrality of the earth is also evident in the creation account, for God created the earth *before* He created the rest of the planets and stars. Why did God create the sun, moon, and stars on the fourth day rather than the first day? Apparently because the earth is the central planet in God's sovereign plan.

U

Virgin Birth

1. *Definition.* The virgin birth is the theological teaching that Christ was miraculously conceived in Mary's womb when the Holy Spirit overshadowed her (see Matthew 1:18,20-25; Luke 1:26-38). This doctrine focuses on the means whereby the eternal Son of God entered human existence. The divine nature of the eternal Son of God was joined, within Mary's womb, with a human nature by a direct supernatural act of God.

In reality, of course, it was the conception of Christ in Mary's womb that was supernatural. The actual birth of Christ was quite normal, aside from the protecting and sanctifying ministry of the Holy Spirit.

2. *Necessity of the Virgin Birth.* Bible scholars believe there are at least five good reasons why the virgin birth of Christ was necessary:

- The doctrine of the virgin birth relates directly to the issue of whether Jesus was a supernatural as opposed to a merely natural being.

- By the virgin birth God kept Jesus from possessing a sin nature from Joseph (see 2 Corinthians 5:21; 1 Peter 2:22-24; Hebrews 4:15; 7:26).

- The Old Testament makes it clear that Jesus had to be both God *and* man as the Messiah (see Isaiah 7:14; 9:6). This could only be fulfilled through the virgin birth.

- Related to the above, Jesus is our Kinsman-Redeemer. In Old Testament times the next of kin (one related by blood) always functioned as the kinsman-redeemer of a family member who needed redemption from jail. Jesus became related to us by blood so He could function as our Kinsman-Redeemer and rescue us from sin. This required the virgin birth.

- The virgin birth was necessary in view of the prediction in Genesis 3:15 (Jesus was predicted to come from the "seed of the woman").

Vows—See *Oaths.*

W

Warfare

The Old Testament is filled with stories of war and warfare. Initially, Israel had no formal army, for God was their protector. But they eventually developed one under the leadership of their first king, Saul, whom the people had demanded (1 Samuel 8–9).

Under the leadership of King David, increasing stress was laid upon military tactics and effective plans for victory. There was emphasis on surprise, ambush, and surrounding the enemy (see 2 Samuel 5:23). As part of David's defensive strategy, he built fortresses in Libnah, Lachish, Gezer, and Beth-horon. When attacking other cities, battering rams and catapults were used.

Under the leadership of Solomon, David's son and successor, a cavalry and chariots were introduced into Israel's army, much like those used by the Egyptians and Philistines. The standing foot army remained the most important component of Israel's army, however, for most of Israel's battles were fought in the rocky hills, where chariots and cavalry were not nearly as effective as on flat land. Foot soldiers were trained in hand-to-hand combat, using swords, clubs, axes, and the like, but were also skilled in using slings and bows and arrows. Soldiers wore armor to protect themselves and used a shield for defense.

Such military preparedness was important for Israel, for pagan nations like the Philistines and Babylonians often attacked. Not only was there loss of life during these attacks, but crops were destroyed, which eliminated the food supply for those Israelites that survived the attack. These pagan nations also stole cattle, plundered the cities, and enslaved the population.

It is interesting to observe that in the Old Testament, God Himself is often portrayed as playing a role in battling against

Israel's enemies (Exodus 15:3; 2 Chronicles 20:15-29; Psalm 24:8). God is even described sometimes in military terms— as the "LORD of hosts" (for example, 2 Samuel 6:2,18 NASB).

Weaponry and Arms

There were a variety of weapons used in biblical times for both offensive and defensive purposes. Some of the knowledge we have about such weapons is from the Bible; other knowledge comes to us from the science of archaeology. Following are some of the more prominent weapons and armory:

- The battle ax was used in hand-to-hand combat and was especially revered for its ability to pierce body armor. This weapon was especially common among the Egyptians and Babylonians (Jeremiah 46:22; Ezekiel 26:9 NASB).

- The battering ram was used to knock down a city's walls (Ezekiel 26:9). It was basically a long pole held by a number of men. Sometimes battering rams were on wheels, making them easier to maneuver.

- Body armor—including a breastplate and helmet— were made of metal, thick leather, or both and served to protect soldiers in battle (see Nehemiah 4:16; 1 Samuel 17:5-6). Soldiers used shields typically made of metal or leather to block arrows or other weapons in battle (1 Chronicles 5:18).

- Bows and arrows were popular weapons in the open field (Genesis 21:20; Zechariah 9:10).

- Chariots, which are essentially rapidly deployed wheeled battle platforms, often had two soldiers aboard them, one to navigate the chariot and one to do battle with a bow and arrow. The first chariots mentioned in Scripture are those affiliated with the Egyptian army (Genesis 41:43; Exodus 14:6-9).

W

347

- The club was a heavy piece of wood used in hand-to-hand combat, useful for battering an opponent. Sometimes metal was added to the club to make it deadlier (Proverbs 25:18; 2 Samuel 23:21).

- The sword was a piercing or cutting weapon designed to kill or maim. Swords were the basic weapons of the Hebrew soldier (2 Kings 3:26).

- The spear was a long shaft with a metal point that could either be thrust with the hands or thrown at a distance (Joshua 8:18-19; 1 Samuel 18:10-11).

- The sling was made of leather and was used to launch small stones or pebbles. These weapons could be extremely deadly, though use of the sling required a great deal of training. (David possessed great expertise in using the sling—1 Samuel 17:4-51.)

Wisdom

The main Hebrew word for wisdom in the Old Testament is *hokmah*. It was used commonly for the skill of craftsmen, sailors, singers, administrators, and counselors. *Hokmah* pointed to the experience and efficiency of these various workers in using their skills. Similarly, a person who possesses *hokmah* in his spiritual life and relationship to God is one who is both knowledgeable and experienced in following God's way. Biblical wisdom involves skill in the art of godly living. This wisdom, which makes for skilled living, is broad in its scope, teaching students how to be successful at home, at work, in human relationships, regarding money, regarding death and the afterlife, and much more (see Proverbs 1–9).

W

Wisdom Literature—See *Poetry and Wisdom Literature.*

Witchcraft—See *Magic and Witchcraft.*

Woe

The Hebrew word for "woe" was used by Old Testament prophets to point to impending doom, grief, and sorrow. It speaks of a dire threat voiced in the face of present or coming danger. Isaiah used the word "woe" 22 times—more than any other prophet. In most instances, he used it in the context of the approaching captivity. Jesus pronounced severe woes on the scribes and Pharisees (see Luke 11:42-44).

Women

1. Oppression of Women ◆ 2. Liberty for Women

1. *Oppression of Women.* The woman is "in all things inferior to the man," said first-century Jewish historian Flavius Josephus *(Against Apion,* 622). A common Jewish blessing was: "Blessed be the Lord, who did not make me a heathen; blessed be he who did not make me a woman; blessed be he who did not make me an uneducated person."

Jewish rabbis in the first century were encouraged not to teach or even to speak with women. Jewish wisdom literature tells us that "he that talks much with womankind brings evil upon himself and neglects the study of the Law and at the last will inherit Gehenna [hell]" *(M. Aboth* 1.5). One reason for the avoidance of women was the belief that they could lead men astray: "From garments cometh a moth and from a woman the iniquities of a man" (Ecclesiasticus 42:13). Indeed, men were often viewed as intrinsically better than women, for "better is the iniquity of a man than a woman doing a good turn" (Ecclesiasticus 42:14).

In view of this low status of women, it is not surprising that they enjoyed few legal rights in Jewish society. Women were

W

not even allowed to give evidence in a court of law. Moreover, according to the rabbinic school that followed Rabbi Hillel, a man could legally divorce his wife if she just burned his dinner.

2. *Liberty for Women.* It was in this oppressive context that Christianity was born. Many people—both men and women—have hailed Jesus a protector of women because of His elevation of them in a male-chauvinist society. Moreover, Paul's statement in Galatians 3:28—"There is neither Jew nor Greek, slave nor free, male nor female, for you are all one in Christ Jesus"—has been called by some the Magna Carta of humanity.

Certainly, from a biblical standpoint, God equally values both men and women. God created both men and women in His own image (Genesis 1:26). Both men and women were instructed by God to exercise authority over God's creation (Genesis 1:28). Christian men and women are positionally equal before God (Galatians 3:28). Jesus allowed women to sit at His feet, the place normally reserved by rabbis for male disciples alone (Luke 10:38-42). He allowed women to accompany Him and His disciples when they traveled (Luke 8:1-3). The early church, following Jesus' lead, did not separate men from women as was the practice in Jewish synagogues.

Even in the Old Testament, we find that leadership is not restricted to men alone. Certainly Miriam played no small role in the Exodus account (for example, Exodus 15:20). Deborah was a judge (Judges 4:4). Lydia was apparently influential in the Philippian church (Acts 16:14,40). And Phoebe may have been a deaconess in Cenchrea (Romans 16:1). Hence, even though the Bible does speak of the husband being the head of the family (1 Corinthians 11:3), and teaches that only males are to be pastors of the church (1 Timothy 2:11-12), women are certainly portrayed in Scripture as participating in various leadership roles. Notice that the great Apollos was trained by Aquila *and* Priscilla (Acts 18:26).

Work Versus Laziness

The Bible has a lot to say about work versus laziness. Solomon, the wisest man who ever lived, addresses the subject often in the book of Proverbs. He points out that the lazy person's home and field is practically in ruins because he never works but sleeps most of the time (Proverbs 24:30-34). Because he does not work, he ends up with nothing (20:4). Lazy hands truly make a man poor (10:4). Such a person has a tough life and suffers the consequences of his laziness (15:19). Yet he continually makes excuses to get out of work, instead of working to make a better life (22:13; 26:13). He also acts like a know-it-all, not listening to the wisdom of others (26:16). This kind of person is a continual pain to employers (10:26). He is always chasing fantasies instead of doing real work (28:19). He may *say* he intends to do a good job, but mere talk leads only to poverty (14:23).

Solomon thus warns against loving sleep too much, because it will inevitably lead to poverty (Proverbs 20:13). Indeed, drowsiness is said to clothe a person in rags (23:21). A wise person works whenever work needs to be done (10:5). Solomon recommends that we learn a lesson from the ant: "Go to the ant, you sluggard; consider its ways and be wise! It has no commander, no overseer or ruler, yet it stores its provisions in summer and gathers its food at harvest. How long will you lie there, you sluggard? When will you get up from your sleep?" (6:6-9).

God Himself is our example, for He worked hard for six days (doing the "work" of creation), and then rested on the seventh day (Genesis 2:2-3). Jesus and the apostle Paul are our examples too, for Jesus worked hard as a carpenter (see Mark 6:3), and Paul worked hard as a tentmaker (Acts 18:3).

W

After God created man, "The LORD God took the man and put him in the Garden of Eden to work it and take care of it" (Genesis 2:15). From the very beginning, it has been God's will that man engage in work.

Worship and Praise

The Bible teaches that God alone is to be worshiped—not human beings, not angels, not idols, not anything else (Matthew 4:10; Acts 14:11-18; Revelation 19:10). Worship involves reverencing God, adoring Him, praising Him, venerating Him, and paying homage to Him, not just externally (by rituals and singing songs) but in our hearts as well (Isaiah 29:13; see also 1 Samuel 15:22-23).

The Hebrew word for worship, *shaha,* means "to bow down" or "to prostrate oneself" (see Genesis 22:5; 42:6). Likewise, the New Testament word for worship, *proskuneo,* means "to prostrate oneself" (see Matthew 2:2,8,11). In Old English, "worship" was rendered "worthship," pointing to the worthiness of the God we worship. Such worship is the proper response of a creature to the divine Creator (Psalm 95:6). Worship can be congregational in nature (1 Corinthians 11–14) or individual (see Romans 12:1). Worship does not stop on earth but continues in heaven when believers enter into glory (see Revelation 4–5).

While it is the Scriptural teaching that only God should be worshiped (Exodus 34:14), Scripture clearly shows that Jesus, as God, is to be worshiped just as the Father is worshiped (see Revelation 4–5). Christ was worshiped (Greek: *proskuneo)* as God many times according to the Gospel accounts—and He always accepted such worship as perfectly appropriate. Jesus accepted worship from Thomas (John 20:28), the angels (Hebrews 1:6), wise men (Matthew 2:11), a leper (Matthew 8:2), a ruler (Matthew 9:18), a blind man (John 9:38), Mary Magdalene (Matthew 28:9), and the disciples (Matthew 28:17).

The most common way of worshiping God is to express adoration and praise to God through songs, hymns, and rituals. But Scripture also teaches that we worship God when we give ourselves totally over to Him on a day-to-day basis. This is taught in Romans 12:1: "I urge you, brothers, in view of God's mercy, to offer your bodies as living sacrifices, holy and pleasing to God—this is your spiritual act of worship."

Offering one's body to God is an act of giving God all that we are. Since the body is the vehicle through which we do all things (both good and bad), the giving of our bodies to God is an act of unconditional surrender to His purposes and will in our lives. Scripture calls this a "spiritual act of worship" on our part.

Writing and Record Keeping

In ancient times, people often wrote on stone (individual stones or the stone walls of caves), clay tablets, and bricks. A chisel was used to make inscriptions on these surfaces (see Exodus 32:16; Job 19:23-24). People would also write on animal skins, leaves, bark, pieces of wood, and potsherds. The ink was generally black, made of soot, oil, and gummy substances.

One of the most popular means of writing in Bible times was writing on a long strip of papyrus, on which the writing was done in columns with a pen and ink, sometimes on both sides (Isaiah 8:1). These sheets of papyrus would be glued side by side to make the scrolls longer, though rarely would a scroll have more than 20 sheets. Biblical scrolls rarely exceeded 30 feet in length (completely unrolled). By New Testament times, writing on papyrus was the method of choice.

After the writing was complete, the bulky scroll would be rolled up and sealed to protect its contents. Such scrolls were quite cumbersome to carry—nothing comparable to a modern paperback. To read such a scroll, one would have to awkwardly unroll it with one hand while rolling it up with the other.

Later, perhaps due to the cumbersome nature of scrolls, the "codex" was invented, which involved pages folded and then fastened together on one side, much like a modern book. During the second century A.D., the codex replaced the scroll as a means of recording.

In biblical times, God often commanded that His revelations to man be written down and recorded. "Moses then

W

353

wrote down everything the LORD had said" (Exodus 24:4). Joshua too "recorded these things in the Book of the Law of God" (Joshua 24:25-26). Samuel "told the people the ordinances of the kingdom, and wrote them in the book and placed it before the LORD" (1 Samuel 10:25 NASB). The Lord instructed Isaiah, "Take a large scroll and write on it with an ordinary pen..." (Isaiah 8:1). Isaiah was told, "Go now, write it on a tablet for them, inscribe it on a scroll, that for the days to come it may be an everlasting witness" (Isaiah 30:8). Today, we possess virtually thousands of manuscript copies of the original documents penned by the prophets and apostles.

Z

Zealots—See *Jewish Sects.*

Zechariah

The book of Zechariah was written by the prophet and priest Zechariah between 520 and 518 B.C. His name means "the Lord remembers" and is appropriate because a theme runs through his message that God will bring blessing to the people because He remembers the covenant He made with Abraham.

Zechariah was born in Babylon in exile, and he and his father, Iddo, were among the first exiles to return to Jerusalem following the exile. Like his contemporary Haggai, Zechariah was a prophet chosen by God to motivate the Jews to finish the task of rebuilding the temple following the exile.

The problem was that when the people first returned from exile in 538 B.C., they made a good start in beginning to rebuild the temple, but now apathy had set in and the whole project had stagnated (Ezra 4:4-5). The people were too busy building their own homes to pay much attention to the temple. Zechariah was one of the prophets chosen by God to encourage the people to finish the task.

The people needed encouragement because they had a defeated state of mind. While they were excited to be home again, they were also despondent over the ruin of their city. They were especially despondent over the fact that it was *their own unfaithfulness* that had brought this ruin. Zechariah and Haggai sought to motivate the people to finish up the temple so worship could begin again.

Instead of motivating the people by rebuking them, Zechariah demonstrated the importance of the temple (Zechariah 1–8). The rebuilding of the temple was important not only because it was the religious center of Jewish life but also because it represented the presence of the one true God among the Israelites before a watching pagan world. For the temple *not* to be rebuilt might give the impression to pagan nations that the true God was no longer interested in Israel and no longer paying attention to the covenants He had made with His people.

It is interesting to observe that there are a number of key messianic prophecies in the book of Zechariah. For example, Zechariah prophesied that Christ would be betrayed for a mere 30 pieces of silver (11:12-13), that He would be pierced on the cross (12:10), and that He would come again in glory (14:4). As such, Zechariah is an important book for Christological studies in the Old Testament.

Zephaniah

The book of Zephaniah was written by a prophet of the same name about 625 B.C. He was the great-great-grandson of the godly King Hezekiah. His ministry took place during the reign of King Josiah of Judah (640–609 B.C.), and his preaching may have been a factor in some of the reform that took place during Josiah's rule.

Zephaniah's message repeated familiar prophetic themes. God would judge the people for not being faithful to the covenant He had established with them. Instead of living the way He had instructed them, the people picked up the habits of the pagan cultures around them. God would not permit this to continue. Hence, judgment was imminent (Zephaniah 1:2-3; 2:2; 3:6-7). Zephaniah continually hammered home the idea that the Day of the Lord was approaching (see 1:7,14-16; 3:8). He affirmed that the fire of God's judgment would have a purifying effect on the nation, melting away their sinful complacency. Yet, he also spoke of the blessing that would eventually come in the person of the Messiah (see 3:14-20).

Z

356

Zion

Zion is first mentioned in 2 Samuel 5:6-9 as a Jebusite fortress on a hill. This fortress was captured by King David and was henceforth called "the city of David." Second Samuel 6:10-12 tells us that David brought the Ark of the Covenant to Zion, hence making the hill a sacred site.

In the Old Testament, Zion is called "the city of God" (Psalm 46:4), God's "resting place" (Psalm 132:13-14), God's "holy hill" (Psalm 2:6), "the holy city" (Isaiah 48:2), and the "holy mountain" (Daniel 11:45). Eventually, Zion came to refer to the city of Jerusalem as a whole.

Z

If you have any questions or comments,
feel free to contact Reasoning from
the Scriptures Ministries.

Ron Rhodes
Reasoning from the Scriptures Ministries
Phone: 214-618-0912
Email: reasoning@aol.com
Web: www.ronrhodes.org

Free newsletter available upon request.